INTRODUCTIONS TO EURYTHMY

INTRODUCTIONS TO EURYTHMY

An Extension of Goethe's Morphological Thinking
within the Realm of Human Movement

Introductions to performances of eurythmy
from the years 1913 to 1924

RUDOLF STEINER

Translated and Edited by Frederick Amrine

SteinerBooks
2025

SteinerBooks | Anthroposophic Press
834 Main Street, P.O. Box 358
Spencertown, New York 12165
www.steinerbooks.org

Original translation from German by Frederick Amrine

ISBN: 978-1-62148-325-0
eBook ISBN: 978-1-62148-326-7

Cover image:
Marie Savitch (Berlin, 1924),
with kind permission of Rudolf Steiner Archiv,
Dornach, Switzerland.

Printed in the United States of America
by Integrated Books International

Contents

(= an excerpt, or a condensed version)*

PART III: A NEW AESTHETICS OF MOVEMENT EURYTHMY AND THE OTHER ARTS INTRODUCTIONS, 1914 TO 1924 195

Introduction

This volume features introductory addresses given by Rudolf Steiner to the first audiences of the newly minted art of eurythmy. Before every eurythmy performance at which he was present, Rudolf Steiner gave such an introduction. His intention, as he remarked on several occasions, was not to elucidate the meaning of eurythmy intellectually—a vain and inartistic endeavor—but rather to orient the audience to this new undertaking in the realm of art. Rudolf Steiner took many approaches to this end, describing in his introductions a range of themes—from the origins of eurythmy as a Goethean art form to its role in pedagogy and therapy. As this volume gathers together a large collection of these introductions, repetition is inevitable but not without value. A slight nuance of expression can awaken new insight.

Though Steiner had hinted at the possibility of a new art of movement at least as early as 1908, eurythmy first began in December of 1911 when Clara Smits, a longtime student of Steiner's, posed the question of whether it was possible to have a healing effect upon the physical body through certain rhythmical movements of the etheric body. Rudolf Steiner affirmed this, saying that he was prepared to teach this new art of movement to her daughter, Lory Maier-Smits, who was eager to study some form of movement or dance. "It will be a matter of *the word*, not [of dancing to] music," Steiner emphasized from the beginning, later calling eurythmy "the art that has grown entirely from the soil of anthroposophy."[1] The first preparatory exercises were given to the seventeen-year-old Lory Maier-Smits in the following months, and the first eurythmy course, the so-called Dionysian Course, was given for Lory in September of 1912.[2]

---

1 Introduction of December 23, 1923.

2 For a more complete origin story, see Rudolf Steiner, Eurythmy: Its Birth and Development, trans. Alan Stott (Rudolf Steiner Press, 2019).

From the beginning, Rudolf Steiner stressed the connection of this new art form with Goethe's conception of art. The following immensely illuminating quotation from the introduction of February 24, 1919, sheds light on the Goethean foundation of the new art form:

> The whole meaning of our art of eurythmy is based upon Goethe's worldview, indeed precisely upon the aspects of Goethe's worldview that, if we assimilate them into our artistic sensibility, reveal themselves to be the profoundest and perhaps the most fruitful for the future evolution of the arts. At the risk of sounding theoretical, I would like to make a few remarks by way of explaining the groups of performers in this regard. Almost everyone knows that Goethe was active not just as an artist: he also provided profound—sadly, today one is not permitted to say "scientific"—"science-like" insights into the inner dynamics and conditions underlying all the processes of nature. We need only recall how it was that Goethe rose up to the idea that each individual organ of the plant should be viewed as a transformation of the other organs that manifest within the same plant. Any one organ within a living organism should be viewed as a metamorphosis of its other organs, and the entire plant in turn (the same thing applying also to even higher living creatures, animals and human beings) the whole organism as a synthesizing metamorphosis of individual organs that are each suffused with meaning. Goethe got that far in his thinking.
>
> If we permeate ourselves with the intuitive insights latent within this view of nature, then it is possible to transpose this insight into artistic feeling and artistic form. That is what our art of eurythmy has attempted to accomplish with regard to certain artistically formed movements of the human body itself. And our way of attaining that ideal is by here transposing into movement what Goethe initially intuited within the realm of form.
>
> If I wanted to provide a comprehensive expression of the

> actual intent of our art of eurythmy, then I would say the following. Our entire human nature is to become a metamorphosis of one single organ—indeed of a preeminent, significant organ, the larynx. The human larynx expresses what lives within the soul through the word, through tone. In the same way, it is possible—by grasping intuitively the forces that are at work within the larynx and its associated organs in the process of forming sounds, of bringing forth tones—it is possible to transpose them into movements that are formed by the whole human organism. The whole human organism can in a certain sense become a visible larynx. We must only remain clear in this process that the things expressed by the human larynx in words, in tones, and harmony, in the lawful succession of sounds and tones, are merely latent tendencies toward certain movements within the air itself. And then in the air the real nature of words is actually given expression within the physical world of the senses.
>
> Hence, I would like to say: We are seeking to bring to expression by means of the whole human organism that which the movement of the human larynx sends forth into a mass of air as a crafted form.

Rudolf Steiner outlines three principal realms in which eurythmy is active. The first is the realm of art; the second, pedagogy; and the third, therapy. In an introduction to a children's eurythmy performance in Oxford, England, in 1922, Rudolf Steiner outlined three attributes of eurythmy through which it had served the pedagogical tasks of the newly founded Stuttgart Waldorf School. The first is its ability to help the children develop a deeper relationship with language:

> First of all, eurythmy is especially important because it is a great aid in the teaching of languages. The children have always been drawn quite naturally to this visible language. They feel pleasure and an inner fulfillment when they enter into something that flows directly out of human nature itself. It is similar to the manner in which children find their way

> into the sounds of speech and into song. When they work their way into this visible language, they feel the essential nature of the language within their inner being. And from there an understanding radiates out into the regular language curriculum.

The second attribute concerns the development of initiative and an active will:

> Even though we fully acknowledge conventional gymnastics in the Waldorf School as a means of physical education, we supplemented it with eurythmy as a kind of ensouled gymnastics, a spiritual gymnastics. And eurythmy reveals itself as especially well framed for the will, for the cultivation of initiative within the will. It gives us the possibility of working upon the soul of the child because whenever a child performs a movement, he feels that he is simultaneously engaging his whole human constitution—body, soul, and spirit. Children feel how body, soul, and spirit coalesce, as it were, and how these are all bound together within this spiritual gymnastics that is eurythmy.

The third attribute is eurythmy's propensity to educate children toward truthfulness:

> Using everyday speech, we can of course say not only what is true, but also what is false. It is especially easy to become untrue, mendacious when speaking. But in the visible language of eurythmy, it is impossible to lie. That is something we have come to experience. Hence eurythmy is also a means for teaching truthfulness. In the visible language of eurythmy, nobody—and least of all children—will find it easy to lie.

Thus, eurythmy, from the beginning of the Waldorf School in Stuttgart, was an integral part of the educational approach. The child is addressed on all levels—body, soul, and spirit—through the right practice of eurythmy in education.

Concerning the third realm in which eurythmy is active—the

realm of therapy—Rudolf Steiner remarked in the introduction of April 14, 1924:

> A third aspect of eurythmy we have developed is therapeutic eurythmy. Because it emerges from the healthy movement of the human organism, eurythmy is able to counteract the fundamental causes of illness and to supplement other medical treatments once its therapeutic potential has been developed. Please note: here, as in all things anthroposophical, we do not allow ourselves to become one-sided. We embrace the multifaceted complexity of life itself. Nobody who knows anything about anthroposophy would ever be tempted to view eurythmy as a panacea. But eurythmy will provide real support for many different healing processes, and that is why we have made eurythmy an essential component of [anthroposophical] therapy. Ever mindful of the qualifications I just mentioned, we introduced therapeutic eurythmy at the Therapeutic Clinic in Arlesheim, which is led by Dr. Ita Wegman in conjunction with the Goetheanum. There the full significance of eurythmy is revealing itself. That work alone is sufficient to demonstrate that eurythmy arises out of the innate needs of a healthy human constitution. But eurythmy had to be modified somewhat for that purpose. What you shall see here today [pedagogical eurythmy], and the art of eurythmy you saw in the theater, are not therapeutic eurythmy. Everything has to be modified in such a way that its influences upon those suffering illnesses are efficacious.[3]

These are but a few of the many ways to approach the open secret of this new art form, inaugurated a century ago but still in its infancy, with applications in the fields of education and therapy. Given as they were to a broad range of audiences, these lectures speak to everyone interested in expanding the possibilities of artistic expression through the greatest instrument of all: the human being.

Clifford Venho

---

3 See also Rudolf Steiner, *Eurythmy Therapy*, trans. Alan Stott (Rudolf Steiner Press, 2009).

Part I: Introductions, 1913–1920

Rudolf Steiner's Words Preceding the First Presentation of Eurythmy: "The Dance of the Planets," "Twelve Moods," and "Satire"

Dornach, August 29, 1915[1]

Before the presentation, I would like to say a few words about how connections can be seen in everything we are attempting—in everything we undertake and in everything that emanates from our undertakings. Without doubt, there is an intense longing in our time to establish a connection between material existence and spiritual life. On the other hand, it is difficult to find places where this is possible. As I have emphasized on other occasions, very few Europeans today have a clear sense of how they might seek the real substance that dwells within the other worlds that are both the foundation of this world and its neighbours. If you consider teachings that are offered today about poetry, about art, you will frequently notice how everything artistic leads back to something higher, and yet how difficult it is for people today actually to feel their way into communion with this higher element. For that reason, let's hope that as the kind of eurythmy we are attempting to develop becomes ever more widely known, it will help to develop in a thoroughly human way just what is needed in order to find a connection with the spiritual worlds. How often you will have heard from this or that group calling itself theosophical that an essential aspect of the soul life is based on becoming one with the Great Cosmic Being that fills all of space and progresses through the ages! But although this longing for communion with the cosmos is emphasized in theosophical circles with great enthusiasm and fervour, there is little inclination to take hold of the reality of this experience. Many today emphasize the kind of mystical "de-individuation"[2] that was sought in the High Middle Ages—for example, by Meister Eckhart or Johannes Tauler[3]—the feeling of being at one with the divinely suffused cosmos. Today, however, we are in a period in which spiritual knowledge must be striven for concretely, within the real. Ours is a period in which something must really be done to lend confirmation to the great truth that human beings in their doing and their being can harmonize with the doing and the being of the universe. That's what we are attempting to do tonight, and you will begin to get to know it by seeing "chapter two," as it were, of the development of eurythmy. I will only direct your attention very briefly to something that can be gathered from today's presentation.

In the second piece ["Twelve Moods"], you saw a depiction of something real within the universe that is both moved and at rest: the "twelveness" that is present within the universe in the form of the Zodiac, and the "sevenness" that is present in the universe as the sequence of the planets. You were also able to see how the resting element within the signs of the Zodiac stood out when juxtaposed with the moving element of planetary Being by the presentation of the figures. Of course, such realizations are possible only when this spirit of communion with the universe suffuses the whole. And so it was that we tried to create something in which there is a complete inner harmony between the spoken word—and not just the spoken word but also the feelings that reveal themselves—and each individual movement. Gradually, you will come to understand that, within the presentation as a whole, the spoken word is there only as an aid. Gradually, you will come to understand that when the movement is performed in all its dimensions,[4] it will be possible to read what is being said out of the movement, in the same way that you can read the meaning of words if you have the letters before you. You don't need anything except to have learned how to read; then, after the system has been gradually developed, you will be able to read what is presented also. But you will be able to read not just literally, not just sound-by-sound: you will be able to read the meaning as well.

In order to do that, you need to have a sense of the inner experiencing that corresponds to the meaning. As an earthly human being—wandering about aimlessly, as we humans do, with the beings who were cast into the abyss, stumbling through the earthly abyss—people generally, as a matter of course, err with their thoughts and feelings during earthly existence. Yet we are able to raise ourselves up out of this erroneous thinking and feeling, to raise ourselves to what becomes for us, out of quiet movement, a firmer thinking or feeling. You see, the cosmos that confronts us to begin with as our solar system is only a special case. "In the beginning was the Word, and the Word was with God, and the Word was a God."[5] And in the cosmos, we see the Word congealed or frozen, as it were, the Word at rest and the Word in its movement. But we must feel the Word within the cosmos. I certainly hope that what is presented here will not be mistaken for any of the many kinds of confused mysticism that are current today. We're not concerned here with imitating the methods of those modern astrologers who outdo all materialism with their methods, simply adding ignorant superstition to materialistic ignorance. We're concerned here instead with introducing the lawful relationships of a spiritual world that manifest in the human being just as in the cosmos. True spiritual science does not try to read human laws out of the constellations of stars; rather, it seeks to discover the laws of both humanity and nature out of the Spirit. Although this spiritual science has been conflated again and again with the nonsensical mystical strivings of recent times, it bears no relationship to them at all. When we draw analogies between certain human expressions and cosmic relationships as the underlying foundation of an expression, we need to state emphatically that spiritual science has nothing to do with the dilettantism of modern astrologers and their crude revelations.

And so we have undertaken to offer a sequence of feeling, sensing, and speaking, which, as it is presented, makes a different case, as it were. It presents an example of the soul's inner feelings vis-à-vis what has flowed into the movements of our solar system. The structure of twelve stanzas, each with seven lines, corresponds, you could say, to the outer framework.[6] If you study this attempt at a "poem of twelve sevens," however, you will see that what wishes to reveal itself is present in every detail.[7] If you take the mood in Cancer, for example, in which, after the ascent has been completed, the descent follows again, where one has the feeling that the Sun comes to rest for a moment—let's simply use this image for now (many others are possible)—the very placement of the words within the "Cancer verse" will allow you to enter into something deeply with your feeling.

You resting, luminous glow,
Engender warmth of life,
Give warmth to life of soul
Toward powerful self-reliance
Toward spiritual self-permeation,
In quiet light-outstreaming.
You luminous glow, gain strength!

Compare this, if you will, with the verse for Scorpio:

Existence consumes the Being,
Yet in Being, existence holds itself.
In activity, Becoming disappears,
In Becoming, activity endures.
In worlds that prevail and punish,
In chastening the shapes and forms,
All-Being sustains the beings.[8]

In every verse, you find exactly the mood that corresponds to the relevant planet in the heavens.[9] This is not all that is attempted, however; if you take certain verses, you will be able to arrive at further feelings in turn. I will take one line from every verse, the line for the planet Mars:

In Aries: Radiate forth, awakening being.
In Taurus: Into worlds suffused with being.[10]
In Gemini: Toward life's mighty ruling.
In Cancer: Toward powerful self-reliance.
In Leo: Toward firm resolve to be.
In Virgo: Actions grounded in living powers.
In Libra: And being, it calls forth being.
In Scorpio: In becoming, activity endures.

In Sagittarius: Wielding within Will's living power.
In Capricorn: Within life's inner resistance.
In Aquarius: May it rise up within the stream.
In Pisces: And sustain itself by sustaining.

Although in every single line the general mood of the verse is maintained, you will be able to discern the Mars mood in each of these lines taken from the sequence of seven lines; you will be able to discern what corresponds to Mars. Thus the ideal would actually be for us, were we awakened from sleep and had one line read to us—"In Becoming, activity endures"—to be able to say, "Ah, yes! Mars in Scorpio!" With another line, we would have to say, "Jupiter in Libra," and so forth. You see, this is the antithesis of any subjective arbitrariness. Being at one with the laws of the universe is really taken seriously. Here we don't merely proclaim that you should commune with the cosmos; rather, it *is* such a communing. We are attempting, at least, to realize this communion in a concrete form. You will also have noticed that the gesture is held, for example, in a certain instance; you will have noticed how, as the Sun circled around, the Libra mood was also beautifully maintained in the gesture, not intentionally but only by virtue of the fact that the corresponding consonant sound is simply there. In the Libra mood, which is expressed here:

The worlds are sustaining worlds.
And being perceives itself within being;
Existence bounds itself with existence
And being, it calls forth being
To pour out deeds that unfold,
In resting world-enjoyment.
O worlds, uphold the worlds!

—you see everywhere the balance of the scales![11] It emerged all on its own that the gesture of Libra was held in just that place. These things occur entirely of their own accord if they are done correctly.

What are we trying to accomplish by doing something like this? Truly, this is not just a game! What we're trying to do is capture, through an actual, inward comprehension, what was carried out cosmically when our solar system was created. We're really trying to enter into it in mood, to enter into it in doing and in everything else. I would say that what you have seen presented here offers the possibility of calling forth inner mobility and mobile concepts out of what can be expressed in the following words:

The Word weaves through the world,
And world-shaping fastens the Word.

Das Wort wallt durch die Welt,
Und die Weltenbildung hält das Wort fest.

In the first piece you saw ["The Dance of the Planets"], we also attempted to connect with the cosmos, only in a somewhat different way. There you will have seen that, captured precisely by the movements, each stanza has four lines, and that the Sun made its twelve movements upon an outer circle. There are also twelve verses. But on the outer circle the Sun is shown moving through the Zodiac.

The two eurythmists who stood in the middle circle expressed the planetary element, and the one who stood in the center expressed the lunar element, the Moon. Thus you had here: the Sun, the planets, and the Moon. And you also had the inner connections among the lines within each verse, and always the relationship of the last line to the first: the first line is always of a Sun-like quality, the last of a Moon-like quality. Just as sunlight is reflected by the Moon, the last line will always be a reflection.

So out of the mystery of the universe comes the form that can be spoken as well as expressed eurythmically in movements. Thus, when the time eventually comes when we have learned to read these things, we will quite clearly know, after seeing such a presentation, just what it is that such a complete system of movement expresses.

Someone might believe it unnecessary to do something like this, but that's just a matter of opinion, isn't it? It's also possible to be of the opinion that human beings could have been mute, and that they don't really need to speak. And if everyone in this world were mute and only a few people began to speak, the others would think that speaking was utterly superfluous. Such views are merely relative, aren't they? As soon as we admit that such views are relative, we begin to realize that we make real progress in human development only by realizing all the possibilities inherent in human nature.

One day, when these eurythmists are also in a position to teach what now comprises the second chapter of eurythmy—in addition to what meets your eye macrocosmically and of course still needs to be developed in that direction—you will see that those "preludes" (*Auftakte*)[12] with which we began will certainly need to have musical accompaniment; today we had only a silent *Auftakt.*[13] Later you will see that a microcosmic element will be added to the macrocosmic and that there will be presentations in which something will be brought to expression just as lawfully as in human speaking itself. Later you will see eurythmy compositions in which you will notice that there arises at precisely the right place a labial sound, and then precisely at another right place a dental sound arises; what really takes place is what arises in another way within the human constitution in the act of speaking, so that we come to know ourselves in what is accomplished in eurythmy. You will also have noticed today that the eurythmists will gradually be able to show us that various aspects of words, their different meanings and senses, come to expression in various ways. You will have noticed today that a concrete word is danced in a completely different way from an abstract word, that a verb suggesting an activity is danced in a different way from a verb suggesting a passive state or a verb suggesting duration, and so on. You will also find presented in eurythmy the connection between the brain and the speech organism.

I hope that the following "Satire" will not be misunderstood. The mood it expresses must not be absent where a serious spiritual-scientific worldview lies at the basis of one's way of life. We're not just toying with serious matters when we try to inject some humor into what is serious. In some circles that fancy themselves "mystical," every frivolity that assumes the caricatured mask of "spiritual profundity" is considered serious, displaying itself in gestures of physical nobility and with tragically elongated faces. But for anyone who really knows life, these are the burlesque somersaults of spiritual life. Whoever wants to be truly serious in the face of seriousness must be able to laugh about laughing matters when the laughable deems itself serious. Anyone who cannot find humor in the humorous will also be unable to be serious in the true sense when confronting what is serious. Especially where knowledge of the spirit is sought, it has to be possible to laugh about the excesses of many "spiritual seekers." Otherwise, they'll make what is serious into something ridiculous among those who laugh because their laughing muscles begin to move whenever they don't understand something; or they'll enrage the folks who fly into a rage whenever they encounter something they haven't ever "seen or heard before."

On Christian Morgenstern's *Humoresques*, I

Dornach, January 15, 1916[14]

This book describes the worldly experiences, and the other profound experiences, the psychological experiences and everything else having to do with Palmström and Herr von Korf.[15] Perhaps some other day, after we have gotten to know both these gentlemen a bit, we can have a conversation about both these men. What we want to do today is to give only a short preface that will characterize them a bit for us inwardly. You have to know this foreword about Herr von Korf, which is called "The Bohemian Village." Now, above all, you have to understand what a Bohemian village is. It's not a village in Bohemia, but rather—well, just what *is* a Bohemian village? It's something that is so totally unfamiliar that, when you see it, you stand totally perplexed in front of it. That's what's actually meant by a Bohemian village. Something like anthroposophy for a professor of philosophy or, hmmm, like the Goetheanum[16] for a modern art historian. Something like that is what's meant by a Bohemian village.

THE PRINCIPLE OF EURYTHMY, AND HOW IT AROSE

Vienna, June 2, 1918[17]

The occasion for taking up eurythmy within our circle came as a kind of stroke of destiny. Our movement does not agitate in any way; rather, in our undertakings we always look to discover what are the needs of the time, coming toward us from this or that direction. We don't proceed programmatically. So it was that a member of our Society[18] asked me one day whether some kind of dance could be instituted within our circles, something that might awaken the interest of our older and younger members. This led to the introduction of eurythmy into our movement. It remains in a germinal state, and it's important to follow eurythmy's development, because it's something avant-garde, albeit still in germinal form.

When the question was posed to me, I had to say to myself: in our circles we can't just cultivate what has been understood as dance heretofore. There are already many such initiatives today, of many different kinds. One needs to keep in mind that, fundamentally speaking, movement as an artistic activity, all spiritual movement, proceeds from human nature itself.[19] At the beginning of a certain epoch, which can even be followed historically, so to speak, with our means of spiritual research, it was the case that spiritual streams flowed from a single source. In the beginning, knowledge, religion, and art flowed from a single source. Within the ancient mythic culture, something was presented that people sought to comprehend through certain institutions, through rituals and such. The same content was set before the people as an object of devotion, of human veneration, of revelation. The arts unfolded within a realm of beautiful appearances. At that time, it was still transparently obvious that these were three branches of the same tree, with a single common source. Art as such flowed from a single source, and the arts today prove that instinctively: in our own time we see the justified tendency to try to unite again what has been divided into separate streams. If a separate art form is to arise, then needless to say it has to arise out of an awareness of the foundation upon which everything artistic rests as a unified whole. And so we asked ourselves: If we are to set the human organism in motion by way of an art of dance, what can we take as the foundation? Nothing arbitrary should be created, nothing that proceeds merely from the personal intentions of a single individual. We do not make programs.

Our first task was to create an art of dance to accompany the word.[20] And this new art will also be developed as an accompaniment of musical tone. For now, we are working on the art of dance as an accompaniment of the word. How can we attain something objective within this realm? Here I must refer to the results of anthroposophical research, of course, if I want to raise this objective basis into consciousness.

Whenever human beings speak, there is a tendency for the whole human organism, and not just the physical organism, to begin to move. Whatever is spoken emerges from the human organism as a whole; the whole of our etheric body, of our body of formative forces[21] is in movement. The basis of human speech, of our habitual way of bringing forth words, is that the movements of the formative-forces body are held back and localized in the region of the breast, the larynx and its associated organs, the tongue, etc. Through this localizing of the processes of movement, which takes hold of the whole organism, the etheric body causes the larynx and the other speech organs to undertake those movements which produce the word and the structures of language. The movement of the larynx is an organic movement of our entire etheric body. But we can redirect that movement into the body as a whole. What we are calling "eurythmy" is essentially the same thing that all of us do in speaking. The movements of eurythmy are those that anyone's speech organs perform in everyday speaking. Eurythmy transposes something etheric that had been localized in the larynx to a physical organ. It turns the whole human body into a larynx. Anyone who has precise knowledge of the realities upon which eurythmy is based generally will not need to hear a poem in order to understand its content: he will be able to read it directly out of the movements. We have only just begun, and we don't have many forces at our disposal; hence the movements are not complete, and we can only allude to them.

Our procedure is to have the poem spoken aloud while being accompanied by the movements that have been spread out over the whole organism. Eurythmy is an expressionistic art. Every human being produces eurythmy; we merely project it onto the whole of the human organism. Actually, our initial attempts sought merely to accompany the movement. Our experience showed that it can disturb the process if we try to accompany the movements without reciting, and because eurythmy is an expressionistic art, while recitation is impressionistic, I believe that these two art forms complement each other. There are two poles, and by combining eurythmy with recitation, something emerges that we envision as a new and special kind of art. Projecting the movements of the larynx and the other speech organs onto the whole human body is something that is represented principally by the movement of each individual eurythmist.

We execute movements that are performed in space, and also group dances, which we are able to present to you only in a primitive form. Whenever you see the arms moving in these dances that are executed within space, what you are seeing performed are the movements of the larynx. Whatever is carried out in space, where the whole organism moves in space, where groups of eurythmists move, they are performing things that are otherwise held back. We never speak with our throat alone. We speak ourselves physically with the whole of our human organism—within our torsos at least. These movements provide only the fundamental tone of speaking. The timbre that we feel through the words is actually restrained movement. We loosen those restraints and perform those movements in space. Part of that is everything belonging to rhythm and rhyme. The spoken word appears in the rhythm; that which is carried out into space, the restrained element, remains only a basic tone, a basic mood. If a sentence is spoken with warmth, or is otherwise permeated with feeling, then that arises through movement within space. We set loose the movement that had been restrained. Nothing is arbitrary here. Anything having to do with pantomime or with mime is strictly avoided. All movements are strictly determined and are conjoined according to laws, as in the art of music. Individual coloration comes into play only in the same way that one person can interpret a sonata in one style, while another plays the same sonata differently. What underlies eurythmy is an art form that follows its own laws in the most rigorous sense of that term. But we are still in the beginning stages, and that's why you will see certain instinctive, involuntary gestures—feelings transposed into arbitrary movement. Eventually that will disappear. The only hint of arbitrariness allowed is a degree of interpretive freedom.

That's what I wanted to say in advance in order to draw your attention to the principle involved.

The Renewal of the Ancient Art of the Temple Dance through the New Art of Movement in Space

Dornach, August 25, 1918

On the occasion of the visit by the Dutch Prince Consort with a presentation of the "Prologue in Heaven" from Goethe's Faust[22]

Perhaps you will allow me to precede the presentations you are about to see with a few words about the meaning and the intentions that we connect with the art of eurythmy. For it is a sample of this art of eurythmy which you will see presented.

We consider our art of eurythmy to be something that is, shall we say, a kind of renewal in a thoroughly modern form of the old art of temple dance. If we imagine inaugurating something of that kind today, then of course we must keep in mind the whole evolution of human art; that is the only way that something intended to be new can be brought into the present. If you contemplate various aspects of the evolution of human culture today, you will see them unfolding in parallel. Art, religion, science—indeed all human cultural movements—have actually arisen out of a single root. In older epochs, in the primordial cultures, so to speak, we are able to contemplate the divine, holy mysteries of humanity. To the extent that they could be gathered from the sensory world, they took the form of art. And when the same worked upon human cognitive faculties, it gave rise to science. And when the same exerted its effect upon human devotion, it gave rise to religion.

And in the same way, the individual arts differentiated themselves as they grew out of religion, art, and science. If you consider an isolated branch of the arts today, and especially if you consider what ideally should be arising at this moment, then you really must situate it within this whole spiritual context, which shimmers and gleams up toward us.

It was something of that sort which we encountered when the occasion arose through destiny[23]—yes, one could say through destiny!—for us to think about inaugurating eurythmy. The point of eurythmy is not to create something arbitrary out of pure fantasy, but rather to place within the world something that is founded in the spirit, something that has been called forth out of the spiritual laws of cosmic existence. But everything that can situate itself in the world can be found in some form within human nature. Truly, human beings are a little world, a microcosm within the great world of the macrocosm. And our eurythmy has been called forth out of the working and weaving of invisible forces that are always exerting themselves whenever we speak or think. (Spiritual science calls these etheric forces.) We have not only this visible, physical larynx, of which anatomy and physiology are aware: behind it stand the invisible forces of the larynx and the other related speech organs. It is revealed to the clairvoyant eye how when we speak, we see at the same time the movements of one locally circumscribed part of this organism.

Our task then is to raise up into art what is otherwise given through Nature, in just the same way that Goethe conceived a view of art that was analogous to his theory of metamorphosis. When he sought to arrive at a conception of Greek art, he said: "There is necessity, there is God."[24] It was there, he believed, that the divine reveals itself within the human being. His view was that in every art form, human beings bring to consciousness their connectedness with the whole of the cosmos. It is in keeping with Goethe's spirit if we transpose artistically onto the whole of our human constitution what is naturally at work only locally within the invisible portion of the larynx.

And so, in this way we transpose into movements of the human limbs what otherwise is performed only by the invisible parts of the human larynx and the other associated organs in speaking, in singing, in music. Nothing here is pantomime; here everything is rigorously lawful. Every single vowel appears again, appears again in its corresponding relationships, sentence structures, linguistic articulations, musical articulations. All of these things should also come to expression within this spatial art of movement of the whole human being.

When we speak and sing, we not only set the invisible larynx in motion: we suffuse the movements of the larynx with our souls, with our heart, with the whole of our human nature. All of that is found only in the undertones—or perhaps it would be better to say, in the "undertoning"—of that which is spoken. Whenever we bring warmth, whenever we bring enthusiasm, or rhythm, or artistic form into what we speak, this is held back, restrained within our speaking. We release it, and it appears in the group dances. The movements that are carried out by the groups, the movements that emerge from the placement of the individuals within the groups, correspond to what is not actually carried out by the individual when speaking. Rather, it is something that is only latent[25] within this invisible larynx, only an "undertoning." The movements that the individual performs as something that becomes visible[26] within space are images of what is performed by the invisible larynx every time human beings speak, and they represent that only.[27] Hence, it's essentially a transformation of the entire human being into a living larynx, a bringing-into-relationship with the individual eurythmist, just as the larynx enters into a reciprocal relationship in spoken conversation. It's Nature that has been raised up into art. Goethe said: art is higher nature within nature.[28] That is just what is meant here in the corresponding art form.

I beg you, please, to take this proffered branch, which is an episode and interlude within our anthroposophical activity, in the spirit in which it is offered. It is something that is at the very beginning. These first trials are just some initial, weak attempts. But everything that comes forth in the world has to enter the world in germinal form, and especially at the moment of the first attempt. We make no great claims for these trials, and we hope you will allow us to make these presentations of individual poems and a eurythmical staging of Goethe's "Prologue in Heaven," the beginning of *Faust*, and receive them in that spirit.

What is the New Art of Movement, and What Does It Hope to Accomplish?

Zürich, February 24, 1919

On the occasion of the first public performance of the art of eurythmy[29]

Please permit me to introduce our performance with a few words. Such an introduction is all the more necessary in the case of this performance—allow me to say this at the outset—because here it is a matter not of some already perfected art form but rather of an intention—perhaps I could even say of a latent intention. And so I beg you, ladies and gentlemen, please understand and receive our attempts today in that spirit. It certainly is not our wish to compete in any way with any other form of dance and such that might superficially resemble what we are doing. We know very well that our contemporaries are able to offer something much more polished than what we can offer within our own specialized realm. But the point for us is not to present something that already exists in some other form. The point is to create a special form of art, called forth by movements of the human body, by the mutual movements and positioning of artists divided up into groups.

The whole meaning of our art of eurythmy is based upon Goethe's worldview, indeed precisely upon the aspects of Goethe's worldview that, if we assimilate them into our artistic sensibility, reveal themselves to be the profoundest and perhaps the most fruitful for the future evolution of the arts. At the risk of sounding theoretical, I would like make a few remarks by way of explaining the groups of performers in this regard. Almost everyone knows that Goethe was active not just as an artist: he also provided profound—sadly, today one is not permitted to say "scientific"—"science-like" insights into the inner dynamics and conditions underlying all the processes of nature. We need only recall how it was that Goethe rose up to the idea that each individual organ of the plant should be viewed as a transformation of the other organs that manifest within the same plant. Any one organ within a living organism should be viewed as a metamorphosis of its other organs, and the entire plant in turn (the same thing applying also to even higher living creatures, animals and human beings) the whole organism as a synthesizing metamorphosis of individual organs that are each suffused with meaning. Goethe got that far in his thinking.[30]

If we permeate ourselves with the intuitive insights latent within this view of nature, then it is possible to transpose this insight into artistic feeling and artistic form. That is what our art of eurythmy has attempted to accomplish with regard to certain artistically formed movements of the human body itself. And our way of attaining that ideal is by here transposing into movement what Goethe initially intuited within the realm of form.

If I wanted to provide a comprehensive expression of the actual intent of our art of eurythmy, then I would say the following. Our entire human nature is to become a metamorphosis of one single organ—indeed of a preeminent, significant organ, the larynx. The human larynx expresses what lives within the soul through the word, through tone. In the same way, it is possible—by grasping intuitively the forces that are at work within the larynx and its associated organs in the process of forming sounds, of bringing forth tones—it is possible to transpose them into movements that are formed by the whole human organism. The whole human organism can in a certain sense become a visible larynx. We must only remain clear in this process that the things expressed by the human larynx in words, in tones, and harmony, in the lawful succession of sounds and tones, are merely latent tendencies toward certain movements within the air itself. And then in the air the real nature of words is actually given expression within the physical world of the senses.

Hence, I would like to say: We are seeking to bring to expression by means of the whole human organism that which the movement of the human larynx sends forth into a mass of air as a crafted form.

Eurythmy also seeks to give expression to what resounds through tone and speech as moods of the soul, as inner feeling—what reverberates in the artistic shaping of speech by way of rhythm, rhyme, alliteration, assonance, and so forth. Our way of expressing them is by forming groups whose individual members add rhythm, pure inner mood of the soul, the weaving of feeling, and so forth, to that which the individual personality expresses through his or her movements.

We avoid—we avoid in principle—everything that might be in any way only a passing expression of the individual personality. The larynx does not bring our inner life to expression through some kind of spontaneously invented movement; rather, a lawfulness within the larynx determines the sequence of sounds and tones. In the same way, this art of eurythmy is informed by a lawfulness in its sequence of movements. All forms of mime, all forms of expression that are merely a matter of gesture, are to be avoided. And should you see hints of mime in today's performance, then I would beg you to understand it as an imperfection that remains within our new art form. We are not nearly so far along as we wish we might be.

As you will already have gathered from these introductory words, eurythmy distinguishes itself from other similar art forms in another regard: the whole of the human body, rather than just the legs, comes into movement. Let me put it thus: here it is of consummate importance to understand that eurythmy is not about dance-like movements of the legs; instead, the key organs involved in this art of movement are precisely our human arms.

So it is that, within a certain realm, we seek to make visible in our art of eurythmy the main thrust of Goethe's worldview. The only way to judge us fairly today must be to receive what we are able to offer as something utterly rudimentary, a beginning that is necessarily still imperfect. And it must be recognized that our habitual expectations of such arts run counter to eurythmy's essential impulse. Here nothing is a spontaneous expression; rather, everything has been submitted to an inner lawfulness—a lawfulness that is based on an intuitive study of the possibilities for movement inherent within the human organism. In music itself, the sequence of tones is subject to a lawfulness; in speaking, in the crafting of verses, the sequence of sounds and words is subject to a very specific lawfulness. Hence, nothing spontaneous or capricious can arise within this art of eurythmy. Rather, when two people, who are perhaps very different from each other as individuals, present something in the art of eurythmy, or when two different groups present something, then the differences that can arise are only such as the differences between the interpretations of various pianists who are all playing the same sonata by Beethoven. So the heart of the matter is that everything subjective, everything arbitrary has been excluded from our art of eurythmy.

Having taken the liberty of speaking these few introductory words, I would ask you please to recognize, to understand that we stand just at the very beginning, that these first steps of ours will necessarily be weak. But please also know that we firmly believe it is capable of being perfected further. And so we beg you, please, to receive kindly what we are able to offer. If you afford us that courtesy, then we can hope that after this first attempt our powers shall grow and that one day perhaps we shall be able to accomplish something better in the realm of such arts than what is possible today.

❀

The Fundamental Thought Underlying the Art of Eurythmy

Dornach, March 13, 1919

On the first public performance of eurythmy at the Goetheanum[31]

Permit me to say a few words by way of introduction to our art of eurythmy, to our eurythmy performance. An introduction is all the more justified in that we will be asking you please to direct your kind attention not to something that has achieved completion or some degree of perfection, but rather something that has yet to attain its goal. The performers themselves share the view that, for the moment, their artistic striving remains only a provisional intention. Perhaps I could even say: an attempt to intend something. What we are offering here as the art of eurythmy will inevitably be compared with various other similar endeavors within contemporary culture, endeavors within the arts of movement and dance and so forth. And we are the first to admit that our contemporaries have accomplished much in this realm, and that much of it has achieved an extraordinary degree of perfection. But if you imagined that we were trying to compete with these neighbors, as it were, then you would be misunderstanding our intentions. That's not the point. The point is to develop a special, new art form—one that, to be sure, we have only just begun to evolve.

What underlies this endeavor shares the same foundations as all our other endeavors: it's a continuation of something that is latent within Goethe's worldview and aesthetics. Eurythmy is a very specific aspect of this larger realm. What we are trying to do is to give Goethe's aesthetics a form that can correspond to more modern artistic viewpoints and sensibilities.

Goethe captured the essence of art—perhaps more profoundly than most others—in his saying: Art is a revelation of hidden natural laws that would otherwise remain forever hidden.[32] Goethe was able to see within the process of artistic shaping and creation something like a revelation[33] of secret natural laws. He didn't mean the kinds of laws that are revealed by the sober, dry, analytic intellect: his comprehensive worldview had already attained a profound intuition of Nature herself and her mysterious beings. Goethe's treatise on the inner dynamics of the organic life[34] of plants[35] is characteristic of his view of nature and significant in its own right, to be sure; it is a radiant example of Goethe's view on the inner dynamics of organic life generally. But his treatise represents only a small excerpt, shall we say, from Goethe's monumental and comprehensive view of nature.

Today I can only mention in passing how Goethe saw that every creature's individual organs mysteriously express the organism as a whole, and how they are an expression of all the other individual organs in turn. Goethe contemplates the plant and its process of becoming, how it unfolds, leaf by leaf, right up to the blossom and fruit. His view is that the colored blossom petal we admire is only a metamorphosis of the green foliage leaf—indeed, that even the more refined organs of the blossom, which look outwardly very different from an ordinary green foliage leaf, are nevertheless only a transformation of the green foliage leaf. Metamorphosis is everywhere in nature. The foundation of all organic form is precisely that: the fact that everything undergoes metamorphosis. And so it is that each individual organ, each individual leaf, is an expression of the whole. Within the individual foliage leaf, within the individual blossom petal, within the individual stamen, Goethe saw a whole plant. But that applies just as well to all living things, above all to the archetype of all living things: to the shaping of the human form and to human movement. That applies to living human activity itself. And that's exactly what eurythmy means to express. It is precisely those mysterious natural laws at work within our human nature itself to which eurythmy lends visible expression.

That was our thought. But it is not our thoughts that matter most here. What matters most is to experiment with actually transposing and dissolving this Goethean view of the inner weavings and becomings of the organism into an artistic sensibility. By revealing the languages of the spoken word and music to our surroundings, we express ourselves through a single organ within our human organism as a whole: the larynx. We speak and we sing with the larynx and the other organs that are immediately tied to the larynx. Just as the individual leaf is an entire plant, there's a sense in which the larynx system—the foundation of human speech—is the whole of the human organism. And the whole of the human organism can be understood in turn as but a more complicated metamorphosis of the larynx.

That is the experiment we performed. We attempted to elicit from the human constitution as a whole movements and configurations in such a way that, just as the larynx speaks and sings, speech and musicality are rendered visible by taking hold of the human organism as a whole.

But this certainly does not mean that the movements we are making should be interpreted in any kind of fantastical way. No, it should be like the art of music itself, in which everything unfolds lawfully and yet is immediately experienced as elemental. We should feel that the art of eurythmy is suffused, like musical harmony and melody, with an inner lawfulness, again without becoming fantastical. Then the artistry inherent in eurythmy will be evident.

The inner life of the human soul, which is otherwise expressed through the organ of human speech, through the larynx, will now be expressed through the whole human being, through our movements, through our positionings. The whole human being is meant to evolve and unfold itself, as it were, before the very eyes of the audience.

Now human speech does not just contain what comes to expression through sounds and sequences of sounds. No, it speaks out of the whole of the human soul: feeling, inner warmth, sensibility, mood, and so forth. Hence our art of eurythmy also strives to present visibly everything that becomes concrete, that comes to expression through the medium of language.

So what we have in eurythmy is an art of movement, with movements performed both by individuals and by ensembles, with movements that are meant to express the moods, the feelings, the inner warmth that both imbue and light up language.

When our pieces feature ensembles, what we are trying to capture is everything expressed in the neighborhood of the larynx, as it were. Rhyme and rhythm are the means whereby language rises up to the level of poetry, to the level of artistry, and that is what these group movements, the mutual configurations of dancing human beings, are striving to attain.

What characterizes eurythmy, ladies and gentlemen, and what distinguishes it from all other seemingly related art forms, such as pantomime, is that we are not seeking some kind of spontaneous expression, just as in music, with its inner lawfulness, nothing like a spontaneous expression is sought—then it would be music-painting. In the same way, eurythmy is something more than a set of spontaneous gestures, and something quite other than the art of mime. Unlike mime or pantomime, eurythmy is grounded in a rigorous inner lawfulness; in that sense, it is more like music. So when two different eurythmists perform the same piece, the difference is more like that between the subjective interpretations of the same sonata by Beethoven when played by two different pianists. The differences will be no greater than that. Everything has been objectified. If hints of pantomime or mime still pop up here or there, should you see some spontaneous gestures, that is because the whole thing is still imperfect. We know that we still really have our work cut out for us before we will be able to satisfy the high demands of our own ideals.

And so it is, then, that on the one hand you will hear poetry or music, and on the other hand you will see the poetry, the music, transposed into movements by solo performers and by ensembles. And this transposition should be done in such a way that the various movements and configurations are meant to have an effect as direct as that of the oscillations in the air, the movement of the air itself. Those emerge from the larynx as an actual movement, after all. It is just that we attend to the audible sounds rather than to the movement itself, which remains invisible.

Our artistic movements, our eurythmy, are meant to make visible in space something of which we remain spatially unconscious, as it were. And that is because we turn our ear only toward the speech that is generated; we do not have an organ to perceive what unfolds within the larynx as a continuation of the larynx's own movement, in the oscillations of the air, in rhythms, and harmony, and so forth.

That is the fundamental thought underlying our art of eurythmy. We are still only at the beginning of our strivings, and I would ask you please to keep that in mind. No doubt our presentation will strike you as imperfect in many ways. But it is a start on something that needs to be developed further in the same direction. And if you will be so kind as to look past what can be presented only in an imperfect form today, your kind attention alone will surely help stimulate us to perfect eurythmy. For our goal is to create something that can take its rightful place alongside the other arts. In any case, we hope that people will begin to have an ever-growing sense that the canon of the recognized art forms remains open. You will be able to capture the essence of eurythmy as a style if you recall Goethe's view on the matter, which is expressed in the following way: "Style, however, rests upon the most fundamental principle of cognition, on the essence of things—to the extent that it is granted us to perceive this essence in visible and tangible form."[36] And it was Goethe who argued that everything we can represent artistically must ultimately refer to those things that can be made visible in terms of human nature itself. In his lovely book on Winckelmann,[37] Goethe seeks to capture the essence of art by saying: The whole world reflects itself within human beings; humanity reveals the most secret laws of nature, and for that very reason humanity represents the pinnacle of all Being and Becoming. Goethe writes: "In that we human beings have been placed at the pinnacle of nature, we see ourselves as a whole nature unto ourselves, within which it is our task to raise up another peak. We climb upward towards that goal by permeating ourselves with all perfections and virtues—we summon all the discretion, order, harmony, and meaning that we can, and eventually we rise up to the production of the work of art."[38]

It is only a trial run that we will be offering you at the beginning today, but—as I said already—a trial run that is aiming for ever-greater perfection. Please lend this experiment your kind attention, and understand that this is only a beginning. For we remain convinced that these first beginnings harbor within them the seeds of eventual perfection. Whether we ourselves are the ones who eventually attain that degree of perfection, or it turns out to be others who carry this artistic initiative forward—that is all a matter of indifference to us. All of us who are bound up with this particular branch of art hold a deep conviction that someone—either we ourselves or our successors—will eventually overcome the imperfections of our small beginnings. One day, eurythmy shall become a branch of art that truly leads us down into the depths of human nature and human possibilities, an art that can take its rightful place alongside other art forms.

The New Art Form in Service to the Life of the Future

Stuttgart, May 6, 1919

For the management and the workers of the Waldorf Astoria cigarette factory[39]

We are presenting a new art to you today, but we beg you to realize that this is only its beginning. It will need time to be perfected, but then it will lead toward the accomplishment of wide-ranging ideals. And yet you can already see, even at this elementary stage, what it intends to achieve for the future of humanity. It is not meant to belong to a small elite; rather, it is meant to serve humanity as a whole. This new art is meant to play an important role in future life.

If I were asked to compare the eurythmy you are going to see here with anything else practiced in the world today, I couldn't! All the other existing arts of movement are only fragments of the greater thing you're about to see. What we are trying to do is to take various elements of human wholeness and pour them together into an activity that will be healthful, invigorating, and artistically fulfilling. If you pressed me hard to make a comparison, I would have to say that in eurythmy we are striving to fill with soul and spirit something that has remained *devoid* of soul and spirit up to now, as in gymnastics, for instance. Gymnastics brings us into external movement in accordance with corporeal laws. Let's have no illusions about it: gymnastics is an art of movement that is completely devoid of soul and spirit. By contrast, you will see here an art of movement that lets the soul and spirit shine directly into the movements of the human limbs. And, on the other hand, you could compare what is offered here with the art of dance. But that is another one-sided expression of an art that strives to be genuinely human. Traditional dance begins with outer things, and then those outer things are translated into dance movements.

Eurythmy does not begin with outer things. What you are going to see represented are movements of individuals and ensembles in various relationships of position and movement, all of which you essentially do yourselves throughout the day! It's just that you don't do it with your outwardly visible limbs, with your arms and legs: you do it when you speak. You do it continually with your outwardly invisible larynx and other speech organs, and with the air that you bring into movement through your larynx. You simply don't notice the way the larynx and other speech organs oscillate, the way the palate and the lungs are in movement, because you are listening, because you are listening to the transposition of the movements into tones. But try to enter deeply into what the larynx, lungs, tongue, palate, and lips are actually doing—and particularly into what the air is doing when someone is speaking. If you can do that, then you can say that in speaking, all of us perform the most artistic kinds of movements! And this is especially the case in the kind of speaking that is intentionally artistic: in declamation. Then the effect of these artistic movements is very similar to that of music. Strange as it may sound, the eurythmy that we will be presenting to you is something we obtained by eavesdropping on the mysteriously artistic creations that we call forth in everyday speech by virtue of being human. When a eurythmy ensemble comes out onto the stage, all of the relationships you see in the way of positionings and relative movements are movements of the larynx transposed into the movements of the performers. The individual performer and the entire group you see there are simply a larynx; everything becomes an organ of speech. So we can play music for you and at the same time show you what is in the music, not by movements of the larynx as it would be if we sang, but by eurythmy movements done by groups of eurythmists. So we can also present poetry, artistically formed speech, through the movements of individuals and the movements and positions of groups. What a single word or sound contains is shown in eurythmy by the movements of an individual, whereas whatever permeates poetic speech with warm human feelings and soul content is expressed by the movements and positions of groups. And all is created in pure rhythm! We can express everything through eurythmy. The part of our human nature that is most thoroughly imbued with soul, and through which our innermost thoughts and emotions[40] are revealed—our organ of speech—this we transpose into the whole human being. We thereby suffuse the human being with soul and spirit; we bring what is formed in the body into the spirit so that in eurythmy we can experience ourselves as soul, as spirit in reality.

People of our time have lost all relationship to the genuine art of poetry. No one today *recites* or *declaims* poetry; they merely read it as prose. In eurythmy, we must recognize that poetry is more than just prose. It is structured, molded speech. Therefore, in the speech, through which you will be hearing what you are seeing in the movements, we are trying to bring back a truly artistic way of speaking, not the prosaic delivery that is the fashion elsewhere where the artistic element has been lost. This art of declamation arises when the speaker expresses what you must express when you are all larynx.

So gymnastics, which lacks soul, is merged with dance, which lacks inner inspiration. The result is something that isn't just watched like stage dance, and isn't just corporeal movement like gymnastics, but rather both together and something new besides. It is an art in which the participant derives health and strength from the forces of the soul and the spirit—something gymnastics cannot do because it does not take hold of the human constitution as a whole.

You have to realize, however, that this is a huge labor. Eurythmy wants to serve the future of humanity, the same future about which I was speaking to you recently over in the factory from the standpoint of our social problems. Then our work will serve liberated human beings if they have entered into it with understanding. By that time, eurythmy will have been perfected, by us or by others. For now, it is the right foundation for that human ideal which looks to the future for its further development.

LANGUAGE MADE VISIBLE BY THE WHOLE HUMAN BEING

Dornach, August 11, 1919

Preceding a performance for vacationing children from Munich[41]

So, dear children! You have come from home to see our beautiful mountains and fields and meadows. And you have found new friends, the kind people who have taken you into their homes. You have been given a warm welcome in beautiful Switzerland!

Yesterday, we showed you what we are doing up here on the hill. Today, we will show you more of it. There was much for you to see. Perhaps someday you will think back and remember what you saw here; perhaps also, you will someday understand the word "eurythmy." Then, I hope this present time will be one of your precious memories.

You know that God gave humanity a wonderful gift: the gift of language. Usually people speak with their mouths. Now, what you have seen here as eurythmy is also a language, but it is the whole human body that is speaking. Someday you will all know what it is that we call the human soul. You don't know yet, you can't know, what it is in you that someday you will call "soul."

But what you saw here yesterday, the movements all those people were making with their arms, the movements they were making together in a circle, and everything else they were doing—that was all speech; it was all speaking, though not so that you could hear it. It was speaking so that you could *see* it. And what spoke was not the people's mouths, it was their whole being; it was the soul in man. If someday you wonder, "Does anything live inside me?" the answer will be, "Yes, that's where my soul lives." Remember then that yesterday and today you discovered how our souls speak through us, through our arms and legs.

And now I am going to look right over your heads and say a few words to the grown-ups in back of you, about what you are going to see in a few minutes, which someday you will understand better. I would like to say that our eurythmy—or what we should call our attempt at it—is actually a demonstration of Goethe's worldview, and of his conception of art, not as they were thought of in Goethe's own time, but as we have to think of them in the first third of the twentieth century.

Goethe saw more deeply than any of his contemporaries—or any of the generations so far following him—into the living being of nature. The depth of his worldview is still not recognized even today. This eurythmy of ours, however, should show how his ideas can be applied to a closely circumscribed field of work.

Goethe sees the entire plant as simply a complicated leaf. For him, every leaf was something in which his suprasensory eye saw the entire plant.

This conception is far from being fully worked out. In the realm of art, it is capable of much further development. Here, it is being applied to a specific, concrete field.

For someone who sees intuitively what takes place in the whole human being when we hear speech, particularly when poetry is recited artistically—for such a person the movements made by the human larynx and the other speech organs are related to the whole human being in the same way that Goethe saw the leaf as related to the whole plant. The leaf is a metamorphosis of the whole plant.

To us here, what comes to expression in human speech through the larynx and the associated speech organs is a metamorphosis of what we as whole human beings are holding back, what we actually want to put into movement when we listen. Anyone who can see suprasensibly knows that it is more than just a theory when we imagine our speech organs bringing the air into movement. Thus, speech harbors an invisible self-movement. This is what we are trying to show in eurythmy. We are trying through our movements to make the human being into an enormous larynx, to make perceptible everything that otherwise remains invisible in speech—invisible for the reason that ordinarily we direct our attention only to what we are hearing with our ears.

To see speech as coming from the whole human being is what we want to achieve by our eurythmy. There is nothing arbitrary about it.

But it has not been achieved completely yet. The art of eurythmy is only at a rudimentary stage. So far, it is only an attempt at a beginning. All pantomime, anything arbitrary has no place in eurythmy. Just as music has laws, just as one tone follows another from the necessity of a musical law, just as music is structured in major and minor modes according to musical laws, in the same way eurythmy is also founded upon an inner lawfulness. If two people or two groups of people present the same piece of eurythmy in two different places, there can be no more difference in the separate performances than there can be when two pianists play the same Beethoven sonata with their two personal interpretations. In both instances, there is a structure based on laws.

That is what we are striving for, trying thereby first to create something artistic, but also something pedagogical and therapeutic. In our artistic endeavor, we must be activated by that great artistic principle which Goethe expressed in this way: "In that we human beings have been placed at the pinnacle of nature, we see ourselves as a whole nature unto ourselves, within which it is our task to raise up another peak. We climb upward towards that goal by permeating ourselves with all perfections and virtues—we summon all the discretion, order, harmony, and meaning that we can, and eventually we rise up to the production of the work of art."[42]

Here, the entire human being becomes a work of art by bringing into play those movements that lie invisible within the whole human being, just as they lie invisible within the human larynx. Now they are to become visible.

The glow that illumines someone's speech, coming from the warmth of feeling in his soul, the power that enlivens someone's speech, coming from the enthusiasm of his personality, all that the poet brings to expression through rhyme and rhythm: these things are made manifest by individual movements and group movements in space. This corresponds to inner laws. There is no more subjective element in it than there is in an artistic program when two individuals perform one and the same piece of music.

Certainly, these introductory words must not encroach upon the artistic program that is coming. After all, true art rests on the fact that it can be enjoyed immediately. Yet, in the spirit of Goethe, it needs to be pointed out that all artistic creation has a suprasensory origin. It is precisely from this source, it seems to me, that we should create a new art form to add to everything else we want to create in conjunction with our building.[43]

The eurythmy will be accompanied by recitation or by music. What we are hearing with our ears will at the same time be presented to our eyes through the eurythmy forms.[44]

Here I would like to mention the art of recitation. It must return again to its good, old style. People today have never really heard a true piece of recitation. That practically ended in the seventies of the last century. Goethe was one person still so permeated by this art of speech that he rehearsed the actors for his play *Iphigenia*,[45] wielding a baton like a choral conductor. That was quite justified, for in recitation it is not a matter of emphasizing the literal, prose content, as is done today from a certain materialistic tendency, but rather of giving expression to the artistic content, the rhythmic elements, the artistic structure and form.

Recitation and eurythmy proceed parallel to each other and show that it is in the very nature of the human being to move inwardly in response to artistic activity. Remember that Schiller, when he conceived a poem, did not at first hold any literal idea of the poem consciously in his mind but experienced a vague melody, a musical content in his soul. He created directly out of the musical inspiration in his soul. So at the foundation of his most important poems lies the rhythmic motion, the inner flow, which he then only afterward embodied in a literal content.

We, too, want to leave the prose content of a poem in the background and bring into prominence the truly poetic qualities of the recitations that accompany the eurythmy.

You will need to be patient, please. Our work on eurythmy is still in its infancy. Above all, it should be pointed out that pantomime, mime, personal gesture will all have been eliminated when our performance is more perfect. We are our own severest critics. We know that in the art of eurythmy we are still at a level of imperfection. But we believe that in the spirit of Goethe's conception, when the whole of our human nature is brought to expression, higher natural laws shine through what is being presented to the external senses. And we believe that on that basis a genuine new art can arise, nobler than any dance form. Also, the aspects of gymnastics that have only a physiological basis and only build up the external physical body are given a soul by eurythmy. The soul is vibrating, the soul is speaking in all eurythmy. Thus, we also want to introduce a pedagogical element into this new art.

I believe I can count on your indulgence in viewing our imperfect offerings. We hope that if our contemporaries respond to these efforts with just the slightest interest, we will be able—perhaps not we ourselves, but those who come after us—to develop this art of eurythmy to such perfection that it will stand beside the other, traditional forms as a fully recognized new art.

✽

Goethe's Worldview and His View of Art

Dornach, August 17, 1919[46]

We take the liberty of performing for you a brief demonstration of the art of eurythmy, which is inspired by Goethe's view of art. Like everything else we have striven to accomplish in this building, and that is connected with it, eurythmy is fundamentally a continuation of impulses latent within Goethe's worldview. Applying what is so grand and comprehensive in Goethe's worldview artistically, but within a certain tightly circumscribed realm—that is what underlies our attempt to create a eurythmy. You will see artists or groups of artists creating movements with their limbs in space. In order to help you understand the meaning of those movements, I would like to sketch out very quickly, in a few broad strokes, the foundations of Goethe's worldview, which remains underappreciated even to this day.

What Goethe's worldview is trying to accomplish does not arise in a one-sided way out of a merely theoretical contemplation of the world. Every aspect of Goethe's work is simultaneously warmed by a real feeling for art. Goethe saw art as illumined by science; and for Goethe, scientific thinking takes on artistic forms. That is why, on every conceivable front, Goethe's worldview allows us to build bridges leading to the shaping of artistic forms.

Goethe's view of the becoming of living organisms in nature is quite simple. He saw a whole plant as latent within every individual leaf, even those with the simplest forms. And conversely, he saw the entire plant as nothing other than a single leaf with a complex structure. And so Goethe thought: The unified living being "plant" consists of many, many separate little plants. This is a view that can be extended to all living things, especially to the summit of the living world in nature, human beings. In doing so, we can think like Goethe the morphologist, restricting ourselves to the metamorphosis of forms; we can think that the overall form of an organism is the more complicated structuring of the form of an individual organ. That is how Goethe himself worked out the thought initially. But we can also think about it in this way: that the function performed by an organ within the living organism latently contains, in miniature, the functions performed by the organism as a whole, and vice versa. We can imagine that the processes of the entire organism are a more complicated revelation of that which the individual organ performs.

It is this thought (the fruitfulness of which, as I said, will be appreciated fully only in the future, by science as well)—this same thought underlies the art of eurythmy.

When we listen to someone speaking, of course our attention is initially directed toward the sequences of sounds, toward what expresses itself in the resounding of language. But for anyone able to see the suprasensory within the sensory; for anyone able to see intuitively and to penetrate the mysteries of nature by means of this intuitive seeing, an invisible movement is present in the larynx and its associated organs in the making of every individual sound. And the sequence of sounds presents itself in the form of invisible movements.

We can also make visible to ourselves how the latent tendency to movement within the larynx and its associated organs comes to expression. You know that when we speak, what resounds from the organs of speech is translated into moving waves within the air. We do not see these moving waves; rather, we hear what was spoken. Clairvoyants see what is carried by the oscillations of the air while we speak. They see it in the mysterious latent movements of the larynx and other speech organs. The larynx is an individual organ within the human organism. Just as Goethe conceives of the entire plant as a complicated leaf, our limbs and every part of our constitution can be called into movements that merely depict for us in a more complicated way what the larynx as an individual organ depicts in the act of speaking. Then, by way of our entire human constitution, something that we can call a visible speech will come to expression. That is what this eurythmy we are striving to create actually is: it is a visible language.

In a certain sense, the movements of human limbs that you will see performed on the stage by individual artists represent the larynx and other speech organs made visible and mobile: through eurythmy, the whole human body becomes a larynx. So we can say that eurythmy reveals outwardly what is otherwise present in suprasensory form in the latent capacities for movement within the larynx.

Or we might put it yet another way. As you surely know, ladies and gentlemen, if you exercise even a modicum of self-reflection, whenever we listen to another person there is always lurking an inner, suprasensory art of imitation. We suppress it, and it's simply the case that we listen by holding back certain suprasensory movements within our organism that resonate with the oscillations of speaking. These movements that we suppress in the course of everyday listening, when standing or sitting still and listening, are placed before our eyes by eurythmy. A listener who has been set in motion, who shows everywhere in his hearing the mirror image, as it were, of spoken words—that is a eurythmist.

I've said that the whole human body becomes a larynx, and now let's add something else to that. Human speech is warmed by the feelings of the soul so that it is imbued with desire, joy, enthusiasm, and also with pain, with suffering. Moods vibrate through it. All of that can also be expressed by eurythmy. We capture it by bringing stasis into movement. We don't just let people begin doing eurythmy wherever they happen to be standing. Rather, we let the individual performer move within space, or we let groups of performers create certain forms in space, or certain movements in relationship to each other. So that when the performers move in space, it expresses what vibrates through language inwardly as enthusiasm, as suffering and desire. The same can be said about everything that is expressed by the poet's artistically formed speech through rhythm and rhyme—all of that is expressed through the movements.

In thinking about the art of eurythmy, please remember that it is not mime, and it is not pantomime; it isn't just an art of gesture, and it has nothing to do with the customary art of dance. In all these other art forms, what lives within the soul comes to expression by means of an immediate gesture or something of that sort, through an immediate movement. Eurythmy is more like music. There's nothing arbitrary about the movement that is performed; rather, the individual movement and the sequence of movements are grounded in something like a law. That is how we can claim that in the same way that the harmonies, the melody, the sequence of tones reveal themselves in music, eurythmy also expresses an inner lawfulness.

That is why what might look like different individual styles will just be the result of different individual abilities. Nothing arbitrary—quite the contrary! A sonata by Beethoven will take on different nuances when performed by two different artists, but the piece that is performed remains the same. It's the same way when two performers or two groups of performers present the same piece through eurythmy. The performance contains a certain personal interpretation, but in principle eurythmy transcends any kind of mere subjectivity, just as music does.

What otherwise reveals itself in speaking, in singing, in music, in any kind of artistically formed speech—all of that becomes a visible language in eurythmy.

Hence you will see two different aspects running parallel. On the one hand, you will see musical pieces that bring what lives within the human soul to expression in a different way. And on the other hand, you will see a parallel attempt to perform recitations that are meant to render artistic, poetic language. What you will see is that, when eurythmy is accompanied by recitation, the recitation has to return to practices that it has lost over time. Recitation has to go back to its good old days. Today people love to recite prosaically, to accentuate the prosaic content. They want above all to render the *content* of poetry. If we go back to earlier periods in the evolution of the art of recitation, then we find that in a sense the content was only an occasion for presenting rhythms and inner movement; those were the things that were felt to be genuinely artistic. We find that in certain primordial epochs the artists who came forth to recite accompanied their recitations with something I would like to call a primitive eurythmy, and that they placed the highest value on the structure of the verse and other aspects of the artistic form rather than the content. In the case of any true poet, we also find that the poetry proceeds from an inner music, which is to say, from the rhythm and form of the tone of the poetry. We know that Schiller composed many of his poems by starting with something other than the content. Rather, the content of the poem might remain very remote from him at first, whereas a melodic element lived within his soul, and he then transposed this still wordless, still thought-free, melodious element and added to it the verbal content of the poem. But today recitation proceeds from the prosaic, from the novelistic dimension. That would not comport with eurythmy.

That is why the art of recitation that has to emerge from eurythmy is so easily misunderstood. This new art of recitation has to emphasize again the dimension of formed speech that is genuinely artistic, rather than the prosaic content that is so beloved today.

Should you see elements of mime or pantomime today, please just view them as imperfections that need to be corrected over time. Now that you have heard these introductory words about the intentions of eurythmy, let me emphasize that we know very well how rudimentary our attainments still are. We know that we are still right at the beginning, and that what you will see might be more like the will to an intention. Within this intention, however, there is a latent art form that is fully justified in taking its place alongside the traditional arts.

It is not just that we can grasp the essence of art in a genuinely Goethean sense with the help of eurythmy. There's another side to eurythmy: it leads us to believe that it has a future in the realm of pedagogy as a kind of ensouled gymnastics, as an alternative to the kind of gymnastics that is founded entirely upon physiology, upon physical corporeality. And this ensouled gymnastics that is at the same time an art form—a ensouled gymnastics that can also be conceived of as eurythmy—is something that we shall gradually introduce into the curriculum and pedagogy of the Waldorf School.[47] We shall introduce an art of bodily movement that is suffused with soul, as opposed to the soulless kind of gymnastics that is oriented only toward the culture of the body. Eurythmy strives to become fruitful in both these directions.

The most essential thing, of course, is to realize that the human being stands at the summit of the hierarchy of the organic world, of the world of living beings. For the time being, we know nothing higher. And we also know that, for the same reason, a most exalted extract of nature's lawfulness really can express itself in him. That is why, if we shape human nature itself into an instrument of artistic performance, it is possible to realize fully Goethe's high hopes for human artistic activity, which he expressed by saying: Because the human beings stand at the summit of nature, they call forth within themselves another summit in turn; they can join measure, harmony, order, and meaning, and thereby rise up eventually to the production of works of art.[48] Goethe sees all this as one solution of the riddle of the universe:[49] in the mirror of art, humanity can regain the mysteries of the cosmos. And if we consider ourselves, as human beings, to be the instrument of this reflection, then clearly we accomplish something that can be understood as a synthesis of a wide range of other artistic intentions.

Once again I entreat you, please handle what we are able to offer with care, because it is only a beginning, and we are already our own harshest critics. We know very well how much remains imperfect, but we also believe that, whether it is we ourselves or others who shall eventually develop it further, this imperfect art shall one day stand among the other established forms of art as fully justified.

GOETHE'S VIEW OF THE IDEA

Dornach, October 19, 1919[50]

[abridged]

It is a realm circumscribed by art, an artistic realm that we intend to develop as the art of eurythmy out of Goethe's worldview. So I do not want to theorize, but I would like to begin with a few words about the sources of this art of eurythmy.

When such an art form first arises within the evolution of culture, it needs to be made entirely clear that—and what I'm about to say is entirely in the spirit of Goethe—we need to understand clearly that what we're enjoying aesthetically actually bears a relationship to the mysterious depths of things, and that we're also attempting to reveal those depths through our knowledge.

It is characteristic of Goethe's thinking that for him art and science were not strictly separate realms. A very typical example would be Goethe's assertion that we actually shouldn't speak about the idea of truth, the idea of beauty, the idea of goodness, because Goethe thought that the Idea unites one and all, that it reveals itself now as human goodness, now as beauty, now as truth.[51] In saying this, of course, Goethe had in mind something much more vital, much more spiritual than the kind of abstraction that many people imagine today when they use the word "idea." In the Idea, Goethe saw something that animates Nature herself, and that human beings can find within themselves in turn if they descend deep enough into the shafts of their own inner nature.

Anyone who wants to understand clearly what we actually mean by the word "eurythmy" here will have to wrestle with the aspects of Goethe's worldview that are most significant and characteristic. The real heart of Goethe's great conception of nature (which also reveals itself artistically, and hence is also the heart of his aesthetics) is far from having been properly appreciated. Mainstream science is essentially a science of the dead, and it has striven more and more to define as scientifically rigorous only attempts to grasp the life-world as something dead, only attempts to think that which is alive as composed of dead elements.[52] Goethe strove to intuit vitality directly. He called such an immediate intuition of the life-world his theory of metamorphosis.

✽

THE WAY TO A REAL CULTURE OF THE SPIRIT

Dornach, November 8, 1919

Performance of eurythmy and lecture for the workers at the Goetheanum[53]

I'd like to be able to welcome you with the lights on![54] But since there's no electricity for the time being, please allow me to offer a cordial welcome to the guests who have honored us with their presence—in the dark! It's always a special pleasure to see guests here, especially now, at this time when our building is actually still a very long way from completion. What's needed most by those of us who are striving to complete the Goetheanum is the public's interest in the activities that this building, the Goetheanum, and the Free School for Spiritual Science,[55] are meant to serve. For we believe that our spiritual movement is addressing what are real human needs at the present time. To be sure, there are still many circles in which people are highly dubious when someone mentions spiritual science, or talks about the possibility of *knowing* the spiritual world. And since the thing we want to demonstrate for you—as soon as the lights come on!—is connected with our spiritual strivings as a whole, let me precede today's performance with a brief characterization of those spiritual strivings. Everything that we do here that is associated with this building is an attempt to reintroduce a genuine knowledge of the spiritual worlds into human culture. I intentionally said "genuine knowledge" because many people will readily admit as an article of faith that the world can be traced back to spiritual causes. But here it isn't just a matter of conveying to humanity some kind of religious confession. The furthest thing from our minds is to deliver any kind of religious creed or article of faith. No, what we're seeking here is a genuine knowledge of that spiritual life which is just as present in the world as the outer life of the external world of the senses.

Now, admittedly, the time has passed (although for many folks it's still at hand!) when people considered it a badge of cleverness if they could say with seeming conviction: It is impossible for human beings to attain any kind of spiritual knowledge; human knowledge cannot prove on its own that we bear a soul and a spirit within ourselves, a soul and a spirit that are connected with the soul-and-spirit which permeates the cosmos. – That was a sort of article of faith for people in the age that many call "scientific." We have gone beyond that now—even though, as I said, many people are still living back then in their minds. A time will come when this worldview will strike people as very antiquated. To be sure, there are still many people today who are either skeptical or who greet with a certain contempt anyone who speaks of spiritual knowledge. But the people who occupy themselves with attaining knowledge of the spirit by following the paths laid out here at the Goetheanum know better. They know that throughout history it has always been the case that when something new is introduced into human evolution, people oppose it at first. People scorn it at first, but then gradually it becomes something that is accepted as a matter of course.[56] And the whole idea that it is possible to know the spiritual world will come to seem natural and obvious relatively soon, in the not-too-distant future.

Using the faculties with which we are born, human beings can perceive the external world. We can perceive what we call "nature"—the outer world that presents us with minerals, plants, animals, that presents the world of the stars above us, the world of the Sun and the Moon and so forth. People who spend their lives seeking nothing beyond what comes to them naturally in this way—anyone who makes no attempt to call forth something within his or her soul—will necessarily come to reject any possibility that there could be a science of the spirit. But to acknowledge the science of the spirit requires a certain intellectual modesty. It feels strange to be talking about intellectual modesty, because people today—especially those who have gotten a bit of an education—think they're awfully clever. But just imagine a five- or six-year-old child standing before a globe or a map. At best the child will run his or her hand over the surface of the globe, or try to tear up the map. You can't say that the child knows the right thing to do with this map. But after the child has developed further, when the faculties that aren't present yet in the five- or six-year-old child have been summoned up out of his or her inner life, then—let's say by age ten—the child knows how to do lots of things with such a globe or map. The child knows how to decipher what is visible there. I mention this only as an analogy, only to show that it is not at all foolish to say: Perhaps the world all about us, with its stones, plants, animals, stars, is like a globe or a map for people who simply make use of the faculties with which they were born and grow up. – We can see something completely different in the world, in so-called nature, if we take our own development in hand and go further. Then something emerges on its own, and what it shows is simply that it's possible for people who have undergone certain developments to see much more in nature than people who haven't undergone such self-development. That is what spiritual science of the kind we are pursuing here seeks to demonstrate.[57]

Anyone who has adopted this perspective knows very well why it is that so many people reject this spiritual science. What people need to do is just admit: It is possible for us as human beings to transcend what can be attained solely by relying upon the faculties with which we are born. If that happens, then we begin to see things with our souls and spirits that we can't see without having undertaken such self-development.

Now there's actually quite a bit to do if you undertake such a path of self-development. In various books I have described what's involved in undergoing such a training. It is a training that opens what Goethe called the eyes of the soul, the eyes of the spirit. What you will find described there are things that every person can work through relatively easily if they have enough patience and time. Admittedly, not everyone will be in a position to make great discoveries in the spiritual world, but it is always possible in principle for certain people to make spiritual discoveries in this day and age. And the point of the book I wrote on this subject—it is called *Knowledge of the Higher Worlds*[58]—was not to sail straight into the spiritual world with flying colors, as it were: rather, it was written for the purpose of awakening a faculty that otherwise slumbers within the soul. It is a faculty that allows you to comprehend what the spiritual scientist finds by doing research in the spiritual world.

So, it is important to make a distinction. Some people really can develop the capacity to make certain discoveries in the spiritual world, to discover things that are intimately connected with our lives as human beings. To be sure, not everyone will be able to make such discoveries. But everyone who employs healthy common sense and then observes what is described in my book *Knowledge of the Higher Worlds* can really understand the assertions of spiritual science. And surely it will be possible to say: Yes, it's true that there will be only a very few people who are able to enter into the spiritual world, but the others will be able to experience through such people truths that are of great value for human life. – In these times especially, people should understand how important it is for human life as a whole that this is the case, and that there should be more and more such people in the future. Today many people are saying that certain new forms of social life need to be widely adopted. But the term "social life" implies living together, living with one another. It implies living in such a way that one person's contribution is accepted by the others, that it is valid for the others as well. It implies that we all work for each other. But we shouldn't work for each other only with regard to material things: we should also work for each other when it comes to spiritual matters. And the right kind of social life shall arise in the future precisely because there are certain individuals who have submitted themselves to the discipline that allows us to make discoveries in the spiritual world and because there will be others who are able to assimilate those developments, and will help others to understand what those who have performed research in the spiritual world are able to communicate. But the things that researchers of the spiritual world are able to communicate are immensely significant for our everyday lives. If there were no spiritual science today and on into the future, humanity would gradually reach a point where it would no longer acknowledge the reality of the spirit at all. What has limited the tremendous damage that results from a lack of any knowledge of the spirit is that certain spiritual truths have carried over from past ages when humanity could still access spiritual truths in a form that is no longer appropriate for the modern world. Humanity works with that holdover today as a kind of heirloom. Unless spiritual knowledge is attained, humanity will not be able to progress within material culture either. I'd like to clarify that last point by making an analogy.

Think about all the tunnels in Switzerland. Those tunnels can be built only on the basis of solid engineering. But that whole art of engineering depends entirely upon the labors of solitary thinkers who weren't imagining at all that their work would call forth anything like a tunnel someday. Without them, the tunnels couldn't exist. And lots of other things couldn't exist. All the electrical lighting that surrounds us everywhere in the world—well, that *usually* does!—simply couldn't exist if it weren't for the thoughts of those solitary thinkers. But what about those thoughts? People don't believe it today; they think that all those thoughts that end up realizing themselves in the practical world just grow from human brains, but that's not true! Those solitary thinkers were able to conceive the thoughts that they thought *only* because humanity has inherited an ancient spirituality. A thinker who takes no stimuli from the spiritual world cannot actually—not even intellectually—do work that is useful to material culture. People do not realize this today only because they fail to recognize the larger context. Our material culture would disappear, nothing new would be added to it, and our cultural inheritance would gradually disappear if spiritual progress didn't find its proper place within humanity as well. But genuine spiritual progress is possible only if spiritual knowledge makes itself ever more widely known again, and only if we finally put an end to a prejudice that prevails in this age of enlightenment: the prejudice that the only way to be clever is to deny the spirit and the soul.

So the important point is that the spiritual world can be investigated scientifically, that beyond the world we see with our eyes and grasp with our hands, there exists a spiritual world. In the modern world, more and more people have come to feel the need for knowledge of the spiritual world, but they've sought to satisfy that need through highly inappropriate means. And today when people hear that something such as our anthroposophical movement exists, and that it has built such a building, then many will reply: Oh, that's just something obscure, like the spiritualists; such folks are looking for the spirit in all kinds of mystical ways. – No, ladies and gentlemen! All those things you run into in the way of spiritualism and vague mysticism—our spiritual movement rejects all that in the strongest possible terms! We have nothing to do with any of that kind of obscure stuff, which claims to be spiritual research and even claims to be scientific. What we are dealing with here is something as clear and distinct as natural science itself. We are dealing with something as clear and distinct as the contributions that Copernicus, Galileo, and Giordano Bruno[59] made to modern science. To be sure, the objects of our research are things of the soul and of the spirit, but we make use of the same methodical ways of thinking that have led to such triumphs in the natural sciences.

You see, up to the time at the beginning of the modern age when Copernicus, Galileo, and Giordano Bruno set to work, people looked up and saw above them the vault of the heavens. They saw the blue vault, like a blue glass bell that had been placed over the earth, with stars painted upon it. And beyond that, people said, lay the eighth sphere. But everything changed after thinkers such as Copernicus, Galileo, and Giordano Bruno intervened. Then people finally understood: Up there, where we seem to see a blue firmament, actually there's nothing, even though our eyes had viewed it as a blue firmament up to then. It is because of the limitations of our vision that we see a blue vault; it's because we cannot see any further. But space is infinite. And what appears to be painted upon the vault of the heavens is actually what's spread out across infinite space. – But now, with regard to space, that has all been overcome. Today people are considered backward if they think that the firmament is a blue glass bell with stars attached to it. But many people consider it a sign of enlightenment to say: "Ah, we can know nothing about what it means to be human except that we are born of a father and a mother, and then we die. Anything beyond that simply cannot be known." Just as people of the Middle Ages said, "Up above us there's a limit, the blue firmament," so many people say the same thing today with regard to cognition: "There's a limit there; we can't see beyond birth and death." There is no more truth in the assertion that we can't see beyond birth and death than there is in the claim that it's impossible to see and think beyond the blue firmament. And just as today it would be taken as a sign of limited intellect if someone were to mistake the blue firmament for something solid, before very long it will be viewed as a sign of limited intellect if somebody says, "It's impossible to know anything beyond the limits of birth and death." As human beings, we bear within ourselves the eternal powers of our existence. And if we just cultivate these faculties latent within us as human beings, then, just as Giordano Bruno pointed the way beyond the firmament, we can find a way beyond birth and death. We can see beyond them in such a way that we can know: just as the stars are embedded within infinite space, our own human existence is embedded within infinite time. We are there before we are born, and we shall be there after we die.

Indeed, that is an article of faith for many people today. But in the future, it shall become a known fact. And a movement such as ours, a movement like anthroposophically oriented spiritual science, is meant to contribute to a process of maturation that would allow such things to be known rather than merely believed. And it's not by means of any kind of outer arrangements, not by way of physical experiments and so forth, that we attain such knowledge. No, we attain it by working upon ourselves, by awakening something within us that otherwise remains asleep, by becoming aware of the power of the eternal within us. At the moment when humanity summoned up the courage to think beyond the firmament, then we all had the great, good fortune to realize that space is infinite. And as soon as you gain the courage to extend your research beyond the seeming limits of birth and death, that will be the moment at which you come to know your own soul as something eternal.

Now, I have just sketched for you in a few words something that is actually a comprehensive science. Indeed, it is so comprehensive a science that all the other scientific disciplines can be fructified by this spiritual science. Only if enough people are able to take up this spiritual science will it become possible to solve certain riddles that weigh heavily upon human souls today. And it will be possible to find many things that people are seeking today—things people imagine can be sought by proceeding from the old presuppositions—it will be possible to find those things only by taking up spiritual science in the way that we understand it here at the Goetheanum.

I would like to draw your attention to one thing. It was a very long time ago now, more than a century and a half, when people came up with the theory that our entire solar system has arisen out of a primordial nebula. People thought that there was a primordial nebula that rotated, turned upon its axis. We call that the Kant-Laplace theory.[60] And then the planets became balls that had become separated from the Sun, and then those planets began to orbit the Sun, etc. And then, over the course of many, many epochs, there gradually arose—primarily upon our own planet, Earth—all the things people now consider the only possible objects of knowledge: plants, animals, human beings, etc. Yes, there have been a few thinkers who also have realized how completely foolish this worldview admired by so many really is. The great art historian Herman Grimm[61] had something good to say about this Kant-Laplace theory. He said: Today people imagine that they can assume on the basis of some kind of science—particularly *this* science—that such a primordial nebula once existed, and that as a result of this balling-up, all the things upon the Earth that we admire just arose on their own. And then they also say that after another immeasurably long series of epochs, everything on Earth will die, the Sun will burn out, etc. Herman Grimm gave us his opinion of all that: A carrion bone circled by a hungry dog is a more appetizing picture than this so-called scientific achievement. In the future, people will find it incomprehensible that such a figment of the scientific imagination could gain currency in our age, or indeed how anyone ever could have found it attractive.

All you need to do is just sit back and think about what it is people are really saying with such a theory. That's asking a lot because people who have been taught this vaunted "science" regard it as a superstition, as something retrograde, if anyone doesn't swear by the existence of this primordial nebula postulated by the Kant-Laplace theory. Now I know very well all the reasons given by the people who swear by this Kant-Laplace theory of the primordial nebula. And it's also easy for me to understand that when somebody talks like me, they label it a fantasy. Or they ascribe it to limited intelligence or even insanity. But you become capable of rendering a judgment regarding such matters by pursuing spiritual science as we understand it here. Then you arrive at the insight that the evolution of the cosmos is like our spiritual biography as human beings. We don't just arise out of matter at birth; what happens is that our spirit and soul bind themselves to matter at birth. And after death, we surface within the spiritual world as spiritual beings. In just the same way, what we recognize as the Earth today didn't arise out of some kind of primordial nebula: No, our planet, our Earth emerged from a spiritual condition, the Earth as something spiritual. That is what preceded everything earthly. Today people are pursuing research to determine how it is that mind—spirit—emerges from matter. But the truth is that everything material is descended from spirit. Spiritual science, as we understand and practice it here at the Goetheanum, delivers refined and clarified concepts such as these.

So now, the thing that people know as "matter" today—what is it actually? Once again, I'd like to explain it to you using an analogy. Let us imagine that a big basin is standing in front of you, and you see chunks of ice inside it. What you don't see is that water is in there also; let's assume that you can't see the water. Then you see chunks of ice. If you see only the chunks of ice, if you never had heard anything about all this but only saw the chunks of ice, then you never would know that ice is something that has arisen out of the water. You wouldn't know that ice is condensed water. Ice is just something that has arisen out of water, something that has arisen through the densification of water. That is our relationship to the material world as human beings. We look upon this material world and believe that it exists independently. The material world has arisen through densification, through a densification of the spirit, in the same way that ice has arisen through densification of water. As I indicated just now, the moment we discover within ourselves the forces that allow us to see the spirit, to perceive the spirit, we begin to see everything material as a densification of the spiritual. Everything ceases to exist independently. And everything that we have to recognize as the Earth, as the material earth, together with everything material upon it—all of that has emerged from a spirit-Earth, and it shall transform itself back into spirit-Earth. We come to know that materiality is only an intermediate state that stands between two spiritual states. What I am describing to you is more or less the result of research. What I cannot describe for you in a brief talk such as this is the underlying methodology, which is just as rigorous as the one employed in the observatory to investigate the outer, material stars, or the one employed in the clinic in order to gain knowledge concerning human anatomy. The methods we employ here at the Goetheanum are spiritual methods, but they lead to something within the human spirit and soul that is connected with the spirit and soul of the cosmos.

You see, when we become aware of our spiritual nature again, we gain a certain inner security. We create a certain inner center of gravity, shall we say. Today there are still many people who are rightly convinced that human souls go through the portal of death and then dwell within the spiritual world. But few people give much thought to the fact that when human beings are born into the world, they come from the spiritual world. What we receive from the material world is only a change of clothes[62] for the entity that emerges from the spiritual world, for the entity that descends from the spiritual world. And just as we have to say: What persists after death is a continuation of the physical life that we lived upon Earth—in the same way we can say: The life that we live here on Earth is a continuation of a spiritual life that we lived previously. This new perspective gives us the possibility of confronting our fellow human beings in a completely different way. We relate to others differently from the way we did when we believed that human beings arise directly out of the material world at birth. Just think what it means to look at a developing child from the moment it is born and to be able to say to oneself: "With each passing day, each passing week, the spirit that has descended from the spiritual world is working its way outward; the spirit is working its way through the material limbs." If that ever became a principle that genuinely informed education and teaching, then you would see what a powerful influence it could exert upon pedagogy, upon the art of education. This is one context in which spiritual science can already become entirely practical. Not long ago in a city in southern Germany, we found ourselves in a position to create something that is meant to become an art of education in the light of spiritual science. In Stuttgart, we founded the Waldorf School, an elementary school. On the one hand, this school intends to meet all the social demands that are now being raised, whereby each person shall be valued as an individual. And on the other hand, the school is meant to meet the need for an education oriented toward the future, one that proceeds from a real understanding of human nature. We will be educating children between the ages of six and fifteen, and at each age—in the child's seventh, ninth, eleventh, fifteenth year—we will be giving special consideration to the pedagogical techniques that are appropriate for that age. That is the only way we can develop all the faculties latent within human nature. Let me tell you just a bit about that. (Ah, now that we have light again, we'll try to get to our performance as quickly as possible!) It is these pedagogical insights that allow us to undertake certain practical initiatives already. And it gives me a great and deep satisfaction to be forming a college of teachers for this elementary school—a college of teachers that is developing a genuine art of education based on anthroposophy. An education that takes the whole of human nature into consideration, and not just the physical body. An education that provides for body, soul, and spirit.

So, you see, all the gifts that spiritual science can give to the human soul can give us another footing within the world that is completely different from the materialistic way of thinking. Humanity still needs to gain conviction in that regard. We are not just playing games with all kinds of pseudo-science. No, we are working sincerely and forthrightly to serve needs that have taken root in countless human souls today. It is just that people have not gained clarity yet about the longings within them. People are already striving instinctively for such a spiritual knowledge. Everything that this building represents outwardly wants to serve that spiritual knowledge. Every aspect of this building's artistic form is meant to show that what we have here is a new spiritual movement, something that should spread and be taken up by humanity if culture is to progress and not retreat, if culture is not to cling regressively to the things that have been handed down to us from the distant past.

So, what I wanted was to characterize for you in a few words the sincere and honest striving for a knowledge of the spirit that is our goal here. I wanted to characterize a bit for you the side of anthroposophy that many people still consider some kind of delusion. Please recall, ladies and gentlemen, that when the first railroad was built in Germany, from Fürth to Nuremberg, a committee of medical doctors were asked for their professional opinion as to whether such a railroad should be built. And the Doctor's Committee replied—this isn't some kind of a fairy tale, ladies and gentlemen, it's a fact, it really happened in 1837, less than a hundred years ago—the Committee replied that it shouldn't be built because it would ruin the nerves of the passengers, because the people riding the train would become extremely ill. And they recommended further that if there really were people who wanted to run that risk, then at least we should erect high, boarded walls so that when trains drove past, bystanders wouldn't suffer trauma to their brains. That is no fairy tale! You can look it up: that was an official document produced by a learnèd society. In the same way, you could ask numerous materialistically inclined people today whether our School of Spiritual Science should pursue the matters it pursues. And these learnèd people today would answer: It should *not* be pursued, because it could—I don't know what—make people crazy or something. And that judgment would be as well founded as the professional opinion rendered by the Bavarian Medical Committee in 1837, who believed that railroads would make people ill. If you listen to people who think like that, then you just can't get any further. People who reject the whole idea of such spiritual progress today belong in the same category as the people who said of Columbus, when they heard that he wanted to outfit his ships: "But that's crazy, to set out like that! Where does he expect to arrive by doing that?!" All he managed to do was to discover America, and if Columbus hadn't set sail, America wouldn't have been discovered. Imagine how different the world would look today! Sure, there are many people who say: What those people are doing is sheer madness. But a time will come when people will see that this "madness" was very necessary in order for humanity to develop further. Sure, there are very many people who say: "You can't eat and drink the spirit that's on offer there!" From a certain elementary perspective, they're right; but from a deeper perspective, they're wrong. Humanity's outer, material culture can only be managed properly if humanity has taken the right stance with regard to the spirit. But humanity can stand in the right relationship to the spirit only if we are really able to enter into the spirit. We don't just *talk* about the spirit here: we strive really to *know* it. It's not enough merely to declare that "spirit is in the world." Rather, spiritual methods should be understood to such a degree that one can say definitively: Our Earth has not arisen out of the kind of primordial nebula hypothesized by the Kant-Laplace theory; it arose out of a purely spiritual state, and it shall return to such a state again—and more along those lines.

You see, the demonstration of eurythmy that we would like to offer you today as a sample of the artistic work being pursued more generally here is something that can be offered only if we view in the light of spiritual knowledge many things that would otherwise be viewed only materially, with our external senses. As human beings we speak through our larynx and the other related organs—the tongue, palate, and so forth. In listening to our fellow human beings, we turn our attention to what is heard via our ears. But while we speak, there is a continuous movement—unseen, or latent at least—of the larynx and its associated organs. Even physics knows that there is movement within speech, for while I am speaking to you, the air in this auditorium is moving in specific forms. By employing those clairvoyant faculties through which we come to see spirit at work within nature and the human being, we can also come to know the spirit within which language is grounded. This same spirit can be applied to the movements of the whole human being, which is what we do in the art of eurythmy. And so it is that today you will see people moving upon the stage, but they won't be making movements that we just thought up. Oh, no! When you hear a poem being recited at the same time, when you simultaneously hear artistic speech, then the performers are executing with their whole bodies the same movements that they naturally make otherwise when they speak. The difference is that otherwise you listen to the language, to the sounds, to what is audible. But here you have a visible speech. The same movements that would otherwise be executed [by the speech organs] are rendered immediately visible here through the whole human being. That is why I like to describe it by saying that we get to know the whole of our human nature as a kind of larynx come alive, a speech that has become visible. Art is always what arises because certain mysteries of nature have been revealed. We named this School of Spiritual Science "the Goetheanum" after Goethe, who penned the beautiful saying: "As soon as nature has begun to unveil her open secret to us, we begin to feel an irresistible longing for her most worthy interpreter, art."[63]

And this is especially the case when we stand before the secrets of *human* nature itself! Oh yes, within human nature itself lurk infinitely many mysteries. If we summon forth the invisible ground of language through the movements of the arms and the movements of the human being as a whole, through the movements of ensembles, then the great miracle of human language is unveiled.[64] Especially in our time, people remain oblivious to the great miracle that is the ground of nature's existence. Anyone who learns what a miraculous organ this human larynx is, anyone who seeks to awaken what lives as a miracle preserved within the larynx and its associated organs, can well understand what Goethe was able to say so explicitly: "In that we human beings have been placed at the pinnacle of nature, we see ourselves as a whole nature unto ourselves, within which it is our task to raise up another peak. We climb upward towards that goal by permeating ourselves with all perfections and virtues—we summon all the discretion, order, harmony and meaning that we can, and eventually we rise up to the production of the work of art."[65]

And if we then turn ourselves into an instrument and reveal what can manifest itself for our own limbs, then mysteries of nature, mysteries of the spirit, mysteries of the soul manifest themselves in an especially profound way for our immediate human feeling.

The gymnastics that is practiced today in schools has been framed entirely for the physical body. Someday, eurythmy will also take the place of this gymnastics. Eurythmy shall become spiritualized gymnastics, a ensouled gymnastics. Children will perform movements in gymnastics not just because the anatomists, the physiologists, the scientists say it is healthy for the body. People will gradually begin to realize that health proceeds from the soul and spirit as well. They will learn how to make movements that are suffused with soul and spirit. And in the Waldorf School, where eurythmy alternates with gymnastics, we see how engaged the students are, how they feel enthusiastic about making movements that have not been conceived strictly in corporeal terms, but rather in terms of soul and spirit. Even in this one small aspect—and indeed it is only one very small part of what we intend with our spiritual science—there appears what we are striving for: namely, to permeate everything with spirit and with soul. And so I beg you please to view everything that is being offered here is a mere beginning. Eurythmy needs to be perfected. Receive it with forbearance as a beginning. But it is a starting point that already allows us to recognize the direction in which the road is leading, so to speak. It leads to a genuinely spiritual culture, one that can become fruitful in all realms of life.

And now, ladies and gentlemen, we would like to show you a little sample of this art of eurythmy. What you will see are movements, performed by the whole human body, that are usually not seen but only heard. You will see a visible speech, and you will hear how the music, as it resounds, expresses the same things that you see upon the stage through the movements of the performers.

You will hear the poems being recited, which express in their language what you will see expressed by the moving performers on the stage: a language that has become visible. You will recognize this language as something that can only be summoned forth out of the mysterious depths of our human nature itself, out of our essence as human beings. Hence I ask you please to make allowances for something that is meant to be only a beginning, just as our building is meant to be only a beginning. We believe that if people would only take an interest in such things, then our initiatives would gradually attract more and more people, so that what many people today view merely as something foolish, something fantastical, shall one day be viewed as something obvious and natural, as genuine art, as something that is an existential need. It shall be recognized as a spiritual light because people need it.

After a short intermission, we want to present two brief interludes from the scene "Midnight" in Goethe's *Faust*.[66] As you may know, the second part of *Faust* is Goethe's most mature poetic work. The manuscript for Part Two was finished right before Goethe's death and was published only after his death. It is fair to say that *Faust* actually occupied Goethe throughout his entire life. The opening scenes of Part One are perhaps some of his very earliest attempts to write literature—certainly they're among the first. And over the course of his long life, Goethe took up the drama *Faust* over and over again, completing it only at a very advanced age. Goethe's *Faust* is a prime example of what it means to live a life of continuous self-development that ascends ever-greater spiritual heights. We know that there are many people today who take their greatest pleasure only in the works of Goethe's youth, works that were written entirely out of the sphere of everyday life. Goethe then went through various stages, ever more mature levels of creativity. When Goethe was in Italy, and he was able to contemplate the great works of art there, he felt that for the first time he had been able to delve down into the essence of art, and it was then that he spoke the great, beautiful, and meaningful words: I have come to know the art of the Greeks and I believe that in creating their artworks, the Greeks were guided by the same laws that

Nature herself follows, laws that I now am trying to track down.[67] Goethe himself understood that his own view of art had ripened over time into something ever more sublime. It is strangely moving to see that even among Goethe's contemporaries there were people who pointed back to the early part of Goethe's *Faust*, after Goethe had already written *Iphigenia*, *Tasso*, and *The Natural Daughter*.[68] Goethe considered all of these to be much more significant works of art than Part One of *Faust*. There were many people who said: "Well, Goethe has gotten old; he can't climb to the same heights any longer." Those people had no idea what was really going on. It was *they* who couldn't climb to Goethe's heights! That's why they kept pointing back to the things Goethe had written in his youth. And we continue to witness the same sad spectacle long after Goethe's death, even in the case of great philosophers of art, people we can otherwise respect greatly. Take, for example, the so-called "Swabian Vischer," the one we call "V-Vischer" because his name is spelled with a "V."[69] He wrote thick volumes about the history of art, but even though he was an important art historian, he said again and again: "Part One is a real work of art, but Part Two of *Faust* is a shoddy patchwork that Goethe just cobbled together in his old age." It is important to point such things out because—you see, just as there are "big wheels,"[70] there are also "big Philistines," and even though I greatly respect "the Swabian Vischer," Friedrich Theodor Vischer, in some ways, with regard to *Faust* he was a "big Philistine." He even tried to write a *Faust: Part Three*! And it needs to be recalled that Goethe often nursed a bitter grudge against people who did not like his later works such as *Tasso*, *Iphigenia*, and *The Natural Daughter*, etc., and were always looking back to Part One of *Faust*. (Part Two of *Faust* was published only after his death; otherwise, it would have suffered the same fate.) Goethe mocked them by writing:

Da loben sie den Faust,
Und was noch sunsten
In meinen Schriften braust,
Zu ihren Gunsten;

Das alte Mick und Mack,
Das freut sie sehr;
Es meint das Lumpenpack,
Man wär's nicht mehr!

They say *Faust*'s pretty good!
And also find
Things in my other works
That suit their mind;

The same old stuff is what
They really like;
The lousy bums believe
I've gone on strike![71]

Goethe would have said the same thing if he had learned what "the Swabian Vischer" and other scholars thought about Part Two of his *Faust*. In Part One, Goethe sought to depict human earthly life: look how beautifully the scenes with Gretchen unfold within the earthly realm! But [even in Part One] there are exceptional scenes in which Goethe raises the world of human sensibility up into the suprasensory world. And then, in Part Two, we peer into the suprasensory world itself, into the world of suprasensory experiences. I have to say, it is difficult to perform this second part of *Faust* with the usual means; it is hard to represent the highest human experiences on stage. I've seen lots of different things: in the eighties of the previous century, I saw the performance of Part Two of *Faust* at the Vienna Burgtheater under the unique, charming direction of Wilbrandt;[72] and I've seen many other productions cross the stage, for example Devrient's[73] interpretation of *Faust* as a mystery drama, with music by Lassen,[74] and so forth. All very nice, but the bottom line is that the usual theatrical techniques one sees employed are simply insufficient here.

With the help of eurythmy, we have tried to represent various aspects of two episodes in which Faust has inner experiences. related to the faculties of the soul and the forces of destiny. Those are experiences that absolutely raise human life up into a higher sphere. And thus we really can say: Goethe really did intend to "occult"[75] many, many things into this life work. All of this has to be drawn out again using appropriate theatrical techniques. We cannot draw them out using conventional theatrical methods. So we're bringing eurythmy to our aid—the performances I described to you earlier, of which you have seen some samples.

And then we shall present the scene "Faust at Midnight,"[76] in which he experiences all the depths and horror of life. The lines Faust himself speaks have to be represented with conventional theatrical means. But when these four figures, the Four Gray Crones, and especially Care appear,[77] then eurythmy shall come to our aid, so that the profoundest impulses and experiences of the human soul, which Goethe "occulted into" his drama so beautifully, might be revealed from out of the depths of human nature itself.

INTRODUCTORY WORDS BEFORE A PERFORMANCE OF EURYTHMY

Dornach, December 14, 1919[78]

(In the presence of friends from England)

We would like to take this opportunity to present a sample of what we call the art of eurythmy. However, this art as we perform it now is only in its infancy. Everything that we strive to accomplish here in connection with this building, which in a certain sense represents our strivings, wants to connect with what I would like to call "Goetheanism." In the same way, this art of eurythmy also strives to connect with the Goethean worldview. While saying this, I beg you not to misunderstand me. Our intention is not to connect directly with the Goethe who died in 1832; rather, we view Goetheanism here like a seed that has been cast into the evolution of humanity and is able to bring forth a variety of blossoms and fruit. We do not speak here at all of the Goethe of 1832—we speak here of the Goethe of 1919, of a Goetheanism that has evolved.[79]

The attempt has been made to develop the art of eurythmy out of the profoundly meaningful sources from which Goethe drew his worldview and his artistic striving, in a way appropriate to the advances which the human spirit has made since then. I would like to say these introductory words are not an attempt to explain this art. Art has to explain itself, art has to reveal everything it contains in the aesthetic impression conveyed by immediate beholding. But I would like to speak about the *sources* of this new form that we call here the art of eurythmy.

This art of eurythmy uses the whole human being as its expressive means. It tries to bring to expression all the movement potentials latent within the human organism. Here on the stage before you, you will see moving human beings and groups of human beings taken hold of by movement. What is it that comes to expression through these people? It's also a language, an inaudible, silent language. But I'm not just employing a simile when I say that eurythmy ought to be a language; it expresses a reality. When people speak so that their spoken words become audible, then at the level of the soul two elements of the human being flow together. From the one side, I would like to say from the side of the head, there is an influx of the element of thought. Then this element of thought in speech meets what exerts its effects through the organs (one can also prove this today physiologically), the element of will. In each single word that we produce, a confluence of thought with the element of will is revealed. Now, when we listen to the spoken word, we at first direct our attention through the ear toward the musical sound, the speech sound and the connections between the speech sounds. But underlying what finds its way to us as speech sounds, as musical sound, as the relationships of musical sound and speech sound, in the singing element, in the musical element and in the verbal element, there are a fundamental set of movement potentials of the larynx and the associated speech organs, the tongue, gums, and so on. We do not pay attention to these movements; we just hear the sound. Through a certain beholding—in the Goethean sense we could speak of a sensory-suprasensory intuition—the person who is able to do this can perceive which movements, especially which movement potentials, which latent tendencies to move, lie at the basis of the spoken word. We have tried to capture these latent movement potentials of the larynx and the associated speech organs. The art of eurythmy has arisen out of the recognition, the observations of the movement that really occurs in human beings when they speak.

In the development of eurythmy, too, we have proceeded in the spirit of Goethe. I do not want to theorize, but I would just like briefly to describe an important principle of cognition and of art in Goethe. You know Goethe's theory of metamorphosis. It isn't sufficiently valued today, for if in its basics it were recognized, it would be the doorway to an important worldview that takes us straight into the world of life.

Goethe is of the view (if I may couch it in more colloquial language) that with everything living—for example, with the plant—a single part, a green leaf, is a simpler expression, a simpler revelation of the whole plant. And the whole plant is only the elaborated form of the single leaf. And what Goethe applies solely to form can be applied to the movements which come to expression in an organism. And it becomes especially meaningful if we apply this view artistically to summon forth from the human being the movement potentials latent within the whole person. Something very interesting comes of this. We can transpose onto the whole human being the movements that can be perceived as the basis of our speech by way of the aforementioned sensory-suprasensory intuition. In the same way that the whole plant morphologically, in its form, is a complicated elaboration of the single leaf, so we can allow our entire human being to move in such a way that we become a living larynx. Then our whole human constitution carries out what otherwise remains invisible, unnoticed, when we listen to speech.

You see that, on the one hand, we create an instrument for an art form. The whole human being becomes an instrument in this art of eurythmy. And because we can call forth the same movements from the whole human being which the organ of the larynx and the associated speech organs create, so the whole human being can become a visible expression of speech. If you think that the human being, as he appears before us in his constitution—indeed, you only have to behold him in order to recognize this—is a drawing together of everything which otherwise is spread out over the whole universe accessible to us, then you recognize that eurythmy uses as its expressive medium the most complicated of instruments. The instrument that contains the most secrets of the universe. If in this way you make the human constitution into a larynx, you really approach what Goethe characterizes so beautifully as his view of the relationship of human beings to nature and to art. He says that if the human being is the pinnacle of nature and feels himself as such, then he brings forth in himself a higher nature so that finally by gathering together discretion, order, harmony, and meaning, he raises himself up to produce works of art.[80] And we especially raise ourselves up to produce a work of art especially when we use the human constitution itself as the expressive instrument.

But, at the same time, something else is attained. The essence of the artistic experience lies in the fact that we immerse ourselves in the work of art, silencing the faculty of understanding, everything intellectual, and everything that lives only in concepts and ideas. The more art contains ideas and concepts, the less it is art. When we immerse our whole being in the revelation of the secrets of nature, avoiding everything intellectual and conceptual, then by excluding ideas, we approach the weaving and power of nature's secrets. Then this perceiving, without idea and concept, this immersing oneself in things is precisely the artistic experience. And this creating within such secrets of the universe—which cannot be laid hold of conceptually but only by excluding the conceptual and what is of the nature of ideas through the immersion of the whole human being into the secrets of the universe—is to the highest degree actually attainable in eurythmy. Now, I have told you that in ordinary speech two elements flow together, the element of thought and the element of will. By transposing the latent movement potentials of the larynx and the associated speech organs onto the whole human being, creating a silent language through this whole human being, you immediately exclude the element of thought and the element of will which are rooted in the whole human being. This is expressed through the movements that you see on the stage.

And so, on the one hand, you will see in the separate presentations something like the whole human being as a moving larynx. You will see groups of people; you will also see movements of individuals in space and relationships in movement among the individual members of the ensembles. When the art of eurythmy is formed as just described, it becomes quite obvious that we want to express what flows through our words as warmth of soul, enthusiasm, desire and suffering, joy and pain, ennoblement, and so on. Everything flows and weaves, as it were, through the element of speech more from the heart, is expressed through the movements of individuals in space and through the movements of ensembles, through the relationships of the ensembles to each other; whereas the actual element of speech, what lies in the speech sounds and their sequences, is expressed through the whole human being by moving the limbs. In this way, however, what is attempted here as eurythmy differs from all the related arts. We absolutely do not want to enter into competition with these related arts, the various kinds of dance. We know quite well that in their way they are obviously more highly perfected than eurythmy, which is only at the beginnings of its endeavors. But eurythmy is also something completely different. The other arts convey a relationship between the gestures of movement and the inner life that one might describe as fleeting. But everything that can be expressed through pantomime, in mime, through spontaneous gestures, is not striven for in our eurythmy. Just as speaking itself is thoroughly lawful, and just as the musical element proceeds according to laws, so too there exists a strict inner lawfulness in that which is striven for eurythmically. If nevertheless something of pantomime, of mime, seeps through, this is something unfinished and will be stripped away later when the art of eurythmy is perfected further. Hence there's nothing arbitrary about it.

If two people or two ensembles were to present in different places the same piece in eurythmy, the individual interpretations would play no greater role than if two pianists were to present the same Beethoven sonata, each according to his individual interpretation. Everything arbitrary is excluded. It is a lawful, silent speech.

Therefore, today, when understandably not everybody can follow the eurythmic element as such, this eurythmy can on the one hand be accompanied by music, which ultimately is the expression of the same thing, but it can also be accompanied by recitation. And precisely with recitation, by placing it alongside eurythmy, it is shown how the one art belongs to the other art. For you cannot recite as people today love to recite. Today, when people recite, it is especially the inartistic element of poetry that is preferred. Today much effort is taken that primarily the prose content is expressed through the recitation. And people love it too. This is something inartistic. You feel just how inartistic this approach is when you recall firstly how certain kinds of primitive recitation held sway in primitive cultures. You could see—those who are now older could still experience this in the countryside—when the balladeers traveled about, how they accompanied their recitation with gestures. These, however, were very natural gestures, not what is called "natural" today, but actually something similar to our eurythmical gestures. They frequently accompanied what they presented in recitation with their whole bodies. And ultimately the real poetry was basically founded not on the prose content as the main thing but on the rhythms, the formulas, the form elements, the meter, the laws in the sequence of what was heard.

In writing the most significant of his poems, Schiller did not have the literal content in his soul, but rather something vaguely melodic, and to this vague melody, still without any trace of literalness, he then added the prosaic content. Everywhere one should feel the formative element that is the basis of each real poem. Most things that are called poetry today are not poems. So much is composed today but actually ninety-nine percent of it is superfluous. But one will not be able to accompany eurythmy with the art of recitation which is so beloved today, which pays attention especially to the prose content of the word. Thus we try here also in the art of recitation to return to the genuinely artistic element.

Goethe himself still rehearsed his verse drama *Iphigenia* with his actors, baton in hand like a conductor. He paid attention to what lies at the basis as the real artistic form, that through which the real artistic element comes to expression—not the prose content, not the literal content of the words. And so one can especially express through the art of eurythmy, through the element of will, that which otherwise is expressed in poetry through the word. You will hear poems recited; you will see these poems in the silent language of eurythmy performed on the stage.

I think that the justification for eurythmy is shown especially with the poems by Goethe. We shall perform for you today, for example, eurythmic presentations of Goethe's cloud poems.[81] Goethe applied his view of metamorphosis to the changing formations of stratus, cumulus, cirrus, and nimbus clouds, externalizing it, but thereby also translating it into the artistic realm. In wonderful verses, Goethe shows how these cloud formations metamorphose into each other, something that came to him after reading the cloud observer Howard.[82] He wrote a very beautiful poem to commemorate Howard, which we likewise will present for you today in eurythmy. But especially in such poems by Goethe, in which the forms of the poems really depend on the shaping principles within nature herself, reflecting nature's effervescence and undulations in the rhythms and shaping of the speech, the eurythmy forms can follow the lead of the poems. And so I believe it is precisely these cloud poems by Goethe that can express beautifully how fully adequate eurythmic expression can be for what is also expressed poetically.

Now there is a poem by Goethe in which Goethe himself expressed his whole way of thinking about metamorphosis, his feeling for metamorphosis, called "The Metamorphosis of Plants." The whole poem lives in the presentation of ways of looking at forms. From line to line we actually feel that we may not cling to the abstract idea but that we have to be obedient with our whole souls to the forms which undulate and weave in the poet's imagination. And that's why the eurythmic presentation of precisely this poem on the metamorphosis of plants by Goethe can be captured so fully by eurythmy. So for today's performance, we have tried to recast this poem into eurythmic form. Precisely where the poem itself becomes like a direct imprint, created through the soul, of the secrets holding sway in nature, there is revealed, on the one hand, the way in which human feeling itself becomes artistic, and on the other hand, the possibility of representing the artistic feeling as it can be brought when the whole human being—as I've indicated—is used as what we can call an instrument of music and speech. So we certainly penetrate deeply into nature's secrets when we explore the secrets in this language of form that we are now endeavoring to reveal in eurythmy.

Now I entreat you to look on everything that we are able to present today is a sample of our eurythmic art, as a beginning—perhaps even as an attempt at a beginning. And in connection with what we are already able to do, we ourselves are our own keenest critics. However, we are also convinced that what lives in this attempt at a new art, either brought through ourselves or probably through others to further development—and very many possibilities of development lie within it—that this art of eurythmy as a fully justified art form will one day certainly be able to take its place alongside the other fully recognized art forms. As I said, we regard very modestly what we are able to offer, and I beg you also to receive kindly what we shall present to you as the beginning of a new art form.

[Untitled]

Dornach, January 17, 1920[83]

Please allow me to introduce our eurythmy program with a few words. I certainly don't want to "explain" the art forms we are attempting here; I only want to point to the sources of this new art.

As a matter of fact, eurythmy has been drawn forth from artistic sources that are quite different from those of certain neighboring arts with which it could perhaps be easily confused. Eurythmy is a kind of silent speech. It is definitely not a system of haphazard gestures, nor does it have anything to do with ordinary pantomime or the art of dance. It is opening up a fresh source for art through the fact that it uses the human body as the medium for its expression—that is, our human constitution with its inner inclinations to movement. The idea that underlies our endeavor comes altogether from what I would like to call Goetheanism, from Goethe's conception of art and his artistic perception. In this regard, however, it will be necessary to accept various laws and facts that few people are ready to acknowledge yet today.

For instance, dear friends, everything connected with the human vocal organs (the larynx and the other speech organs) is in a remarkable way a miniature image of the entire structure of the human organism. In the system of the larynx, we find a microcosm, formed of cartilage, of the whole of our human organism. But the amazing thing about it is that the organs of the larynx do not continue inward and become muscular, as do the other organs of movement: instead, what rises out of the larynx as an impulse for movement goes out immediately into the surrounding air and sends forth tone or speech. Anyone who has the faculty of sensory-suprasensory intuition (to use Goethe's expression) can study the movements the human larynx makes in order to send forth what becomes our speech and song. These movements are completely unnoticed by us while we are listening to speech or song, but whoever does observe them can then transfer them to the entire human being.

Sensory-suprasensory intuition reveals that this possibility of transference has a certain relation to the fact that an animal's vocal sounds reveal the character of its connection to surrounding nature and also to its own form. Whoever has intuitive perception will have no difficulty recognizing in the roar of a beast of prey a certain imitation of its form and, more particularly, of the movements coming from its muscular system. Similarly, he will recognize in a bird's song a wonderful expression of the bird's movement on the waves of the air and will observe that certain birds pour forth their particular pattern of song with certain definite accompanying movements.

To study such things carefully brings us to the moment when we are able to translate what normally remains invisible—the movements and inclinations to movement of the larynx and its adjacent organs—into visible movements of the entire human body. We then have brought about a kind of silent speech of which the instrument is the entire human being.

This, then, is what you will now see, with individual eurythmists making gestures as they move their arms, or groups of eurythmists moving in space in definite relations to one another. In all that you see, there will be as little personal slant as you would find in a succession of tones forming a melody, or a structure of tones forming a chord. Eurythmy is in very truth a kind of music that is carried through space by physical movements, and when two eurythmists, or two ensembles, present the same eurythmy piece, there is no more personal aspect in the two presentations than when two pianists play the same sonata with their individual interpretations. Thus, any indulgence in play of gestures is here out of the question. Whatever personal expression you may see is due solely to the imperfection that still clings to our eurythmic art.

Human beings, particularly as they speak, are really an expression of the entire universe. The fact, therefore, that here the entire human being becomes the medium for an art—usually, as you know, it is some musical instrument or other, but here it is the whole human being in movement—this fact fulfills what Goethe said so beautifully about human nature and human artistic activity:

> In that we human beings have been placed at the pinnacle of nature, we see ourselves as a whole nature unto ourselves, within which it is our task to raise up another peak. We climb upward towards that goal by permeating ourselves with all perfections and virtues—we summon all the discretion, order, harmony, and meaning that we can, and eventually we rise up to the production of the work of art.[84]

It is significant that we rise up to this height when we use our own organism as the means for our artistic expression.

Although eurythmy is still in its infancy, we believe that we have been able to achieve the beginning of a most important new art form. What is being attempted here now will be subject to constant further development.

You will see this silent speech of eurythmy accompanied sometimes by music, sometimes by recitation. For what language expresses through the art of poetry can also be expressed by eurythmy in a completely parallel fashion. In eurythmy, the movements meant for the air when the larynx makes them are in eurythmy given over to the muscles and, due to the fact that the entire human organism has now become the instrument for the movement, these movements that normally happen in the larynx at tremendous speed are now made in eurythmy comparatively slowly.

In the recitation, too, you will find a rather different style from what is customary at the present time. Eurythmy wants to bring out poetry's truly artistic content. It is good to remember how Goethe rehearsed his *Iphigenia* and his other verse plays with the actors, holding a baton in his hand. Today people believe—wrongly!—that the essential task in recitation is to accentuate the prose content. In Goethe's time the more artistic natures—Schiller, Herder,[85] and others—all knew that beat, rhythm (in other words, the style underlying a poet's structuring of his language) is the real element in poetry, and that this must be our primary concern in recitation.

So we try here in our art of recitation to practice something I would like to call an invisible eurythmy—that is, to handle our speech in such a way that what we do with our sounds and words parallels what you see the eurythmy doing on the stage.

You can see, I'm sure, that in our work here it is especially the eurythmy that requires a return to certain fundamentals of art. These are the very fundamentals that are practically ignored in artistic circles today. Often today people who consider themselves to be exceedingly artistic are actually far from it, for the reason that they are not laying the elements of true artistic style at the foundation of their work—elements of space, time, movement, for instance—but rather bringing into the foreground, even in poetry, whatever constitutes a prose content. People get up to recite as if they wanted to impart a bit of prose information. They completely ignore the inner pulse of the poem.

So we believe that precisely through such performances as these, attention can be drawn in our time to true art.

In conclusion, dear friends, I would ask you to accept our program with good will. I feel I must say once more that eurythmy is in the first stages of its development. We are convinced that it will be carried forward by us and by others from this simple beginning to ever greater perfection. It contains many varied possibilities for development, and it will eventually take its place as a fully recognized art alongside the older arts

Impressions of Nature

[Dornach] On the Programs of January 17 and 18, 1920[86]

[abridged]

Today we shall attempt to show you a series of poems that are particularly well-suited to this kind of eurythmic presentation because to some degree their authors already felt the inner eurythmy that is within them. Or because, as is the case for example with Goethe's "The Metamorphosis of Plants," they have been fashioned in a way that is true to nature, so that the eurythmy seems to arise all by itself. That is the extraordinary thing: in the case of bad poems, it is hard to accompany them with eurythmy, but in the case of poems that have been felt in a genuinely artistic way right from the beginning (a sense that has nearly disappeared in our age), we find that they are easily accompanied by eurythmy—especially when they are what I want to call "impressions of nature," which presupposes a deep empathy between the human soul and nature in the process of composition.

The reason why transposing the otherwise unconscious movements performed by the larynx and other speech organs is so interesting is because for an observer of both the sensory and the suprasensory aspects, something important becomes clear. It becomes clear in a certain sense how the relationship of a creature to its environment and to its own bodily form is revealed in the sounds, in the voice[87] of that creature. Anyone who has attained a degree of intuitive apprehension will have no trouble hearing in the howling of predators a certain imitation of their outer form and especially of their movement as it arises right out of their musculature. And likewise someone who possessed the appropriate degree of sensory-suprasensory intuition would be able to see how the song of birds, the modulation in the songs of birds is a wonderful expression of the movements of the birds themselves upon the undulating air. On the other hand, one can observe how certain species of birds express the modulations of their tones, the shaping of their songs, using accompanying movements.

If you study such things carefully, you will come to see that it is possible to transpose what otherwise remains invisible in the capacities for movement of the larynx and other speech organs into the human body as a whole; we really can call forth a kind of silent speech in that way. Only the organ for this silent speech is the whole human being.

Those esteemed members of our audience who have attended our performances many times will be convinced that we have made quite a bit of progress over the last few weeks, especially in making sentence structures visible within specific forms, artistic structures, the structures of rhythm, of rhyme and so forth, in the whole way in which the stanzas are put together.

We are working very hard to make progress month by month. But everything is still very much at a beginning stage.

❁

THE PEDAGOGICAL AND CURATIVE SIGNIFICANCE OF EURYTHMY

Dornach, March 21, 1920,

Presented to physicians, with presentations by children[88]

For those of you who are present today who were not here earlier, I would like to begin briefly with only a few words. (We don't want to go on so long that—God forbid!—the children who are helping us out today start to become impatient!) I would like you to know that what we call the art of eurythmy in no way consists of arbitrarily invented gestures. No, they have been called forth from the capacities for movement within the human larynx and the other speech organs, all of the organs that are otherwise active in the act of speaking. The result is simply that latent tendencies in the larynx and other speech organs are transposed into the rest of the human organism. You could say in a sense that the whole human being becomes larynx in this silent speech of eurythmy, which is accompanied by recitation or music. The whole human being becomes a larynx in what you see performed before you upon the stage. Groups of performers likewise become larynx. That is why it is somewhat harder to orient yourself in eurythmy: it's because nothing arbitrary is there; you are not seeing configurations of impromptu gestures, but rather what underlies spoken language in the way of unnoticed movements. It is precisely those movements that have been represented and translated into a visible language. That is all I want to mention for our friends who haven't seen it before by way of justifying eurythmy, this approach to art that we are cultivating here.

Let me add also that our esteemed physicians will see hardly any of what I characterized yesterday as the therapeutic side of our art of eurythmy. Only a few things could be performed that were already prepared when we arrived. Frau Dr. Steiner[89] was able to take up only a few of the things that had been rehearsed. In the few days since we have returned from Stuttgart, it was hardly possible to shape an objective program. So I would beg those who wish to know more about this art of eurythmy please to be patient a while longer. The next time we have a performance of eurythmy, very soon, I'll explain the whole nature of eurythmy to you in a somewhat more complete introduction. For today, I would ask you please to make do with the little that we can offer you given the short period of time since we returned from Stuttgart. So that is all I would like to say about the performance today.

In her capacity as the children's eurythmy teacher, Fräulein Hollenbach took on the task of teaching the children choral singing while hopping the tones. We begin with a song called "Joviality" by Löwenstein, with music by Hiller. It was she who taught the children the movements in eurythmy and how to hop the tones. What you are seeing is a gymnastics that has been suffused with soul through and through, something that can take its place as a complement to regular gymnastics. And let me stress that the art of eurythmy in no way diminishes regular gymnastics. But precisely because it is a way of bringing to children movements that are imbued with soul, it will become clear that this art of eurythmy will also have a significant role to play as therapy within pedagogy. If gymnastics is a strengthening of the physical body, less so of our whole human nature, then it is eurythmy in particular that will be able to strengthen initiative in the will. Hence, for that reason, regular gymnastics is supplemented with children playing through movements imbued with soul, which is a goal of eurythmy.

❀

On Goethe's Prose Hymn "Nature"

Dornach, April 17, 1920, before the intermission[90]

[abridged]

Now there will be a short pause and after that we will perform for you, among other things, Goethe's "Hymn to Nature."[91] Goethe's prose hymn is a kind of foreshadowing of his worldview. Goethe conceived it, one might say, at the beginning of the 1880s—I attempted to depict the whole history of its composition in volume 7 of the publications of the Goethe Society—and he did not write it down immediately. Rather, he mulled it over in his soul and discussed the thoughts with the Swiss writer Tobler,[92] who was staying in Weimar at that time. Goethe spoke freely to Tobler, reciting the hymn, and it exists in Tobler's handwriting also in the so-called *Tiefurt Journal*, which is still extant. Tobler then wrote it down immediately after the conversation. In my earlier publication, I tried to prove that this had been the history of its genesis. As I said, you will find an essay on this in volume 7 of the publications of the Goethe Society. And having researched the history of its composition, nothing could persuade me otherwise, and especially not what was published here recently.[93] Goethe himself recognized that the hymn had been the starting point when, later on, he elaborated the thoughts in the hymn in his *Metamorphosis [of Plants]*, etc. He called everything that came later in his worldview a kind of comparative, of which the hymn was the positive.[94] Hence we can say: within this prose hymn is contained everything which we then encounter in a metamorphosed form, intensified to the highest degree, as in Goethe's worldview.

And then, in the second part of the program, we will present, in addition to Goethe's prose hymn, other pieces by Goethe, including some that reveal the magnificent humor of Goethe's worldview in which everything—including everything of a philosophical nature—has really been experienced in the depths of the soul.

Three Aspects of Eurythmy

Dornach, May 15, 1920[95]

Ladies and gentlemen, permit us to offer you another sample of the art of eurythmy today. Through this art we want to contribute something to the spiritual evolution of humanity, something that can be viewed from three different perspectives: first, from a purely artistic point of view; second, from a pedagogical perspective; and third, from a curative point of view.

As an art, eurythmy represents a kind of silent, visible speech. Although it takes the form of gestures and movements, either in groups or individually, you should not confuse it with mime or pantomime or with traditional dance. Eurythmy uses the entire human being as its language; this visible, silent speech is the result of having studied the laws of audible speech.

The spoken word is indeed a way of expressing what dwells within human nature itself. Schiller got it exactly right when he was led by a significant intuition to write: "If the soul should *speak*, then—alas!—it is no longer the *soul* that is speaking."[96] In a certain sense, that's true. Language bears the human soul out into the external world, or at least it should, but it is also the means of communicating between one person and another, and hence it becomes something conventional. And language is also the bearer of the thoughts people use to make themselves understood. In a certain sense, language is a social phenomenon. The more language is made to serve as a means of communication and of expressing thoughts, the less it can serve as a means of artistic expression. For art must arise out of the wholeness of our human nature.

Language has two sides. The first is the social side. We must bow to the social world when speaking. Only in that way does language retain something that is intimately, inwardly connected with the entirety of our human nature. Language is not learned by adults; children learn it from their dreams, as it were. They learn it during that time when they want to adapt their entire being to their surroundings. This natural adaptation protects language from being used just as a means of communication.

When a poet—that is, an artist with words—wants to express something by employing everything that hovers behind language, he needs something besides. A poet needs pictures and, above all, musicality. True poetry—that is, the artistic aspect of a poem—isn't found at all in the literal content of the words; rather, it is the way the content is formed that is essential. More than anywhere else, in poetry we need to take into account what Goethe said so beautifully in *Faust*: "Consider the what, but even more so, the how."[97] The way the poet shapes the poem is what is most important in poetry.

This becomes much clearer when you want to express yourself in a thoroughly artistic way. Instead of reaching for an expression that is too strongly permeated by thoughts, you engage the whole of your inner nature. For this reason, we have used both sensory and suprasensory observation[98] to study the movement potentials that are latent within the human larynx, tongue, and other organs of speech when people reveal themselves through voiced speech. We studied the movements that are transformed into sounds, into trembling movements, into oscillating movements in the air through normal speaking. We transferred those movements to other human organs, particularly those that are most comparable to the primary organs of movement within the organs of speech: the arms and hands.

When people first see eurythmy, they are often surprised that the performers use their hands and arms more than their other limbs. You can see this as an obvious outcome if you consider that even in everyday speech, if someone wants to express more than simple conventions; if someone wants to express his or her own individuality or perception or feelings through speech, that person finds it necessary to transfer expressive movements to these more freely mobile organs. Of course eurythmy takes the whole person into account, not just the arms and hands. Above all, eurythmy uses the expressiveness of movements in space, especially by ensembles, but also by individuals. The most important thing to remember is that those movements, whether they are done by individuals or groups, are not at all arbitrary. They are movements along lines that are the same underlying foundation of what we express through voiced speech, but now transposed onto the whole person.

That is why I need to emphasize again and again that what we see on stage is essentially a kind of larynx, represented through the whole person. That allows us to summon forth rhythm, meter, the musical dimensions, and the pictorial dimensions as well—that is, the actual poetic element, where poetry is art. We can summon that up either through solos or through ensembles.

Eurythmy's mute, visible speech is also accompanied by music or recitation. Since music and speech are just other forms of expression for what lives in the human soul—other than eurythmy—we need to use that good old-fashioned form of recitation that Goethe had in mind when he was working with the actors. Like a choirmaster, he kept a conductor's baton in his hand so that they would not only understand the content of the words but also learn their iambic meter. In our case, we need to avoid precisely the things that our inartistic age sees as important in recitation—namely, the emphasis upon the literal content of the words. We need to go back to what was genuinely artistic in more primitive recitations. That is rarely seen today, especially if you live in a city. However, much of it is still alive in people my age, who can remember the traveling speakers of their childhood who recited their street ballads. They drew pictures on a blackboard and then spoke the text. They never spoke without tapping the measures of the verses with their feet and when a particularly dramatic passage was reached, they marched up and down, in this way indicating that it was not so much the content of the verses that mattered to them but their pulse beat, the dynamic of the poem.

You will see that we therefore try, whenever we can, to foreground this genuine artistic element. Even when we try to represent through eurythmy the humorous, grotesque, or comical aspects of poetic language, we do not aim at transmitting the literal content by means of gestures or miming. Using forms made visible only in space—and not in time—we render what the poet, the artist, has *made* of that content.

Those are a few of the indications I want to give you with regard to the artistic element of eurythmy. Just because the eurythmist herself becomes the instrument—neither the violin nor the piano, neither colors nor forms and so forth—by making use of the forces that drive the cosmos, eurythmy becomes an eminently suitable means of giving form to what is latent within human beings themselves as a microcosmic expression of those same powers.

The second aspect of eurythmy is its educational side. I'm convinced that mere gymnastics, which came into being in materialistic times, is limited too much to the laws of anatomy and physiology. In times to come, when people will view these matters more objectively, it will be understood that although gymnastics makes you stronger in a certain way, it does not strengthen your ability to develop initiative in the soul and the will. When we began employing it in education, the art of eurythmy also became a kind of ensouled gymnastics and a way of playing through soul-imbued movements. When you watch our modest beginnings today, you will recognize that every movement performed by the children is carried by an inner mood of soul. Through eurythmy, something I would like to call initiative in the life of the souls and wills of growing children is being developed over and above any training of their bodies. It is this nurturing of initiative that is needed so much today in the life of the growing human being, and that gymnastics alone cannot cultivate. It is important for people to recognize how we are attempting to carry this out in the curriculum of the Stuttgart Waldorf School.

Before showing you this eurythmy demonstration, which will be performed by local children, I have to mention that these children received eurythmy training outside of school hours, and that we feel this is not right at all. One of the aims of Waldorf education—which grows out of our work here in Dornach and has been put into practice in the Stuttgart Waldorf School—is that children should not be overburdened. We try not to impinge upon their free time by giving them any extra-curricular lessons.

That is why it is so important for the contribution eurythmy can make to the children's education as a whole to be recognized and valued highly enough that this subject will become part of the established school curriculum. That would make it possible for the pupils to receive everything that promotes the normal development of body, soul, and spirit in just those ways that eurythmy has helped us to understand it.

The third aspect concerns the hygienic effect of eurythmy. As human beings we're a microcosm, and all illness is fundamentally caused by our being torn out of the great harmony of the cosmos. I would like to describe illness metaphorically. As soon as a finger is cut off from the rest of the human organism, it ceases to be a finger, for it will wither away. The finger fulfills its proper function only as a part of the entire human organism. In a similar way, human beings have been able to develop their true inner being only in conjunction with the entire world. Through what is taking place within us all the time, we are directly linked with the whole world. You only need to consider the most superficial things to recognize how dependent we are upon the whole world, how we are by no means enclosed within our skins. Just think: the very air which is moving through your body was part of the outside world a moment ago. Yet, after having been inhaled, it became part of your organism. The air which is in you now will be exhaled and from that moment on, it will again form part of the external world. That is how we are living within our surroundings, not just as far as the air is concerned but also with regard to the forces permeating the entire cosmos.

We can derive the causes of illness by observing the ways in which someone cultivates and employs language. If that is not in keeping with the spirit of our times or our full human nature, we fail to contribute to the harmony that must prevail between human beings and the world as a whole. But just because all movement in eurythmy naturally comes forth out of the entire human organism, just as the movements of the larynx and its associated organs do for normal speech, everything done in eurythmy can bring the human being into harmony with the world, with the entire macrocosmos.

We can certainly say that what a person, even as a child, can gain from the movements of eurythmy has a healing element. Of course, it has to be performed properly and not clumsily. This is something we can certainly consider part of the hygiene of body, soul, and spirit.

These are, then, the three perspectives from which we should see eurythmy, and from which we have situated it within our spiritual movement.

Therapeutic Eurythmy[99]

Dornach, October 4, 1920[100]

Excerpt from a Q&A session during the first anthroposophical university course[101]

There is a question regarding the causes of speech impediments (stuttering) and their treatment.

Gradually people will come to see that eurythmy can provide significant therapy to combat such ailments of the physical body. Eurythmy can be pursued in two different directions. One is the side of eurythmy to which I am always drawing attention in the introductions I give before the performances. In those introductions I try to show how the movement potentials latent within our present speech organs become conscious through sensory-suprasensory intuition, and how those are then transposed onto the human body as a whole. But the converse has no little meaning. For, you see, in linguistic development, which was covered very well for you in today's lecture by Dr. Treichler,[102] there is no doubt whatsoever that a kind of *Ur*-eurythmy,[103] which developing human beings perform, plays a very significant role. Things do not have the sound within them in the sense of the "bim-bam theory,"[104] but because all things are interrelated, there is a relationship between this microcosm, the human constitution, and the macrocosm as a whole. It is fundamentally the case that all outer occurrences can also be imitated through gestures in movement. Hence there exists within us at all times a fundamental, latent tendency to imitate outer phenomena with our own organism. Only we don't carry out those movements with our *physical* bodies but with our *etheric* bodies. Our etheric bodies continually perform eurythmy. The bodies of primordial human beings were much more mobile than ours today. As you know, one artifact of this evolution from mobility toward rest is that in certain circles today it is viewed as a sign of cultivation if one behaves as phlegmatically as possible while speaking, if one makes as few gestures as possible while speaking. Certain speakers have come to see it as the height of respectability always to have their hands in their pockets, so that they don't make any gestures with their arms. It has come to be viewed as an expression of eloquence when people just stand there like clods. But that is a caricature of the general evolution from mobility to rest, and we have to determine[105] that one foundational principle of human evolution is that there was a transition during primordial times from a gestural language, a kind of eurythmy, to a spoken language. What came to rest within the human organism became localized within the organs of speech; indeed, that was what actually called forth the organs of speech in the first place. Just as the eye was formed by the light,[106] the speech organs are formed by a language that was initially mute. And if one understands all these connections, then one knows how to introduce eurythmy into pedagogy correctly as a way to counteract the forces creating impediments. Up until now, eurythmy has been developed more fully in its artistic and pedagogical aspects, but if we had just a bit more leisure, it would be a very engaging task to extend eurythmy further in the direction of healing, and to create a therapeutic eurythmy. And then we would want to look particularly at the kinds of therapeutic demands that were just brought up. I don't know whether this answer is comprehensive enough, but I wanted to say at least a few words along these lines in response.

There is a question about the relationship between the movements of eurythmy and the etheric body. Does spiritual-scientific research show that the etheric body has the same form as the physical body?

Let's have no misunderstanding about this: eurythmy allows us to perform movements in the physical body and through the physical body that are otherwise performed solely by the etheric body today. [But] just because eurythmists perform with their physical bodies the movements of the etheric body they have studied, it does not follow that when they have some kind of horrible thought, for example, they don't then perform this horrible thought with their etheric bodies. They can perform the most beautiful movements with their physical bodies, but then under certain circumstances, following their *emotions*, their etheric bodies can dance along in a way that is quite caricatured. Let me add just the following.

It is generally the case that when you look at a resting human being, his or her etheric body is at rest, and somewhat larger than the physical body, correct? But that is only because—drawn schematically—the physical body has a "spiritualizing"[107] effect on all sides from the etheric body.[108] If it were not retained in its form by the physical body, if it were not captivated[109] by the physical body, the etheric body would be a completely mobile entity. In itself, the etheric body is fully capable of moving in all directions. Moreover, in the waking state it is subject to the continual influence of the mobile astral body, which follows the soul in every way. So that the etheric body in itself is something completely mobile. As a painter, for example, when you want to paint something etheric, you encounter a great difficulty: it's like trying to paint lightning. You have to translate motion into rest. And so in the moment when you leave the physical world, at that moment the concept also gains distance, and all these things that actually refer only to static space cease to exist, and a qualitatively different thinking begins. A thinking begins that can actually be characterized only by saying: It stands in the same relationship to the everyday thinking that is framed for spatial objects as a vacuum effect stands to positive pressure. Instead of touching objects, you get sucked into them, as it were. That is how it stands with the relationship between the etheric body and the physical body

WRITING WITH IMAGES – WRITING – EURYTHMY

Dornach, October 30, 1920[110]

[abridged]

What you will see on the stage is a moving performer, or you might also see moving ensembles. The movements they are performing are fundamentally different from gestures, or mime, or any kind of dance. No, what you will see is really visible speech, a *real* language, one that's gained not by interpretation of the word or anything like that. Rather, it's based on a careful study of the nature of speech sounds themselves.

In spoken language, we have to do with movements that the larynx and other speech organs want to perform but that do not come out as such. What happens instead is that they are arrested *in statu nascendi*,[111] so that they metamorphose themselves into the movement of the air that mediates the tone.

By employing sensory-suprasensory intuition—that's a Goethean term—in a careful study, we actually can form a concept of the ways in which the larynx and other speech organs intend to move. We can intuit the qualities of that inner movement at its moment of genesis, before it transforms itself into sound. And then, by moving an individual organ or a group of organs within our larger human organism, we can use the human body as a whole to call forth a visible language. So that the whole human body, and especially the arms, move the same way the speech organs want to move when speaking but do not because they are restrained by the will so that sounds arise out of that latency.

Now we can say that, in transforming the whole human body into a larynx, or ensembles into a single, great organ of speech, we become able to open up genuinely artistic sources and an artistic language of forms. This is also true with regard to what otherwise comes to musical expression, or especially what comes to expression as poetry. That happens in the following way.

The poet necessarily expresses himself via language. In cultures that have advanced further, language becomes more conventional, on the one hand, and, on the other hand, it becomes more and more the expression of abstract thought. Neither conventional nor abstract thought can ever hope to exert an artistic effect. Thus it really can be said (allow me to put it a bit trivially) that poetry becomes ever more difficult in the civilized languages, unless other modes of expression come to our aid.

One way of understanding what I mean by calling eurythmy a "visible language" is by referring to its antithesis. Let me characterize eurythmy, about which we will say more in just a moment, by contrasting it with the other pole, the inartistic pole within the development of language.

There's a sense in which the language we fix on paper can also be seen as a metamorphosis of speaking. Written language is a kind of visible speech. But writing evolves in a different direction. We can trace writing back to the original stages of its existence. Then we see how the thought, the mental picture of an external object that our ancestor formed is still immanent within the written sign. We see how the element of thought becomes a kind of mute speech within the script, how it becomes a visible language.

And then this script that was originally ideograms or signs turns into entirely conventional alphabets. That is the one pole.

You might say there's a way in which language's thought-life becomes submerged within written language. Writing renders language mute. The element of thought disappears into the script. Writing also becomes a kind of visible language thereby. The further a civilization progresses, the less we are able to recognize in the written language how it is that this script once welled forth from the life of language. In the primordial languages, one still would have noted this individualized, human, personal element in their scripts. There, too, you would still feel that a kind of mute, visible speech was still alive within the written language if you looked at the oldest surviving remnants. But then, over the course of human evolution, the element that lives within language gradually becomes intellectual and conventional—which is to say, inartistic. And the more we try to take hold of thoughts within language, the more inartistic language becomes. That's why stenography is so inartistic. Stenography is already terrible because it is the antithesis of anything artistic.

And now we can move to the other pole, in which we look not to the intellectual content of the language but to the element of will. Whenever we speak, the intellectual element, which is borrowed from the external world, and the will element flow together—our engagement with the external world flows together with what wells up out of our inner life. That which flows into writing is completely pushed aside. When we study spoken language in order to turn it into eurythmy, then we take up into eurythmy what gets externalized in writing, what is thrown out, so that we have what is written before us and there is nothing personal in it; it is completely separate from the individual. Eurythmy takes that up into itself, as it were. By virtue of our movements, the whole of our human nature, as a totality, becomes the expression of that which is the element of will within language.

That is how we can assert the following. Whereas written script, which is also a mute language, separates the element of language from us as human beings, when we cross over to eurythmy we connect with it more intimately again. Eurythmy dwells deep within our human nature again, in the place where we do not fix what comes to expression in language in a separate sign. No, in eurythmy we make ourselves into the artistic instrument of all that lives in language, for example, in poetry. So that we can say: language splits into two separate poles. On the one hand, into the inartistic element of script, which becomes completely separate from us. And if we study language inwardly, through sensory-suprasensory intuition, in such a way that we then metamorphose it into eurythmy, then we take it all back up into our own being again. Then all the aspects of poetry that live within the will, within the soul,[112] come to life again in the movements of eurythmy. That is why, on the one hand, everything that can appear within eurythmy in the form of artistic movements can be nuanced musically. But, essentially, it is poetry's real, inner artistry that eurythmy is best able to express.

Poetry's real, inner artistry is not the prose content of the poem; rather, it's what lives within the rhythm, the meter, the musicality—all those things that move forward as though the words were riding upon waves. Or it is the images within language. Both aspects, the pictorial aspect and the musicality that lives within language, within poetry, assert themselves especially strongly in eurythmy. They do so because the human will manifests itself, brings itself to expression, by means of the instrumentality of the human body itself. We really can say that. When we watch eurythmy movements being performed, the effect is the same as when something within our souls expresses itself in spoken language. We have before us something that we directly intuit; something that does not need to be comprehended.

To be sure, people are not accustomed to eurythmy yet. Hence many things remain incomprehensible. But the more people become accustomed to it, the more people will experience every movement within eurythmy, every sequence of movements as the direct expression of that which resounds simultaneously in the recitation of poetry. And then people will view the whole human being as the instrument of the soul, and in the same moment they will have the soul indeed. For people naturally suffuse eurythmic movements with the life of their souls—the same inner life that poets are able to express only imperfectly, because the inartistic element of thought enters in.

So the "prosaicizing,"[113] so to speak, that people experience in the civilized world, where the more one writes, the more and more prosaic one becomes, leads to the outcome that often people no longer have a genuine, inner experience of spoken language. It reaches a point where people no longer hear language; rather, they transcribe it directly into written language, with the result that our human nature flows right out into prose. Poetry shall enter again into human sensibilities, into human emotions, if we take up eurythmy, and thereby take language up into our inner lives, into our movements.

That is why we cannot accompany eurythmy with recitation of the kind practiced in our inartistic epoch, in our wooden age. Eurythmy can be accompanied only by a recitation that allows you to hear the rhythm, the meter, the musicality, to sense the underlying image that lives within the poet—a recitation that is simply the occasion for revealing the deeper levels, the real artistry of poetry. What lives within eurythmy is the words themselves, not the words that are heard. Thereby the inartistic element of thought evaporates, so to speak; only the remnant that is actually artistic lives on in eurythmy.

We have launched many initiatives recently that strive to give artistic form to things that otherwise remain only latent within our feeling for language. In the kinds of pieces that we will be performing for you today, you will see that, on the one hand, the "how" of the artistry[114] comes to expression in the serious, solemn poems. And you will see how we express the poetic style of the humorous, the comical pieces through a different style of forms. That is one side of our work.

Eurythmy has other sides as well: it has a therapeutic side, for example. But I won't speak about that today. And then it also has a pedagogical side, which really has demonstrated its many benefits already during its first year as an obligatory subject at the Waldorf School in Stuttgart. There we have already seen how the children receive from this ensouled gymnastics something completely different from what they are given by mere gymnastics, which cultivates only the body. With eurythmy, the children don't just perform the movements that physiology dictates, even though such movements might be beneficial for the body. Rather, the children imbue each of their movements with soul. That is something that adults who engage in performing eurythmy no longer can feel, something that has no great meaning for the grown-ups. But in the children, we can see how very much it is the case that eurythmy connects us with our fundamental humanity. Because we regain a revelation of our soul being through eurythmy, then when everything is employed pedagogically, we shall once again obtain a means of cultivating truthfulness. The more abstract language becomes, the more it becomes untruthful. And it is precisely in the more "advanced" languages that we find the most clichés, because language loses its connection with the human being.

In eurythmy, everything in language that has lost its connection is taken back up into the human being once again. Whenever we must enter completely into what we ourselves experience and feel, by making ourselves into an instrument, we cannot be untruthful. And when we have the children perform eurythmy, then they develop a natural antidote to clichés; they develop a sense for truthfulness. That is the pedagogical outcome that people will find as soon as they begin to consider the whole matter more objectively.

For a long time now, the question that has occupied me has been: How can we give expression to drama, for example? To date, we have been able to express epic and lyric elements, and also dramatic episodes that represent suprasensory experience. That is what you will see presented today: drama that gives expression to suprasensory experience, in a piece from one of my Mystery Dramas.[115] The suprasensory elements within drama can also be expressed adequately by eurythmy. But conventional drama, which plays upon the stage of the sensory world, so to speak, is a problem that I have set myself. We shall find those forms as well. You see, everything is still in flux.

❀

Part II: Introductions, 1921–1924

On Christian Morgenstern's *Humoresques*, II

Dornach, April 3, 1921[116]

If you are patient, you will also see what we have done with more serious poems, and you will be able to compare what we've attempted to do with more humorous or picturesque poetry. You will be able to compare the treatments and see how eurythmy resonates completely with the forms of these different styles. You will see, on the one hand, how the extraordinarily complicated ideas of Fercher von Steinwand[117]—verses that, one might say, resonate with the mysteries of the cosmos and trace out hidden cosmic forces—are brought to expression through the forms of eurythmy. And on the other hand, you will see how we've attempted to capture the style of Christian Morgenstern's[118] *humoresques* by using special forms of eurythmy. It is entirely possible to do this with eurythmy, to capture Morgenstern's intentions without taking recourse to mime or pantomime. Morgenstern was led to write his humorous verses, the *Gallows Songs*, the *Songs of Palmström*, etc., by the philistinism he experienced and suffered with humor. Christian Morgenstern was especially sensitive to the philistinism that is endemic now in our culture, which has become prosaic. The smug provincialism, the platitudes that philistinism sends out in all directions wounded a nature as sensitive as Christian Morgenstern's whenever he encountered them. But that is what made his thoughts begin to dance. On all sides his thoughts were beaten back by the platitudes of the philistines—especially the kind of philistinism that tries to pass itself off as so brilliant today, that wants to seem brilliant and then puts on airs of brilliance. This cringing of his thinking, Morgenstern's thoughts beginning to dance in response to the platitudes of the philistines, calls on us to develop yet another special variant of eurythmy.

❁

Three Addresses at the Summer Art Course
I. Introductory Words Regarding Eurythmy (pedagogical)

[Dornach], Monday, August 22, 1921, 5 p.m.[119]

The eurythmy that you will see performed here today and over the next few days is based upon a visible language that has been shaped out of human nature itself. This language reveals itself in movements performed by the bodies and limbs of individual eurythmists, or by ensembles. To that extent, what will be presented here looks similar to expressions through gestures, through mime, and through dance. And yet eurythmy is as distinct from these other kinds of expression as lawfully formed human speech itself. We are not trying to conjoin subjective experiences, sensations, feelings with a gesture or a movement yielded by some spontaneous and arbitrary urge. Rather, eurythmy's individual gestures and movements stand in the same relationship to our potentials for inner experience as do the individual sounds of language or the individual tones of song. And eurythmy's gestures and movements have a syntax of the kind that sounds and tones exhibit in sentences and in speaking.

Just how it is that such a visible language raises itself up to the level of artistic presentation is something I will have to tell you before the performances over the next few days. Today we are concerned with a different side of eurythmy. Children shall appear before you. For them, eurythmy is a kind of spiritualized, ensouled gymnastics. For that reason, we have introduced it as a required subject and as a complement to gymnastics in the Stuttgart Waldorf School founded by Emil Molt and led by me.

The justification for this is that eurythmy guides the human organism over into a special kind of mobility. This mobility is a natural, temporary manifestation of our human *Gestalt* itself, of our own inner being, mobile or at rest. Consider the human arm and hand. Their very *Gestalt* already contains the mystery of their mobility, of their employment. You cannot look at the hand and arm at rest without at the same time seeing in the spirit the movement potentials latent within them, just as you cannot view a placid, mute countenance without its form and *Gestalt* betraying that it only needs to open its mouth in order to make the soul audible. And likewise, you cannot observe a moving hand or arm without inwardly sensing a striving to attain the state of rest, just as speaking human beings reveal the mystery of their physiognomic expression.

But just as language itself springs forth out of the human soul in a lawful way, it is also possible to translate the soul's inner formations into movements, which can then be elaborated from gesture and mime all the way up to the full articulation of a visible language. And then we experience through our movements an expressive capacity that is similar to speech and song. The whole range of our human nature reveals itself through such a visible speech in body, soul, and spirit.

And children sense this possibility for self-expression. Our inborn urge to move is realized again in the child's activity. The child feels its innate humanity, summoned up out of its own inner being and out of its general sense of bodily well-being. All real education is based on such a summoning-up. Eurythmy in its guise as a spiritualized ensouled gymnastics is a significant means of education. After they have abandoned many of today's prejudices, future ages will realize that gymnastics requires eurythmy as a complement. Gymnastics takes its laws from a knowledge of human corporeality. We do not wish at all to gainsay what gymnastics has been able to accomplish in that way. But our ensouled gymnastics will be able to accomplish things that purely corporeal gymnastics cannot. For example, it shall summon up initiatives out of our wills. It shall educate the whole child in body, soul, and spirit, without neglecting the body in any way. For when we are fully human, body, soul, and spirit are one. And anyone who teaches movements that flow from the *living* spirit—not the abstract, nebulous "spirit" that is invoked almost exclusively today—will also be cultivating in the best way what is suited to the body, what is natural.

That is why children feel that eurythmy is something they just naturally want to do. It just wells up inside them, in the same way that an inner impulse makes them want to speak.

The justification for eurythmy as a means of education will be felt by anyone who seeks educational methods arising out of a genuine, objective knowledge of human nature. That is why we can hope that in the future, educators will make this ensouled gymnastics a part of every curriculum. They will do it to increase the children's inner engagement in their own education, to cultivate their full humanity through education.

THREE ADDRESSES AT THE SUMMER ART COURSE II. INTRODUCTORY WORDS BEFORE THE PERFORMANCE OF EURYTHMY

[Dornach,] Wednesday, August 24, 1921, 5 p.m.[120]

Last Monday we had the honor of presenting for you a performance of eurythmy as a kind of gymnastics for the spirit and soul. We wanted to give you a picture of eurythmy as a means of educating and teaching. Today we would like to present eurythmy to you as a freestanding art form. Seeking to explain such a performance is an inherently unaesthetic undertaking. Real art has to be compelling as a direct experience, and the audience will consider artistic only what immediately feels complete in itself.

So it follows that my reason for giving this introduction cannot be to explain the performance. I'm doing it for a different reason. Eurythmy draws from hitherto unaccustomed artistic springs, and it employs a grammar of forms that is just as unfamiliar. So it does make sense to say a few introductory words about those springs and that grammar of forms. Eurythmy is grounded in a visible language. Its forms of expression are the movements of the limbs of the individual human body, or the movements of groups of performers.

These movements did not arise like everyday gestures, or like mime or pantomime—and least of all like traditional dance. Rather, they arose out of the study of the movement potentials inherent in the human organs of singing and speaking, a study that employs sensory-suprasensory intuition. Here it is a matter of movements that have not been completely formed: singing and speaking are grounded in such unfinished movements. When we sing and speak, these movements have only just commenced when they transform themselves into that which can be mediated by tones and the sounds of speech. That is why we need to take hold of singing and speaking right when they first arise (*in statu nascendi*). The movement potentials that we grasp in this sensory-supersensory way must then be transposed onto the human being as a whole, which becomes the organism of singing and speaking.

What is being raised up into the realm of artistic creativity here is the principle of metamorphosis which Goethe held up as the goal of morphological intuition. Goethe sees the entire plant as a more completely structured individual leaf, and he sees the individual leaf as transparent to the underlying idea of the plant as a whole, which reveals itself in a simpler way merely for the sake of the senses.

In human speech, thought is bound up with the will. Thought is the inartistic element. That is why the more that language becomes civilized, the more it is robbed of its artistic quality. Language becomes the handmaiden of thought. It becomes, on the one hand, a servant of cognition and, on the other, a servant of social conventions. Poets who are real artists fight against this inartistic element of thought within language. Real poets seek to form configurations of sounds and words that are grounded in rhythm, meter, harmony, rhyme, alliteration, and thematic motifs that are musical or imagistic. In this way, poets make language into an expression of the will, which is to say: of the whole of human nature.

This element of will is what holds sway within eurythmy, and pervades it as the essence of eurythmy. Through eurythmy, we reveal in visible form what the musician strives to attain by shaping tones, the poet by shaping speech. All the dimensions of a poem that transcend its prosaic content and are the ground of its artistry are rendered visible by eurythmy.

Eurythmy is accompanied on the one hand by music. Then it is visible song. On the other hand, by recitation and declamation. Then the content of poetry that is actually artistic and poetic can come to visibility.

But one cannot accompany eurythmy with the kind of declamation and recitation that has become all too common today, the kind that thinks the point is to highlight the prosaic content of a poem. The techniques of recitation and declamation deployed by speech formation[121] need to transcend the prosaic content. Speech formation needs to see the elaboration of meter, rhythm, harmony, rhyme, musical and imagistic themes as the essential thing. The task is to summon forth the *invisible* eurythmy that is hidden within the poetry, which then steps forward as *visible* eurythmy in performance.

Eurythmy still stands at the very beginning of its development. We know this, and we ourselves are the harshest critics of our own accomplishments to date. But anyone who understands what we are trying to achieve has to see eurythmy's unlimited possibilities for further development. Goethe discovered: "As soon as Nature has begun to unveil her open secret to us, we begin to feel an irresistible longing for her most worthy interpreter, art."[122] And now eurythmy can paraphrase Goethe, saying: "As soon as human nature itself has begun to reveal the mysteries of the human constitution, we begin to feel an irresistible longing for the kind of artistic forming that is the goal of eurythmy." For eurythmy makes use not of an external instrument, but rather of the human being himself as the most worthy instrument. On another occasion, Goethe said: "In that we human beings have been placed at the pinnacle of nature, we see ourselves as a whole nature unto ourselves, within which it is our task to raise up another peak. We climb upward toward that goal by permeating ourselves with all perfections and virtues—we summon all the discretion, order, harmony, and meaning that we can, and eventually we rise up to the production of the work of art."[123]

This "raising up" necessarily must be most successful when we take in hand the order, harmony, measure, and meaning of our own human nature and shape a work of art of and through ourselves. For within ourselves as a microcosm, all the mysteries of the macrocosm lie hidden in one way or another.

With this goal in mind, we dare to hope that, even though eurythmy stands at the very beginning of its development, one day it shall be able to take its place as a fully justified art alongside the older, fully established sister arts.

Eurythmy as a Means of Education

Dornach, December 28, 1921[124]

Please permit us now to add a performance featuring the pedagogical aspect of eurythmy to the other performance that you saw recently.[125] Today's performance will be presented by children. At the Waldorf School in Stuttgart—founded by Emil Molt and directed by me—we have supplemented gymnastics with eurythmy as a required subject. Now, after having employed it for several years, we can already see that eurythmy can make a significant contribution to the development of the child.

Conventional gymnastics has been set up in such a way that only the laws of human corporeality, of the physical body, are taken into consideration. Now I don't want to criticize gymnastics in any way. We are not getting rid of it; we just want to complement it with what eurythmy brings over and above conventional gymnastics is a kind of spiritualized ensouled gymnastics. I won't go so far as a certain German physiologist[126]—a very famous man—who once attended a performance of eurythmy right here in this hall. He listened to my introductory remarks regarding the relationship between eurythmy and gymnastics, and then said to me afterward: "So you want to characterize eurythmy as something that is justified pedagogically with regard to the human physical body? For me"—as a physiologist, he meant—"gymnastics is not pedagogical at all. It is a barbarity." As I just said, I wouldn't ever want to go that far myself. That is not my own position, so I do not feel any need to justify it.

As opposed to gymnastics, children always experience pedagogical eurythmy—in their feelings, in their will-impulses, in every movement, with each movement-form—children experience eurythmy as something suffused with soul, as something spiritual. The movements are performed in such a way that the child allows them to flow into his or her soul and spirit. The children open themselves up to this influence in such a way that they are seized not just by the general sense of having made a gesture, but rather by the meaningful experience of a truly enlivened language, of a visible language.

We can observe clearly something else that happens when eurythmy is employed as a pedagogical principle. Older children definitely take up this language in a way that is as elementary and natural as their assimilation of spoken language and song at an earlier age. For eurythmy is as much a kind of singing as it is a kind of speech.

Moreover, a real knowledge of the human body or of human nature as a whole can lead us to understand that the artistic shaping of thinking isn't something that depends solely upon the human head or the human brain: it is something that proceeds from our human nature as a whole. We learn to think not just in accordance with our brains, but also in accordance with the ways we can move our arms and hands! As soon as we understand that, then we also begin to understand that it is not just in the utilization of the organs of speech, of the head, of the chest, that we see this when we speak or sing. We can note something else besides. We can note how something is cultivated within us by this ensouled gymnastics, by this spiritualized gymnastics. Something is cultivated that this current generation and the following generation will need above all: initiative in their souls, and especially initiative in their wills. And with regard to the development of the will, eurythmy is an important addition to the school's curriculum. Gymnastics contributes to flexibility and coordination, but it does not look to the soul in developing the body. And for that reason, eurythmy is better able than gymnastics to foster real cultivation of the will.

And so it is that we can develop an appreciation for the employment of eurythmy as a pedagogical technique if we begin to view human nature in its wholeness again, as consisting of body, soul, and spirit. We would like to show you a few examples of that today, and to persuade you that eurythmy is a great fit for the bodies of young children. And I believe that something else will become immediately visible, and that will call forth in turn the feeling: This art is something that animates our very humanity, something that can be experienced with joy and inner fulfillment—and please keep in mind, my dear friends, that joy and inner fulfillment, pursued seriously as educational ideals, always yield excellent, significant results. Perhaps you will begin to see that, ladies and gentlemen, as a result of our performance today.

MUSIC; LYRIC, EPIC, DRAMATIC POETRY STYLIZED BY THE NEW ART OF MOVEMENT

Dornach, March 26, 1922.

Dramatic performance with eurythmy fromthe Mystery Drama The Guardian of the Threshold, Scene Six[127], [*abridged*]

It is really true when we say that in eurythmy the whole human being becomes a visible larynx—one great, visible organ of speech. What is available today is only the beginning of the artistry; it is a speaking that awaits artistic treatment. And ultimately what you see is not really all that different from the rhythms, the musical themes, the images conjured up by the sounds in speech itself. So it is not especially important which individual movements or gestures correspond to this or that sound, this or that sentence, this or that tone. Rather, what is especially important is the way that one movement-form transitions into the next, the sequence of the movements within the work of art as a whole. There is a sense in which we can speak of the same kind of lawfulness within the movements that we see in the ordered sequences and recurring structures of music.

That is what makes eurythmy a third art form, one that can be raised up to the level of music and poetry themselves.

When music awakens our feelings, what we are actually feeling is the mood of our own souls. It is the inwardness of feeling itself that we are feeling once again in the tone. The spiritualization of feeling comes to expression in musicality. When we turn to poetry, then what reveals itself in poetry is the spiritual shaping of the ideational element. That leaves perception itself. In perception, the sensory world lies before us, but that which presents itself in the outer, sensory world is also grounded in something spiritual. This spirituality can be expressed only through the human organism itself. And this representation of the perceived spirit through the human organism, hence through expressions of the will—that is eurythmy. So we can say: Music is the spirit of feeling, poetry is the spirit of ideation, and eurythmy is the spirit of perception.

Thus eurythmy as an art form is justified in taking its place alongside both the others. Moreover, we can also say: When we see performers moving upon the stage, when we see how they become the medium of expression for poetry and music, then the moving performer is like sculpture itself having been brought into movement. Or we might also say: Eurythmy finds its niche as a separate art form alongside sculpture, alongside the art of sculpture.

There you have some initial thoughts about the artistic aspect of eurythmy. The representation of poetry is quite straightforward in this way when it comes to epic and lyric poetry. Eurythmy allows a higher degree of stylization than the kind of mime conventionally employed by actors. That is why, when it comes to drama, we employ eurythmy not when purely naturalistic scenes from everyday life, from the world of the senses, are represented on the stage, but rather when such facts are represented as reveal our human connection with the spiritual world, with the suprasensory world. For it is precisely those things that encompass the relationship of human beings, of the human soul, to the suprasensory world which call for a stylization that conventional, naturalistic theatrical techniques cannot provide. Then we see how eurythmy can give expression to suprasensory episodes in drama by means of its higher, lawful stylization, in which language itself is summoned forth out of the human organism.

Today we will be able to present only a short scene from one of my *Mystery Dramas*,[128] but perhaps you will be able to gather from it how it is possible to make such a thing visible precisely by employing eurythmy. The presentation will show how a number of human souls actually live out in dream form what they have assimilated from all sorts of mystical and otherwise suprasensory experiences. For suprasensory cognition is indeed able to enter into human souls with inner truth and vitality. But this possibility presupposes that we are already able to meet this suprasensory knowledge with inner truthfulness, inner honesty, inner uprightness. We must first cultivate those virtues within ourselves. This is the ideal of anthroposophical self-development: that we all work upon ourselves to cultivate total inner truthfulness, total inner honesty and uprightness.

Upon that path, many souls who are otherwise thoroughly good and kindly show that they have fallen prey to a certain sentimentality, to a certain inner untruthfulness that arises in the course of pursuing suprasensory knowledge. They assimilate that knowledge, but they do so only with a certain—what shall I say?—a certain lack of inner vitality. It has not taken hold of them completely; they are just dreaming, as it were, because it gives them a kind of gratification. We have to be clear with ourselves about that; we have to attain clarity through a kind of irony. We need to see clearly how untrue souls can become who have not first cultivated this inner truthfulness—untrue to themselves—when they assimilate various kinds of suprasensory knowledge. Such souls will be portrayed here, souls showing the widest range of inner nuances.

Then the souls are confronted by that figure whom I have often called Ahriman. It is a figure who actually represents everything that is pedantic within us, something within ourselves that actually pulls us down into the gravity of the world, as it were.[129] Having assembled such a chorus of more or less honest, more or less dishonest, mystical souls, one can then show how that which pulls humanity down[130] takes joy and comfort from this, from seeing how something that otherwise functions to bind us to the Earth can also be effective precisely within such souls who want to fly off, as it were, who want to flee the Earth in a kind of inauthentic and spurious mysticism. That really is an accurate depiction of something that unfolds within our inmost souls, that represents our relationship to the suprasensory realm as human beings. So it is precisely that scene—one that has been torn out of the context of my *Mystery Dramas*—which we will perform for you in eurythmy today. In Ahriman, you will see a figure who will remind you a bit of Mephistopheles in Goethe's *Faust*,[131] but the figure of Ahriman recurs in every epoch of human spiritual evolution. And he can be felt to be very much alive in our own times. He is, shall we say, the spirit who takes his joy and his advantage from souls who *seem* to be inwardly "very deep," "very mystical," "very occult"—but actually are not truthful.

Introduction

Vienna, June 2, 1922[132]

Underlying the art of eurythmy there is a visible speech created out of human nature itself. This is revealed in movements that individuals perform with their entire bodies or with their limbs, or that are carried out by ensembles. It is *not* concerned with the kinds of movements one sees in traditional gesture, mime, or dance; rather, it has to do with a real language that is as far removed from dance, mime, and gesturing as are singing or speaking themselves. We do not arbitrarily conjoin inner experiences, or a perception, or a feeling, with the form of movement. Instead, we shape the potentials for movement that are latent within the organic structuring of the human body as a whole, whereby they become a means of expression. The same thing happens in accordance with the laws of nature within a single set of organs when we speak or sing. The individual movements in eurythmy follow as naturally as musical tones and speech sounds in acts of singing and speaking. The movements that are ultimately revealed through eurythmy are also latent in singing and speaking, as organic and volitional intentions; but as they arise, they are instantly transformed into those movements which the singing and speech carry out. These *potentials* are captured in eurythmy through sensory-suprasensory intuition, and in that way the whole human being is made into an organ of singing and speaking that is expressing itself visibly.

In human speech, thought and will come to expression. Of these, it is thought that is the inartistic element. In the poetic treatment of speech, the power of the thought is led back into the will-like element, into stress, rhythm, imagery, and so on. Eurythmy carries this transformation through to its conclusion. Performers moving in space become the manifestation of the soul and spirit. On the one hand, eurythmy can be accompanied by music. Then it is visible singing. On the other hand, it can be accompanied by recitation and declamation. Here the truly artistic, poetic content is directly intuited. When they accompany eurythmy, recitation and declamation must refrain from any kind of (prosaic) accentuation of the content of the poetry, and instead allow the pictorial and musical element to come to the fore—that is, the truly artistic element. Along with the artistic aspect, eurythmy has a healing, therapeutic aspect and a pedagogical aspect, in which the artistic forms of eurythmy have been suitably transformed. We believe that this art form, which remains in its infancy, is capable of unlimited further development because its instrument is human nature itself, and that in a more comprehensive sense than is the case in other art forms.

❀

Eurythmy's Pedagogical Element

Oxford, August 19, 1922

With presentations by children[133]

Yesterday I took the liberty of speaking a few introductory words before the eurythmy performance, so as to explain what distinguishes eurythmy from the other arts. I don't want to say anything else about eurythmy as an art form today. The same words I spoke yesterday would have to be spoken again to introduce the second part of today's performance. Today's first part consists of a presentation by children who have studied eurythmy here for a short period of time. So please allow me to say a few words about the pedagogical aspect of eurythmy.

Above all—and we always have to bear this in mind—eurythmy is intended neither as gymnastics nor as dance: it is meant to be an art form. Because it consists of an actual visible language that has been drawn forth from the healthy human constitution itself, eurythmy can be elaborated in such a way that it can be employed as a kind of spiritual gymnastics in teaching and in education. When the Waldorf School was founded in Stuttgart, we immediately introduced eurythmy as a required subject, accompanying gymnastics. Now, after a few years of having eurythmy at the school, the great pedagogical value of eurythmy has become completely clear to us.

First of all, eurythmy is especially important because it is a great aid in the teaching of languages. The children have always been drawn quite naturally to this visible language. They feel pleasure and an inner fulfillment when they enter into something that flows directly out of human nature itself. It is similar to the manner in which children find their way into the sounds of speech and into song. When they work their way into this visible language, they feel the essential nature of the language within their inner being.

And from there an understanding radiates out into the regular language curriculum.

Moreover, eurythmy is of special help in the education of the will. Someday folks will exhibit better judgment in this regard than today, when conventional gymnastics—I'd like to call it *bodily* gymnastics—is somewhat overvalued. I really do not want to say anything more today about this bodily gymnastics, which flows from the laws of physiology; I freely acknowledge its merits. I would simply like to mention—to adduce in passing—something that happened once when I was introducing the didactic and pedagogical aspects of eurythmy within our Waldorf curriculum at the Goetheanum. A remarkable thing happened: I was approached by a very famous contemporary physiologist,[134] who had been in the audience when I said among other things that I completely respect gymnastics, and that I view eurythmy as a kind of ensouled gymnastics and hence an important complement to the things that bodily gymnastics are able to accomplish only in a one-sided way. He replied: "You regard gymnastics is educational? In my view as a physiologist, gymnastics is barbarous."

Again, that is not me talking: that is a famous physiologist. Nevertheless, even though we fully acknowledge conventional gymnastics in the Waldorf School as a means of physical education, we supplemented it with eurythmy as a kind of ensouled gymnastics, spiritual gymnastics. And eurythmy reveals itself as especially well framed for the will, for the cultivation of initiative within the will. It gives us the possibility of working upon the soul of the child because whenever a child performs a movement, he feels that he is simultaneously engaging his whole human constitution—body, soul, and spirit. Children feel how body, soul, and spirit coalesce, as it were, and how these are all bound together within this spiritual gymnastics that is eurythmy.

And then—here's a thought that might perhaps strike you as paradoxical, and yet it is true, especially in advanced cultures such as those of the West today—using everyday speech, we can of course say not only what is true, but also what is false. It is especially easy to become untrue, mendacious when speaking. But in the visible language of eurythmy, it is impossible to lie. That is something we have come to experience. Hence eurythmy is also a means for teaching truthfulness. In the visible language of eurythmy, nobody—and least of all children—will find it easy to lie.

I have just described to you certain pedagogical aspects of eurythmy. Let me add just one more thing. Often it is possible to observe one or another challenge to a child's physical, psychological, or spiritual well-being.[135] Then the teachers of the Stuttgart Waldorf School usually come to me and say: this child is experiencing one or another psychological or physical challenge. In such a case, all that is necessary is to employ a certain suprasensory power of seeing, to recognize with clairvoyant intuition what kind of eurythmy exercises should be prescribed for this particular child—eurythmy or eurythmy-like exercises. And indeed, we have sometimes attained astonishing results in the overcoming of corporeal or psychological challenges when we have been able to recommend eurythmy exercises for that particular child and they have then been carried out by the teachers in the Waldorf School. So there you see that everything needs to be elaborated on the pedagogical side. It is first and foremost an art form, but eurythmy can also be placed in the service of pedagogy.

Let me mention in conclusion that the children you will see in the first part of the program have been studying eurythmy for only a short period of time, so please extend them special consideration and forbearance. The teachers have been able to give these children only a few lessons, and then after we arrived, we added a few numbers to our program as a kind of improvisation. So you should not expect to see anything polished in this children's performance. As is the case with the other performance, we ask your forbearance regarding something that stands at the very beginning of its development. Please look past the surface to the principle, to what is essential here. I believe that will be evident even in this children's performance in the first part of today's program. After an intermission, we will show you what eurythmy can become as an art form.

✽

[UNTITLED]

The Hague, November 2, 1922[136]

It is my pleasant task to introduce our eurythmy performance, but forgive me for not speaking in the language of this country. I hope you will excuse my inability and allow me to use the language to which I am accustomed.

The eurythmy you are going to see will be performed by individuals and groups. The movements they will be making are not gestures in the usual sense of the word, nor are they pantomime or mime or any other art of movement. They are movements presenting actual visible speech. I do not say this in order to explain the artistic content of the performance. Art must speak for itself through its immediate impact; any explanation of a work of art is itself inartistic! Our eurythmy, however, springs from artistic sources that today are still unfamiliar, and it uses an artistic form that likewise is unfamiliar. Perhaps, therefore, you will allow me to say few words about them.

In ordinary human speech and song, we have to do with something that has evolved quite consistently according to certain laws out of the human organs for speech and song. We have the human will coming forth from the deepest core of our human nature, and also thought that is poured out of the nervous system in a most complicated way into the speech organs. These two elements flow together in speech, and a third element, feeling, unites what thought, on the one hand, and will, on the other, want to bring to expression.

Now, it is really the thought element in speech that produces the most obstacles for any poet—any *real* poet. Thoughts are an inartistic element. But thought can be studied, and everything you are now going to see of the eurythmic art of movement is based entirely upon careful study employing—if I may use Goethe's expression—sensory-suprasensory intuition. We can observe, for instance, the movements that the larynx and its neighboring organs are making at the moment when a word or a singing tone is being given over to the air. We gradually discover that even ordinary speech actually arises by virtue of a transformation of gestures—not the everyday gestures by which we normally accompany our conversation, but rather gestures that live within us while we are speaking and that do not come into external, physical view at all. The human brain is such a complicated organ that it is extremely difficult to see what happens when someone speaks or sings. Actually, for every vowel, for every consonant, a specific gesture is produced, but it is held back and transformed. Through a complicated expedient of the nervous system, each specific gesture is made into a picture, and an after-image of the gesture is, so to say, entrusted to the vibrating air that in speaking or singing streams out from the human organism. It is just this—the gesture that is held back when we speak or sing, and then by a mysterious human power is committed to the air stream—it is just this that is brought out and revealed by the art of eurythmy. Every vowel, every consonant, the complete structure of a word, of a sentence will now appear before you in the movements made by individual eurythmists and groups of eurythmists on the stage.

It is especially the arms and hands, the most expressive part of the human body, which speak to you in this visible speech. We should not, however, try to link single gestures that the eurythmist makes to single words, to the soul content of single words. In music, for instance, we should listen for the way the tones follow one another to form a melody; so also in eurythmy we look to the sequence of movements. It really is possible to say that we are talking about a melody of movements. We hope you won't try to interpret single gestures; rather, a sweep of movement should have the power, at the moment that it is being seen and artistically enjoyed, to evoke the impression, the mood, that the poet or composer wanted to create.

For some time, we have been working to make the entire staging relate to the eurythmy as it is being performed on the stage. In particular, we have tried to develop the stage lighting so that the entire staging is, as it were, an extension of the eurythmy itself. Thus, it is not a matter of separating or conjoining individual lighting effects, but rather what is important for us is to create a melodious, harmonious, artistic sequence of lighting effects.

So eurythmy can accompany a piece of music with visible song, singing visibly as one would sing with tones, and it can make visible what the poet expressed in artistic language.

It is extremely important that when eurythmy is accompanying a poem, the recitation and declamation should also capture what is being expressed in the visible speech, the eurythmy. In the work of a true poet—in the structure of the language, the formation of the sentences, the way that meters and all the other artistic elements of language are employed—there already lurks a hidden eurythmy. Since here our recitation and declamation will always parallel the poetic content of the eurythmy, you will realize that we place less value on the literal prose content of a poem than on the true artistry of the language, the melodic quality, the imaginative, pictorial element that real poets put into their work. Some future epoch that is more artistic than our own will, among other things, return to the fine art of recitation and declamation, and will emphasize the musical, sculptural, colorful elements in poetry instead of accentuating its prose content, which is the usual practice today. Here, the recitation and declamation must sound forth in harmony, in a parallel mood, with what happens visibly on the stage.

In that way, my dear friends, we achieve a higher degree of style than is possible with the ordinary art of mime. That will be especially evident today because you are going to see eurythmy and acting on the stage at the same time, in a scene from the second part of *Faust*: "Care and the Four Gray Crones."[137] You will see Faust presented quite naturalistically, as a character is usually portrayed expressing his normal soul life. That can be represented by using ordinary acting techniques. But then Faust is confronted by the Four Gray Crones and Care, who are actually the embodiment of suprasensory powers, suprasensory forces. These forces are rendered physically perceptible, and we see what relationship an individual human soul can have to the suprasensory, spiritual world. In such an instance, where something spiritually perceptible, spiritually experienced is to be put on the stage—something not physical, not earthly—there eurythmy can be especially useful. In this scene from *Faust* that we are showing today, you will see Faust presented in the usual theatrical style. What the Four Gray Crones and especially Care bring to Faust, however, you will see presented by eurythmy accompanied by recitation just for the eurythmy.

We can say, therefore, that particularly when a subtler style is needed for something on the stage that goes beyond the usual naturalism, the art of eurythmy can be experienced in its true character.

Today, as always, I must beg you to be charitable! We are our own severest critics and we know that our eurythmy is still in its infancy. It will be perfected greatly over time. While we ourselves are only involved in its beginning, we know that the possibilities for development are open-ended, because eurythmy employs the human body itself as its artistic medium, rather than any external instrument. In the human being all the secrets, all the laws of the cosmos are gathered together. We are a microcosm. By revealing our human nature through the visible speech of eurythmy, by drawing forth from our own inmost nature what moves the soul, what awakens the human spirit, we really draw forth from the whole human being all cosmic secrets in miniature. Goethe said about art: "In that we human beings have been placed at the pinnacle of nature, we see ourselves as a whole nature unto ourselves, within which it is our task to raise up another peak. We climb upward towards that goal by permeating ourselves with all perfections and virtues—we summon all the discretion, order, harmony, and meaning that we can, and eventually we rise up to the production of the work of art."[138]

Likewise, one can say that in eurythmy, order, harmony, measure, and meaning are taken not only from the surrounding world but out of human nature itself, because all cosmic secrets are contained in us as a microcosm. The cosmos can tell us its most intimate secrets through these human movements; through them the soul can most purely, most profoundly, most intimately reveal itself. For the very reason that eurythmy uses human nature itself as its medium, we can hope that, although today it is still rather unusual, in the coming years eurythmy shall arouse more and more interest, and also shall become ever more perfect as it develops, so that one day it shall be given a place beside the older sister arts as a fully acknowledged young art in its own right.

GESTURE IN PANTOMIME, IN DANCE, AND IN THE ART OF SPATIAL MOVEMENT, EURYTHMY

Dornach, April 14, 1923

During the pedagogical course for teachers at the Goetheanum[139]

We are now going to present a short program of eurythmy. This new art must be distinguished from the art of pantomime and from the art of dance. Certainly, we would not raise the slightest objection to those arts. But eurythmy is intended to be something entirely different. In mime, one makes gestures to indicate something, to call attention to something, while in dance, one uses overflowing gestures in which the soul loses itself. Eurythmy uses gestures, too, and movements of the body; but eurythmy's gestures are neither indicative nor overflowing. Perhaps one could call eurythmy's gestures expressive, in the sense that words themselves are expressive, indeed, that everything coming from a human being by way of speech is expressive.

Speech, too, has to do ultimately with something like an art of gesture, only in speech the gesture is performed by the stream of air coming from the larynx. This outgoing stream of air takes on exactly what lies in the words and sentences. If you could see it, you would see that this is so. In the stream of air, the speaker's will and thinking are flowing together out of the soul. Will is the element that gives the air a radial direction, so to speak, while it is the thought which creates the cross-section of undulation within the airstream. In the artistic shaping of language to create a poem, we see the poet striving as far as possible to overcome the element of thought that predominates in prose. Already in the art of rhetoric—in speaking that aims to use beautifully flowing speech—the intention is to give a form to the language itself. A poet's chief endeavor is to overcome the purely prosaic thought element by making every possible use of the musical or the sculptural-painterly elements of language in order to express what is meant to be expressed.

When, therefore, it comes to reciting the poem, a real art of recitation and declamation—something that certainly is not being cultivated properly in today's inartistic world—a real art of recitation and declamation has the corresponding task of shaping the words in a musical, sculptural, and painterly way again. If, for instance, a poem describes the passion that is moving a soul, this will have to be expressed in the recitation by a rhythm in the flow of words that is different from a rhythm which might express sorrow or the soul's retreat into itself.

Language has become so prosaic that it pretends to capture the content of the inner experience within the content of the words. In poetry, by contrast, our task is to reveal by various artistic means what in prose is found only in the lexical content. So it is not real recitation and declamation when somebody merely accentuates the prose content of a poem, as is usually done today. Genuine recitation or declamation requires that the speaker take pains to bring out the hidden eurythmy that the poet has placed into the language. As soon as we become aware of the musical element and the sculptural and painterly elements in speech, as soon as we realize that these musical elements can be represented by certain self-contained, expressive gestures that are to be found in the natural structures of the human body, then we have reached the possibility of creating an actual visible speech. This visible speech can already be seen in the indicative gestures made by rather temperamental people who feel they can't capture what they want to express through the sounds of speech alone, so they help their speech along by making gestures. But such gestures are a mere babbling, so to speak. Just as young children learn to speak by babbling and then advance to articulate speech, so the ordinary gestures we make while speaking are related to the eurythmy gestures you are now going to see on the stage. Eurythmy has indeed come about in this way: sensory-suprasensory intuition was able to observe the forms that are created by the air streaming out from the larynx and its neighboring speech organs while speaking and singing.

This shaping that is usually framed for inner experience is now transferred to the limbs. The most expressive human limbs are the arms and hands, but the rest of the body can also make eurythmy movements as well, even though the other limbs are less characteristic for eurythmy. The inner experiences that otherwise flow out into the shaped stream of air when speaking or singing now flow into the expressive forms of the arms, the hands, and the other bodily members. Then we can have an experience, and the art of eurythmy is meant to provide that experience. When music is being played or something is being recited or declaimed, initially one hears the tones or speech sounds that the artist has formed. But the hidden eurythmy that underlies such things can be transposed into visible singing or into visible speech, and that is just what eurythmy is: an individual in movement, or a group of individuals in movement, or ensembles relating to one another, all revealing the human soul from the stage by translating speech or song into movement.

So eurythmy is not an invention of arbitrary gestures that have been added spontaneously to a poem or a piece of music. Just as you cannot embody what you want to say in any random collection of speech sounds, for the reason that every single state of soul has a specific sequence of sounds corresponding to it, so also a soul experience cannot be expressed by some spontaneously invented gesture, for the reason that every soul experience has a definite gesture corresponding to it. So when you find a series of vowels in a poem, you can be sure that the poet has used it to express something in a musical-painterly way. It follows of course that when you recite, you need to treat that sequence of vowels accordingly. You cannot express the poem with certain sounds one day, other sounds another, because the sounds relate to the harmonies existing between our physical organism and the life of our soul. In the same way, there are only unambiguous sequences of movements to be made in eurythmy. For a certain motif, you will always see the same gesture. Yes, down to the smallest vowel or consonant, everything has its own fully determined gesture. In speech, "I" [ēē] is a very definite sound; in eurythmy, too, it is a very definite gesture. But then, just as in reciting poetry an "I" [ēē] can be spoken brightly or dully, loudly or softly, long or short, so also in eurythmy the specific gesture for "I" [ēē] can be made in various ways. So you can see that in eurythmy it is of prime importance that when a gesture is being shaped, it should be shaped in a genuinely artistic way. Every movement must be formed artistically. Then something will have been created that is a truly independent art able to take its place alongside the other arts, an art of movement in space.

Admittedly, eurythmy stands today only at the beginning of its development. But it holds promise of many, many phases of growth because it makes use of what we might call the most perfect human instrument, the human organism itself. The human organism contains all cosmic secrets and all cosmic laws. It is a little world, a microcosm, reflecting the great world, the macrocosm. Eurythmy makes more perfect use of this microcosm than does the art of mime with its indicative gestures. These are only guessed at, so to say, which means that an intellectual element is forced to enter in. Eurythmy also makes more perfect use of the organism than does the art of the dance, which overflows in its movement into space. Eurythmy can also overflow into space in its movements, but it should not do so in such a way that it flows out into the movement, as it were. Its movement should always be kept under control by the inner structures of the human organism itself. In eurythmy, no movement should be performed that does not show by its very nature that an element of soul underlies it.

If, indeed, eurythmy is occasionally called upon to express something similar to what we stoop to convey in our everyday speech by mimicking facial expressions—for instance, smirking to show that we consider ourselves above something or other, or drawing the corners of our mouth down to mock at someone, and so forth—that is, if we express a certain kind of bodily feeling through mime, then eurythmy can stoop to mimicking, too, if that is what the poet wants. But if eurythmy falls too far from its own impulse into mimicry, then it has become impure.

Similarly, eurythmy can fall into dancing when, for example, it has to convey that one person is hitting another or that someone is rushing about in a passion. But then this overflowing, this exaggeration must be held within the bounds of eurythmy itself, for when eurythmy becomes dance-like, the effect is brutal. Eurythmy must stay clear of these two extremes, mime and dance. It must regard them as strict boundaries; otherwise, it will fall into impurity or vulgarity.

Obviously, then, eurythmy must be recognized as a distinct and separate art. This is easiest to see when you watch tone eurythmy. The eurythmist is not dancing to the music but rather singing to it, singing-with-movements. If we cultivate a sense for the difference between dancing to instrumental music and this "singing-with-movements," we will then have the right feeling for the place eurythmy holds between the art of mime and the art of the dance.

Eurythmy uses the human organism more perfectly than either of these two arts, and we can hope that, because the human organism is the most perfect instrument, eurythmy shall become ever more perfect. We stress that continually. Let me add something else. We have been trying recently to perfect our coordination of stage lighting and eurythmy in order to attain an ever-perfected staging. So we can hope that eurythmy will someday be ready to take its place alongside the other arts. I should add also that unfortunately Frau Dr. Steiner[140] will not be able to perform the recitation in the usual way tonight. Ms. Mitscher[141] shall replace her. We hope that everyone present tonight will have the opportunity to hear [Marie] Steiner herself perform next time.

And so I have tried to indicate with these few words how it is that eurythmy seeks to take its place as a separate art alongside the established arts—not as something derived from this or that other art, but rather an art that draws from heretofore unknown springs, and makes use of an unaccustomed grammar of forms.

❋

On Indicative Gestures

Dornach, April 15, 1923[142]

[abridged]

If you want to let eurythmy create the right effect within your soul, then you must not confuse eurythmy with its sister arts, the arts of mime and dance. Eurythmy is neither of these. To be sure, these other arts deserve all praise, and the last thing we want to do here is to dispute their significance. But eurythmy wants to be something completely different. The only excuse for pushing eurythmic expression to the point of mime is if there is something in the underlying poetry that signifies contempt, condescension toward something. Something in the poetry implies that the corner of the speaker's mouth has turned up into a sneer, that the speaker is winking, as it were, etc. Everything that tends toward mime has to be considered in that way from the standpoint of eurythmy. If someone just wants to be a mime, then that is entirely justified. What I'm saying now does not apply to the art of mime as such, but rather to situations in which eurythmy changes into mime in a way that is not justified. Then eurythmy becomes impure.

What I want to say applies just as little to the art of dance, to dance itself, but rather only to moments when eurythmy changes inappropriately into dancing. To be sure, eurythmic movements can modulate into dance movements: for example, if something occurs in a poem in which one person hits another, does something to the other, where a powerful passion comes to expression. Then, indeed, the eurythmic movement that otherwise would have remained localized entirely within the realm of our bodily nature can modulate into dance movement. But if eurythmy changes into dance when that is not justified, if dancing for its own sake appears within eurythmy, then the effect is brutal. I'm not saying that the art of dance is brutal; what I'm saying is that when eurythmy changes into dance, it has a brutal effect. So if you really listen to what eurythmy itself is saying, then you can say: eurythmy is not pantomime; it is not any kind of mime. Those other artistic forms employ gestures that indicate something. Dance movements make use of overflowing gestures; they arise when passion flows out, so that the dancer in a sense no longer holds her movements back within the compass of consciousness. Eurythmy stands right in the middle of that encompassing consciousness. It does not have wild, dancing gestures. Eurythmy also has indicative gestures, but they always indicate understanding. We have need of indications; we need gestures that indicate something. Eurythmy has expressive gestures that want to indicate, and whose indications should have an aesthetic effect, an artistic effect. Eurythmy has such gestures that are neither intellectual constructs nor wild displays. They are not meant to be interpreted allegorically, nor are we meant to be overpowered by them. Rather, the immediate form of their lines, the whole way of moving, is meant to be pleasing and to be experienced as beautiful.

You can get a good sense of eurythmy by viewing it as singing brought into movement. Today you will also hear musical pieces; we do eurythmy to them. This "eurythmizing" is not a dance. When it is done properly, it is fundamentally different from dance: it is a singing brought into movement, not a dancing. And it is just this quality—eurythmy as singing brought into movement—that allows us to distinguish eurythmy from its sister arts. And by thinking about eurythmy in that way, you will be able to get a feeling for what I have just said.

❀

[Untitled]

Dornach, June 10, 1923[143]

From various comments that have been made recently concerning our eurythmy performances, we are starting to realize what a long time it takes for people to reach an artistic understanding of what eurythmy is meant to be. We have noticed that ordinary people who simply give themselves over to aesthetic pleasure let the eurythmy affect them through their immediate perception, and this naïve openness soon leads to a sense for eurythmy. But people who are accustomed to pondering for long periods over art—art critics, for example—have a really hard time accepting eurythmy from a genuinely artistic point of view. They often say that eurythmy has too much intellectual content, that it is extraordinarily clever—this is the latest comment heard—but there is so much intellectuality in those movements!

As a matter of fact, there is not one iota of intellectual content in them! That is the amazing fact about eurythmy: that it contains nothing intellectual at all, and you will understand it best if you do not pile up a stack of thoughts about it but, instead, simply open your artistic eye to it. For eurythmy is really just to look at and accept through a direct, visible impression. It is meant to be taken in as simply as you take in speech. With speech, you simply let it come to you. We learn it so early in our childhood that it is just there without question. It has been pushed up out of the unconscious; it is not formed by intellectual forces. It would be sad indeed if children had to think through the forming and pronouncing of words, and the learning of their meanings, before speaking. If that were so, a child would never learn to speak. Fortunately, we don't learn speech that way. Children experience speech while imitating it, in the same way that they grow. Children do not work up their growth out of thoughts: they simply respond to their human nature and grow. And so it is with speech. Children do not build it up intellectually; rather, speech arises out of their complete immersion in their surroundings.

It may look as though there must be more to eurythmy than what is there when we learn to speak. But really, there is nothing else at all. With eurythmy we have to do with a genuinely visible speech that is summoned forth from our inner nature in just as matter-of-fact a way as ordinary speech. Actually, we do something similar to gesturing whenever we speak, but we are not aware of it; we don't notice that we are sending gusts of air out on our breath continually like gestures.[144] Our stream of breath is in a certain state of vibration because of the element of thought that permeates it. As we send them outward, the gestures are transformed into audible speech sounds. These audible speech sounds originate in the head.

The human head has the important characteristic that it holds itself still, while the rest of the organism is built for movement and mobility. Just as a person sits still in a moving train or carriage while the horse or the carriage wheels move, so our human constitution—to the extent we are not head—is a kind of a carriage, a kind of organism for movement, and our head sits motionless on top of it all. Everything we experience in our head is movement of that other part of our organism that has been brought to rest. Modern physiology knows this in an external way, but only in relation to speech. It knows that there is a connection between right-hand gesturing—that is, movements of the right arm and hand—and the speech center in the left hemisphere of the brain. Unless we are totally phlegmatic, we always accompany our speech with gestures—northern people less, southern people more—and what we express through gestures comes to rest, is stopped and fixed in stillness, by our speech.

If I may turn today more particularly to those in the audience who are acquainted to some degree with anthroposophy, or who are anthroposophists, I would like to say the following. Speech takes its impulse from the human head, from organs that are directed by the head. Even if some of the organs are not in the head, they nevertheless receive some of their impulse from it. Speech is movement that has been arrested by those organs. Speech is chiefly an expression of the human I, and insofar as it is an expression of the I, it is in constant danger of being egoistic. It is in constant danger of being reduced to the vehicle of our wishes and appetites. If we were not restrained to some degree by our whole experience of speech in relation to our organism, we would give expression only to our inner experiences. We would be like children in the first, primitive stages of speech, when only inner emotions, impulses of will or of feeling can find expression. But adult social relationships compel us to orient our speech within a whole environment. Speech receives a general character thereby; it is torn away from the individual I; it becomes the common property of a culture, of an entire human group. The fact that we do manage to transcend the natural sounds that only bring egoistic tendencies to expression, and that we do manage to adjust ourselves to the speech rooted in the genius of our language, shows that there is a constant striving away from the egoistic element. This very effort to subordinate the egoistic state to a common element has its darker side, which the poet has rendered into the beautiful words: "If the soul *speaks*, alas! the *soul* speaks no longer!"[145] It is nothing other than the soul speaking when a child begins in his inarticulate way to express what he's experiencing inwardly, even though it is merely instincts and desires. Finding himself later in unegotistical speech, in a human community with speech as its common ground, spiritualizes him for this earthly life. The soul element is spiritualized by speech.

When we accompany our speech with gestures in mime, we take what is I-activity in our speech and push it back again into our astral body, into our soul. We should try to feel what is happening there, how when we accompany our words with gestures—words that, naturally, we must take from common language—we obviously need to bring some of our own personality, something individual, into the common speech. Gestures push speech back again into the soul—that is, into the astral body, into the personal.

But for this reason, you can also feel a kind of shame about the gestures—except for those that simply accompany ordinary speech in general—a feeling of shame because what they communicate belongs so particularly to our individual personality. We lay bare our souls, so to speak, through our gestures. So when we turn to mime—this holds good as an element of dramatic art—it means that what had become more spiritual in speech is now pushed back again into our soul, into our individual personality.

Consider another way that we reveal our humanity. At the pole of the head we reveal ourselves through speech, while at the pole of the foot, the pole of the leg, we reveal ourselves through dance.

If dance is really beautiful, it must be because the dancer is no longer suffusing it with his or her own egotism. It must be a total rhythmic offering. It must, so to speak, have had all personal aspects stripped away from it. When someone dances with élan,[146] the spectator has a perception of the rhythm itself as an objective thing moving as the sweep of the music directs it. In dance, we are no longer contained within ourselves; we are carried out of ourselves completely. Our body has become entirely body; it dances among other bodies and makes movements as if there were no soul in it. What one likes in dance is the verve and the perception of the sweep of movement. If the *poet* said, "When the soul *speaks*, alas, the *soul* speaks no longer," then for *dance* one should say, "When the body dances, alas, the soul is no longer there." In dance, the soul is stripped away. Speech lives in the I; mime pushes the general content of speech into the astral body. In a similar way, dance lives in the physical body, and when dance is transposed into the etheric body—that is eurythmy. Eurythmy is the transposition of the bodily movement of gymnastics or of dance out of their purely physical, bodily sphere back into the etheric body, which is something that stands near to the soul. Movements are given a soul content again by the eurythmist. In eurythmy, human movement in the physical world is transposed into the spiritual, etheric world. The movement is suffused with soul, and if eurythmy is done properly, everything—whether single movements or group movements—is drawn from what is inherent in human nature itself. The movements have the same lawful origin as all the speech sounds—A, I, L, M, and so on—that arise out of the human organism. In eurythmy we express ourselves visibly through movements, just as in speech we express ourselves audibly through speech sounds. An A and an E are absolutely specific sounds in the area of human hearing, and any eurythmy movement is just as specific an expression in the area of the whole human being, since the eurythmy movement originates in the etheric body, within our own inner being.

You might say that in our everyday speech we express ourselves as earthly beings. In the movements that are intimately related to our etheric body and that become visible speech when we do eurythmy, we reveal what the gods wanted us to be: not an earthly but rather a wholly divine being who has a dwelling place in the human form. So when we look at eurythmy, we are no longer just enjoying the sweep of a dance form and the rhythm of dance movements, but we are receiving what is said to us by our cosmic selves. We are made soul by the spirit—who does have something to say! So if a poem is recited or declaimed, or a piece of music is played, and eurythmy accompanies it, then that is really like an orchestral ensemble.

Artistic feeling and perception are all we need in order to gain a simple impression of what is happening on the stage. Usually a few words of introduction are offered, but that is only so as to point out that what appears before the audience in complete simplicity is summoned forth from the whole of our human nature—yes, from our cosmic stature. What is seemingly simple is in fact drawn from the profoundest secrets of our soul life as we live in the world. Nothing is loftier or wiser than the unconscious utterances of a tiny child. In eurythmy, the wisdom has been drawn out more or less consciously, but this makes no difference for the immediate artistic impression.

There is no basis, therefore, for the idea that eurythmy has some sort of intellectual basis. Just as in mime what originates in the head is pushed from the head down into the arms, so in eurythmy invisible movements from within the human being are pushed up into the movement of the arms. Through eurythmy we can gain an impression of our inner nature as beings of soul, of how the whole of our human nature expresses itself in the world through our truly human nature.

Of course, all of this makes it necessary that speech artists reciting for eurythmy be aware that every real poet performs a certain hidden eurythmy in the shaping of language, in what we can call the imaginative, musical element of language. A hidden eurythmy that lurks within the poet's language—that is what you have to be able to hear if you are reciting and declaiming for eurythmy. Audiences don't enjoy that today; our time is too inartistic for that. Frau Dr. Steiner[147] has worked for years to develop a style of recitation that returns to the genuinely artistic foundation of speech. It will be through eurythmy that we rediscover the artistic character of speech once again.

There are always people who come and say, "Yes, I know, we've been told that eurythmy is visible speech, that it is neither dance nor mime. But what we liked best in the performance"—and again, these are not laypeople speaking but rather intellectuals who have spent a great deal of thought on how the arts are evolving—"what we liked best were the pieces that were danced to music." My dear friends, nothing was danced to music! Just because there was music, people think that the eurythmist was dancing. Things are regarded so carelessly today! Eurythmy does not *dance* to music; it *sings* to it—in movement. Eurythmy is singing-in-movement. Because eurythmy is chiefly movement and speech is chiefly song, what you see accompanying the music is not dance, but singing-in-movement. You have to feel this distinction as you look at it; only then can you entertain a correct judgment about it.

We have to gradually cultivate an understanding of the importance of eurythmy. The art of eurythmy was drawn from artistic springs that remain unfamiliar today. People need to understand the significance of eurythmy as it develops in the midst of dance, mime, and speech.

True speech is raised up out of human movement, but it is not raised up as far as the head. If it is raised up as far as the head, it becomes everyday language. If speech is kept down in the arms and hands, which lie between the twin poles of head and feet, then we become able to express our real nature as humans standing on the earth without slipping into one extreme or the other. We might also say that it is only in speech that our temporal nature expresses what it feels about things. In eurythmy, our outer nature expresses through movements what we experience in outer events. Eurythmy is still in its infancy today; it is still imperfect. We know that quite well because we are our own severest critics! But it will evolve further. Eurythmy's medium is human nature itself, which is a microcosm containing all the secrets of the macrocosm. Eurythmy shall evolve further and shall one day take its place as a fully recognized art alongside the other, traditional art forms.

On the Genius of Language
The Human Body of Formative Forces

Dornach, June 16, 1923[148]

In the course of my lectures, I have spoken about the genius of language in various contexts.[149] In saying various things about the genius of language, I wanted to allude to a certain discovery that we can make by undertaking research into relationships that are inherent within language itself. Those relationships turn out to be entirely inward ones. What you will find is that language actually has a kind of a soul of its own living inside of it. It is a soul that comes over us, a soul that cultivates us. By growing into language, we cultivate ourselves. A kind of objective spirituality—that is what I mean by the term "genius of language."

Now I'd like to point out briefly just one example to show what can come of such a turn toward the genius of language.

When we think about something ever so cleverly, and feel we are able to reconcile it with other thoughts we've had, we say that we *grasp*[150] it. When using the German language at least,[151] we say that we *grasp* one or another thing.

Now let's turn to that word "grasp." Just what do we mean by that? We mean that we take hold of it—"comprehend" it. I *grasp* the watch by picking it up. Hence we characterize the relationship that our thoughts have to things with an expression that actually signifies an outer action, through which we enter into a palpable[152] relationship with external objects.

So why is it that language brings us something so very peculiar? From the clever, enlightened perspective of today, language is just crazy. It speaks just as though we were taking hold of something with our hands when we comprehend the meaning.

Language isn't talking nonsense, however. And it is one of the most beautiful experiences we can have when we realize that, in such a case, language isn't talking nonsense at all. For when we do the thing that we describe when we say that we grasp something, we really are grasping something—just not with a physical hand. We are grasping with a hand that forms itself out of the so-called etheric body or body of formative forces. And language is right. When it comprehends something, the etheric body carries out a movement that signifies an indicating gesture and a rounding of the specially formed limb; that is what happens if something has been "grasped." The expression "grasped" is meant in quite a literal way! It is just that what is grasping is the etheric body rather than the physical body.

So we have to ask ourselves: What is the source of a wisdom as great as that which dwells within language?

That wisdom has been passed down to us from epochs in which people felt in a more vital way what it is that we are actually doing when we think. If only the expression did not sound so paradoxical! But it is correct; it only sounds paradoxical. And so I do not want to make any apologies for the expression, but I almost feel the need to apologize for saying it. Phenomena such as this come down to us from the times in which people still felt inwardly how active we are when we think.

Today we think least of all when we think. Today we feel least of all when we feel. Actually, we have no idea what we're doing when we think. We are most asleep when we think.

If we take hold of something, then we feel that we are moving our arm, our hand. When we think, we no longer feel anything. But back when people formed their comprehension out of the innermost recesses of their souls, then it was the case that people still felt they were performing an action, that they were grasping with a body subtler than the physical body.

And back when people still had the feeling that when we think, we reach out, we touch and feel something with our etheric body—back then people knew how intimately speaking is connected with this grasping that is inside of thinking. They knew how intimate the relationship is between breathing and comprehension. People knew how the brain sucks up out of the breathing process what it uses as a kind of subtle substance in the act of comprehending. They did not know it in the way that people know things today—but that's not worth much anyway! When people said, for example, "The day is clear, the night is dull," then in saying "clear," what they were feeling was that their gropings were meeting no resistance. When it is clear, the etheric body or body of formative forces meets no resistance; it can feel its way about. When it is dull, then it meets resistance everywhere; then it is not possible to feel our way around; then we bump into things everywhere; we cannot feel our way around.

So you see, back then people felt how breathing is at work within speaking, while in thinking, on the other hand, something that is used in order to comprehend is drawn out of the breath, as it were. They felt how speaking is a denser form of grasping, a grasping that proceeds within the air. And if you realize that the act of comprehension is indeed a gesture, an action, a pointing at things that we do with our etheric bodies, then you will also grasp how the denser breathing in speaking is actually a gesture, how it is only the condensed gesture of thinking.

Why is the gesture condensed? Because as a result of this condensation, thinking is brought down to the level of feeling. It is because thinking is immersed in feeling.

So, in our thinking we withdraw our formative-forces body somewhat from our physical body, from our corporeal movements, and we make invisible movements with it.

Eurythmy goes in the opposite direction. Now it seeks not abstract thought but feeling: How do we *grasp* things? And in particular, how do we grasp things that have been taken hold of in a genuinely artistic way? And eurythmy pushes the gesture of the etheric body back down into the physical body again. Eurythmy makes it possible to perform what the poet also has in giving shape to a poem, what happens in musicality: a subtle, artistic comprehension that is in the nature of feeling and will. Eurythmy allows what lies within the activity of the soul to fall back down into bodily movements again, so that then the physical body moves in the way that is natural for the etheric body to move.

In that way we follow the steps that our souls take, what our souls experience in moving from comprehension to speaking. We take further steps along the same path. We descend more deeply into our bodies than we do in speaking. We proceed from aeriform things to those that are fixed, half-fixed—in short, to that within the body which then becomes the basis for external movements.

And because these external movements have no utility, it is precisely such gestures as are summoned forth in that way from the etheric body that come to light in eurythmy. They allow us to achieve a high degree of freedom—freedom in the inner sense. Our souls are borne out into the external, visible world.

You see, we can distinguish between the outer and the inner human being. Many things can be explained that way. So just imagine—don't worry, you don't need to be like Demosthenes,[153] you don't need to go put stones in your mouth[154]—simply imagine that you had just taken a bite of something; and now you want to speak, but you are hindered from speaking. The speech apparatus needs to be completely mobile for us not to be hindered in speaking freely. Many people often have a bite of something in the mouth of their thinking. Then they cannot comprehend; then they are hindered. We could describe those hindrances in detail. There are hindrances in regard to thinking, hindrances to our inner life; and we can be hindered in speaking by a bite of something or a wad that we stick in our mouth—hindered in the making of gestures that have already been pushed down into the air.

As a boy, I was taken to the church fair. Something peculiar happened. Oddly, the boys—I don't think there were any girls—the boys were tied up in sacks and then we were supposed to keep walking inside our sacks. Everyone kept falling down. Helpers were posted every five feet who would lift us up, and then we would continue on our way inside our sacks. Now that is what you would call trying to walk with an external hindrance! In such a case, we carry out only the limited movements we are able to perform despite the hindrance.

But in all aspects of life, the human physical body is just such a hindrance to the continual movements that the etheric body wants to carry out in understanding the external world. Now, if we liberate the etheric body completely, and ask it what it senses when confronted with this or that object in the outer world, and then let that flow out freely into the physical body, the opposite arises: unhindered movements of our inner being.

Just as someone can tie up your physical body in a sack and hinder you externally, so is the physical body a kind of sack that hinders the free movements of the etheric body. And by studying the movement potentials of the etheric body, we can train the physical body until it's no longer a sack but rather something that follows these movements of the etheric body. We can reach the point where, in fact, the life of the soul, to the extent that it runs its course within the etheric body, comes to expression through the physical body, not just as with the air, as with audible speech, but the point at which a real language arising within the physical body itself gives expression to something which otherwise originates within the etheric body as well—as here language is indeed a reflex of the etheric body out of the astral sensing.

In this way, it actually becomes possible to call forth a genuinely visible language in eurythmy. Eurythmy really is not something thought out. Rather, it has been summoned forth from of the inner life of nature; it is something that has been transposed onto the external physical body, just as that which still lies enclosed within even subtler organs during the tender age of childhood is carried over into the larynx and its associated organs and then becomes gestures within the air. Just as conventional singing unfolds in the form of gestures within the element of air, eurythmic speaking and singing unfolds in gestures that are then executed by the physical body.

I would go so far as to claim that, no matter where you begin contemplating human nature, it is possible to find a way from there to an explanation of eurythmy.

You see, that is the difference between [what we are trying to do] and the sorts of aesthetic programs people favor today. People start with definitions, and then they try to make reality fit their definitions. And when they talk about it, then they just rattle off their program. But we can speak about eurythmy from any number of perspectives because it is not just an aesthetic program. It is something living that can be illumined from many divergent angles. No matter how many times I have tried to illuminate eurythmy from every imaginable point of view, in the same way that you can photograph an object from all sorts of different angles, it always remains the same object. But ever and again it must be said that eurythmy is a kind of revelation of human nature itself which makes use of articulated gestures—not mime or dance-like movements—to express what resonates through musical motifs, on the one hand, or is recited or declaimed, on the other. As for declamation, it should exhibit qualities that allow the genuinely artistic elements to shine through. That means looking to the formation of the speech, to the shaping of the sounds, at the way in which one sound colors another—that is to say, we listen to the timbre of the language,[155] or to the musical elements in the language—meter, rhythm, melodic theme, and so forth. So that the mode of recitation and declamation that merely dramatizes the prosaic content, which is so avidly pursued in our rather inartistic age, should gradually yield to the genuine art of recitation and declamation with the help of eurythmy.

Frau Dr. Steiner[156] has worked for many years to cultivate this art of recitation. More artistic epochs used to have an innate feeling for it. You simply cannot accompany eurythmy with the arts of declamation and recitation that are favored today, because eurythmy has to dig right down to the actual artistic foundations of poetry.

And if you pursue eurythmy's musical side, then you do not dance. Actually, you are singing visibly. It is a visible singing! You will need to gain a feeling, a new sensibility for the difference between visible singing and actual dance. Only then will you be able to see and understand the difference.

In any case, nobody should believe that eurythmy is about any kind of interpretation. It is a matter of sensing through an immediate perception, not through explanation or interpretation, how the harmony that wells forth out of our inner nature as human beings calls forth its effects as beauty, as artistry.

The Mood of the St. John's Festival
Living with the Festivals

Dornach, June 24, 1923[157]

The art of eurythmy is not trying to be any kind of dance or mime. That is something I have often taken the liberty of emphasizing when speaking introductory words such as these before the performances we have attempted. What you really have in eurythmy is an attempt to create visible speech or visible song. The same lawfulness that underlies the genesis of everything associated with sounds and tones in speech and song underlies eurythmy. It is a lawfulness that has been called forth out of the deepest recesses of our souls and of our connection to the world. It underlies eurythmy when you project it not onto the larynx and its neighboring organs, as in audible speech and song, but rather onto our human organs of movement. If you consider that audible speech and song are, at bottom, a kind of gesture, a gesture of forming and shaping of the exhaled stream of air—if you keep that in mind, then you will already be quite close to understanding that just as speech represents a kind of gesture on the part of the air that we set in motion and that streams within us, something speech- or song-like can also be revealed, can also come to expression through the movement of the human limbs or of the whole human being.

In framing this analogy, we have to remain clear about one thing, however: that we have no hope of understanding how language of any kind arises if we stop short at our physical nature, the systems of our physical bodies. What we have to do instead is attend to the ways in which a higher, suprasensory organism is at work within the systems of the physical body. And we have to begin by saying that those forces which give shape to the air that take form in audible speech and in song are stimulated within our suprasensory organism, within our etheric bodies. What lives within us as human beings in that way can be studied,[158] which leads us to the insight that underlying speech and song is something that lifts us up above our earthly existence as physical beings. To be sure, in everyday human intercourse and also in scientific communications, the organs of speech and all that they conjure up are initially placed at the service of earthly life. But the capacity to speak and to sing is something that does not proceed directly from the physical organism. On the contrary, it streams into our physicality, if you will allow the expression. For it is simply the case that human beings who have lifted themselves up out of their physical and sensory existence, people whose suprasensory nature commands their physical and sensory nature, are living within speech and song. This is the case even though speech and song, as they express themselves in the earthly element of air, initially reveal themselves by shining into the earthly element. Hence it will be possible to bring to expression, in speech and song, something that corresponds to a universal human longing: the longing to escape the physical and sensory worlds and enter into spiritual relationships. Indeed, such a correspondence is present in every art.

Just as language—let us say, colloquial speech—represents the adaptation of an unearthly element to an earthly one, our movements, our gait, our running are likewise the adaptation to the earth of our suprasensory nature as it streams into our limbs. But we can strip away from this earthly existence the movements that have arisen through adaptation to the earthly. We can do this by giving form to the movements of the feet and legs, and also especially in the gestural movement of arms and hands—which are, after all, the part of our nature that is most expressive with regard to spatial expression. We can, so to speak, represent what lives purely within our souls, what does not allow itself to be overpowered by the earthly, which is the case with walking and running, and also with the arms, to the extent that they serve everyday movement. We can represent what does not allow itself to be dominated by the earthly, what wants instead—and I mean this in the strongest possible sense now—to give expression to what lives within us as the most exalted earthly creatures.

If you take all this into consideration, then you will admit that an extraordinary amount has flowed into language in the course of this adaptation to earthly circumstances. This is particularly the case with the so-called "civilized" peoples. And progress within the historical evolution of language actually does result from language adapting itself ever more closely to the earthly realm.

But if today, on the contrary, we can tear the movements of our limbs away from earthly service, so to speak, and make those movements into the pure expression of the otherworldly, transcendent [forces] dwelling within the human soul, then we have created a far greater possibility for bringing our purely human inwardness to expression through this kind of gesture than would be possible through language. For language, especially where it has "progressed," has so accommodated itself to earthly concerns that it is no longer easy to bring it back into the transcendent element.

A prime example of this, ladies and gentlemen, would be an attempt to embody through the visible language and the visible song of eurythmy something like—if I might put it thus—a particular solemn festival mood.

Today we would like to undertake the experiment of trying to reveal the mood of St. John's through eurythmy. In modern life, we have utterly lost any understanding of the aspect of human life that involves communing with the cycle of the seasons. We really do experience diurnal rhythm strongly. We eat breakfast, lunch, supper, and often at other hours of the day. We are conscious that the position of the Sun relative to the Earth has some meaning for our daily lives as human beings. We are not fully satisfied if we are not able to participate in the cosmic life of time.

Although it might strike us modern people as quite improbable, or even paradoxical, in earlier epochs, participating in the cycle of the seasons was felt to be every bit as significant as our own experience of daily rhythms. In the past, people were conscious that they needed to participate in the diurnal rhythms for the sake of their physical bodies: people need to eat at the appointed times of the day. But our ancestors were also well aware—and this is something to which conventional intellectual historians devote far too little attention—that we as human beings do not have merely that abstract construct people still call "soul" today—even though nobody has anything like the right idea about it. Certainly most do not go so far as Fritz Mauthner,[159] who wanted to get rid of the word "soul" altogether, and introduce the word *Geseel* ["soulings"][160] in its place. He cannot imagine a "soul" any longer. Its promptings have become so vague for him that he wants to create a new term that is analogous to *Geschwister* ["siblings"]—not "brother" or "sister," but instead a generic term for people who belong together somehow. In the same way, once the concept of a real soul disappears from the background, once thoughts and feelings and will impulses have all just run together, you just coin a generic term like "soulings." I really hope that in the future people will not talk about the sensibilities of my "soulings" instead of the sensibilities of my *soul*! But very clever people are already working hard at that. Even though it might sound paradoxical to us—because everyone knows how much more clever we have become than in the olden days—our ancestors were conscious that there needed to be a care of their souls. And so people believed that they would have to attune the needs of their souls to the course of the year, just as people needed to attune the needs of their bodies to diurnal rhythms. And it was from such a lively human consciousness that the festivals of the year arose: Christmas, the feast of the winter solstice; Easter, the festival of spring; and above all the feast of the summer solstice, St. John's. And again, Michaelmas in the fall. The various comprehensive rituals that were instituted in ancient epochs, and then later all the actions that recall those rituals, penetrated into our ancestors' consciousness, into their feeling, into their sensibility. People considered it just as necessary to nourish their souls as it was to feed their bodies with physical substances. As the time of high summer approached at St. John's, people felt a hunger to experience those days in festivities that released them from their ties to the earth. Those festivities engaged them in all kinds of ritual games of movement, one might say, in all kinds of activities that made them aware they were not merely bound to the earth, but rather able to raise themselves up and gaze outward into the wide-ranging cosmos, into the ether.

It was just such an exaltation into the etheric sphere that was celebrated at St. John's. The experience was lived unconsciously. It was not actually spoken in words; rather, it lived unconsciously within the people. If they had expressed it in words, however, then we might imagine an elder saying: The physical body has a hunger that is satisfied by the day; the soul has a hunger that is satisfied by the year.

And then there is the spirit with its universality. The spirit does not undergo changes as powerful as those of the body and the soul. Our physical body needs nourishment every day. In the course of our lives, our souls often experience hunger, and they often need nourishment. And in ancient times, the year did indeed give souls both hunger and nourishment, whereas the spirit was something that remained constant over long periods of time. But in ancient times, our ancestors also knew that dawning mornings, high summers, and evening dusks of the life of the spirit were present within the unfolding epochs of human evolution.

We did not need a Spengler[161] to tell us in a dilettantish way what earlier epochs knew out of ancient, deeper insights, even though those insights may no longer be appreciated in the present. They were deeper than many of our contemporary insights. We did not need all this recent controversy in order to know that in the course of its historical epochs, the human spirit experiences a kind of progression through morning, noon, and evening, through spring, summer, autumn, and so forth. As human beings, we feel ourselves to be placed into the cosmos with body, soul, and spirit.

We can gain just the right insight into the festivals of the year by looking to this older life of the soul that was not defined abstractly, but rather directly *felt*. If we hope to overcome materialism, what we need again today are much more concrete ways of bringing the soul to life than a philosophy or anything else of that sort can give us. It is an artifact of the materialism that dominates our age that our last connection to the cosmos is through our physical bodies. If we are looking for materialism, no need to go all the way to the scientists or the monists.[162] We can find it—indeed, we can find it in a much more comprehensive form—in people who still experience the course of the sun only in their physical bodies, people who care only to observe the times of the day with breakfast, lunch, five o'clock tea, and supper, people who no longer participate in the course of the year with inner intensity. Strong evidence that our consciousness of the inner life of the soul has disappeared, that materialism has our consciousness in its grip, is provided by the conventionality of our festivals. We are no longer able to enter into the moods of the festivals.

That is why an art like eurythmy, which is striving to create out of new artistic sources, turns to such festivals again. Please understand: it is not an attempt to warm up cold traditions, but rather to create something new.

But at the end of the day, nature remains constant. The mood of St. John's remains the mood of St. John's. And especially since the goal of eurythmy's visible language is to represent not what binds us to the Earth but rather what takes us out into the cosmos, into the wide etheric worlds—for that reason, these moods of eurythmy are an especially apt way to give form to the festivals of the year.

Whenever I introduce our eurythmy performances, I always say that we stand at the very beginning. We are our own worst critics; we know that it has to be developed further. But it really does have limitless possibilities within it. May our performance today be judged in that spirit! We have tried to evoke the mood of St. John's in selecting the program, and especially in the staging—everything that imbues and resounds through the performance. So today's performance is yet another occasion on which we must beg your kind indulgence. It is just a beginning, but it is something that just has to be tried. It is important that humanity should regain a sense for participation not just in daily rhythms, but also in the periodic formations of cosmic existence. Human beings must participate in the diurnal rhythms of the cosmos with their bodies, the annual rhythm in the cosmos with their souls, and the rhythms of the great, historical epochs with their spirits.

Perhaps it will seem odd to you that we are launching such an experiment in fostering human progress from an artistic perspective. But art *always* has collaborated intensively in pushing humanity forward, epoch by epoch. Thus eurythmy is warranted in its attempts to contribute to the overcoming of materialism. We need to escape from materialism and enter into a more spiritual atmosphere. That should be the actual goal of the St. John's mood. It was ever so that the mood of St. John's sought to lift humanity up out of earthly life through the warmth poured out by the Sun as from the cosmos itself. It evoked the light that reached its highest point at midsummer, when humanity could become aware how it is that as human beings we are enclosed within something that streams in from above, and not just what rises up from below. This mood of St. John's, which was ever deployed to awaken a consciousness that we as humans are cosmic and not merely earthly beings. That same mood can be employed by humanity today as a way of striving out beyond the earth. That can best be accomplished through means that already began as a spiritual deepening of the life of our contemporary civilization, and eurythmy is intended as one such means. Please allow us, therefore, to try to conjure up the mood of St. John's through eurythmy today.

Let me conclude by drawing your attention to the artwork on your programs,[163] and to our programming, through which we have attempted to capture the mood of St. John's by choosing pieces of the right artistic timbre. The mood of St. John's is difficult to describe in words. What we can do is stimulate what lives within it as a human striving to escape from the earthly into the cosmic. A striving to escape our own earthly, telluric nature and to enter into our cosmic nature. Calling this mood of St. John's to life: that is something we want to achieve by suffusing every aspect with the St. John's mood. That is what I wanted to say with these brief, introductory words.

The Origin of Language and Eurythmy's Language of Gesture

Dornach, July 1, 1923,

On the occasion of the pedagogical conference at the Goetheanum[164]

Let me begin by expressing my particular pleasure and satisfaction that we are again able to present a eurythmy performance to the teachers gathered here. I already sought to characterize the essence of eurythmy during our dear friends' last visit. Today let me just precede our performance with a few words of introduction.

Eurythmy can assume three ways within contemporary life: firstly, as art, as artistic eurythmy; secondly, viewed from the perspective of pedagogy, as a kind of spiritualized ensouled gymnastics, as pedagogical eurythmy; and finally, as a certain branch of therapy, as curative eurythmy.

Eurythmy as an art form is rooted not only in the fact that, as human beings, we are able to reveal what lives within our inmost souls through audible speech and audible song, but also in the possibility of creating a real, visible language through the movements of our own bodies, our own limbs, or through the movements of individual performers or groups of performers in space. It is not our physical bodies that speak and sing, after all: we sing and speak from our souls. And we discover the real origins of everything having to do with speaking and singing only when we trace them back to the suprasensory aspects of our own human constitution. The outer, physical, corporeal aspect of our human nature that we see with our eyes is grounded within the so-called formative forces or etheric body, which represents a connection between our actual spirit and soul and the physical body. If we reveal ourselves through speech or through song, then this arises because both the elements that remain separate within us due to our current stage of evolutionary development, breathing and thought, coalesce. The exhaled air is shaped, and it is thoughts, ideas, that do the shaping.[165] And the result when the exhaled stream of air is shaped in this way is that a kind of gesture shaped by thought manifests itself in the sounds of speech and in musical tones. In making these gestures shaped by thought, our human organs of movement remain—for the most part, at least—motionless. Only when we have the feeling that we are unable to give full expression to things that we wish to communicate by way of the mere sound that is shaped by thought do we take recourse to gesture. And we use customary, everyday gestures to support our speech, which adds to more conventional language a kind of augmented revelation of inwardness. Those are merely indicating gestures, however. Such indicating gestures never actually signify anything more than a kind of babbling.[166] Our speaking begins with babbling and then becomes cultivated, articulate language, and so it is also with gesture: babbling in everyday gesticulations—something all of us do to some degree—can be cultivated as articulate, thoroughly artistic *gesture*. That is what happens in eurythmy.

In everyday speech, breathing and thought coalesce into a unified whole. But the rhythm that lives within the circulation of the blood and the movements of the human limbs can also come together as another such unified whole. The same relationship that prevails at the one pole of our human constitution between breathing and thought also prevails between the circulation of the blood, which dissolves material substances, consumes them, and the movements of the limbs. When we reveal ourselves by joining thought and breathing in speech, we bring to expression more of what lives between human beings. In the same way, we can reveal what we as human beings experience in our relationship to the cosmos, to the whole universe (although, to be sure, it is something that we often experience only unconsciously in our ordinary consciousness). We can [bring to expression][167] those mysterious inner processes that play out between the gestures of our movements and our inner metabolism.

If we allow our knowledge of human nature to lead us back to the etheric body, then we find within movement the same thoughts, feeling, and will that otherwise reveal themselves by way of the physical body.

But please understand, ladies and gentlemen, that the lines between thinking, feeling, and willing are not hard and fast. And so, although it might sound paradoxical, it is the case that in the etheric or formative-forces body, the will thinks and thinking wills. Both these activities, willing and thinking, can shade over into each other; feeling always stands between them. Language flows from feeling. It flows forth from feeling into the breath, and then thought forms what is spoken. Feeling flows into the circulation of the blood as well.

As you know, "blood is a very special fluid";[168] it contains the innermost aspects of human nature as they relate to the cosmos. And movement—[artistic] gesture—can give form to something that exemplifies the relationship corresponding to a rhythm. That rhythm is actually macrocosmic, and it finds microcosmic expression in the circulation of human blood. Everything that the macrocosm would speak within human beings, within the human microcosm, can be spoken via the visible language of eurythmy, through expressive gesture. Nature brings forth audible language unconsciously out of the child. Similarly, with the knowledge of the relationship between the will and the circulation of the blood by way of the etheric body, we can call forth meaningful gestures—gestures as meaningful as the sounds of speech. These gestures will be like an alphabet in which each movement corresponds to a specific expression of the soul. In this way, we can obtain a visible language that contains nothing arbitrary, that consists not of spontaneously devised gestures, but flows rather, like speech or song themselves, from an inner lawfulness of human nature. Thereby we become capable of using the "movement-circulation pole" of our human constitution to perform what had been set forth originally by the "respiration-thought pole." That is the source of this orchestral collaboration that presents itself to you in the art of eurythmy. You can see upon the stage how it is that human beings speak the language of the cosmos.

On the other hand, poetry will be declaimed and recited—you will hear poems performed using certain techniques of declamation or recitation. The way that happens is something like the harmony of two instruments in an orchestra. In our time, which has become rather inartistic, little feeling for genuine declamation and recitation remains. Latent within all genuine poetry there is a declamation or recitation that is already an inner eurythmy, so of course one of eurythmy's tasks is to express it.

For many years, Frau Dr. Steiner[169] has striven to bring this art back to life. Genuine declamation, genuine recitation, can still be easily misunderstood. Whenever recitation and declamation are to accompany eurythmy, you will see how necessary it is to reveal the pictorial-imaginative dimension, on the one hand, and, on the other hand, the musical-thematic, rhythmic, metrical dimension—in this particular recitation and in all genuine recitation and declamation. Not the kind of prosaic accentuation that leads every dilettante to think that he can also declaim and recite, but rather the kind of artistic forming of speech that is the essence of actual poetry. That is what I wanted to say about the artistic aspect of eurythmy.

And then there is eurythmy's pedagogical aspect. It asks us to perform movements, but each and every movement is suffused with spirit and soul. For that reason, it situates us within the world and within life in a way that mere gymnastics cannot. Gymnastics arose at a time in which materialism began to hold sway. People rightly saw that gymnastics is a means of exercising the will, but that was a time when they had become accustomed to focusing solely upon our physical body. Hence the question they always asked was: What movements ought to be performed in keeping with the laws of the physical organism? But such an approach fails to grasp human nature as a whole. I certainly do not want to criticize gymnastics. We even introduced gymnastics into the curriculum of the Waldorf School[170] as soon as we had the financial means to do so. And today we still pursue gymnastics enthusiastically—physical gymnastics—together with our pursuit of the more spirit-infused, ensouled gymnastics that is eurythmy. What must be kept in mind, however, is that, whereas conventional gymnastics always looks only to the human physical body, and actually suppresses the spirit and soul in that process, pedagogical eurythmy brings our whole human being—body, soul, and spirit—into movement. Each and every movement bears the stamp of the soul; eurythmy flows as from the lips of our speaking souls.

That is why school-aged children (and, indeed, children of all ages) find their way into eurythmy as naturally as young children find their way into speech. If they are properly instructed, the children feel that doing eurythmy is a natural and obvious revelation of human nature itself. Just as it is natural for human beings to pour out their souls in language, to send them forth into the air in song, it can come to feel natural for us to orient our souls more toward our wills in gestural movements of our limbs and in spatial movement. These movements have been fashioned so as to reveal themselves outwardly while also working inwardly through strengthening, ensouling, and spiritualizinng.

And thirdly, eurythmy represents a kind of therapy. We certainly do not want to dream up cures in some dilettantish or amateurish way. But it is the case that when eurythmic movements of an artistic or pedagogical nature are transformed so that they reflect back in a certain way into our human constitution itself, then certain organic conditions can improve. So with movements that have been transformed, metamorphosed to a degree—not with the same movements you see here in artistic eurythmy—you get something that can have a healing, a therapeutic effect in the case of certain illnesses and other debilitating processes. In our Arlesheim Clinic,[171] headed by Dr. Ita Wegman, and also in our clinic in Stuttgart, we practice curative eurythmy as an integral part of our therapeutic regimen. This treatment is already yielding good results that are entirely demonstrable—just as the Waldorf School has demonstrated that pedagogical eurythmy is likewise bearing good fruit.

Nevertheless, today I would like to beg your forbearance, ladies and gentlemen, as I always do before such performances, or "attempts at performances." We know all too well that in every aspect of eurythmy we still remain at the beginning of this art. We know that the pedagogical aspect, the therapeutic supplement—all of that will require much further development. But anyone who takes up this matter can be sure that unlimited possibilities for development are latent within it because it makes use of the most perfect instrument available, the whole human being. No other art makes use of this most perfect instrument in the same way, not even the art of mime, which makes only partial use of the human body as a kind of adjunct to language. And so we dare to hope that eurythmy will perfect itself continuously, and that one day a time will come when it is no longer necessary just to beg indulgence because eurythmy stands at the beginning of its evolution. We hope for a time when eurythmy will be recognized as an entirely valid younger sibling who can stand with her older, fully established sister arts.

Overcoming Gravity through Eurythmy

Dornach, July 8, 1923[172]

I have always preceded these performances with a few remarks about eurythmy. Today, I would like to speak about eurythmy from yet another, very specific point of view. We need to be completely clear about one thing: eurythmy is an attempt to create a visible speech, a visible speech that is a kind of sculpting and that will be able to reveal the experiences of the human soul more vividly and therefore more artistically than tone and speech themselves are able to do. In order to accomplish this, we need to have a genuinely anthroposophical command of the process of speech development and speech formation. We need to understand fully how that process is rooted within human nature itself.

Speech is, first of all, an expression of what human beings bring forth out of the depths of their souls and communicate outwardly with the help of physical organs. If you think about speech and song as expressions of the human soul, you can come to see that song offers a deeper, more inward expression of human soul life than speech—especially the speech of our civilized languages. Speech imprints some particular meaning on tone, and the tone becomes a speech sound thereby. A speech sound is a tone that bears meaning. But because meaning—in other words, thought—has entered the sound, speech has taken on an inartistic cast. The term "artistic" can be applied only to something that offers an image of human experience to immediate perception. Hence we see that song becomes more artistic the more it succeeds in eliminating the words and getting back to musicality. With language, a poet must struggle to overcome the intellectual element by which speech serves merely as a means of communication, the element through which it expresses abstract thought and meaning. Any true poet must be willing to try to reveal soul experiences either by an imaginative play of language—making one sound brighten another, a sound illuminate or darken itself, and the like—or by a musical play of language, making rhymes and alliterations, using rhythms and beat, creating motifs that are like melodies.

From this point of view, of all the poetry that travels around the world today, at this rather inartistic time, ninety-nine percent certainly is not poetry at all. One percent at most! A poet's calling is not to make poems *about* the spirit; it is to allow the spirit to flow *into* language. The tone color of language, the musicality of language—that is the revelation the poet should be seeking.

Now we can trace language back to its fundamental elements, as it were. With the help of spiritual science, we can readily observe how speech as we know it, and particularly the kind of language that is spoken today, is utterly determined by our nervous systems. Everything that our nerve-sense system experiences flows into the shaping of our breath, which then becomes a kind of airy gesture. Just as in ordinary life, when we feel our speech is inadequate, we already help it along with gestures that can be really expressive, so too are invisible gestures being formed in speech, in the air that is pushed out on our breath—gestures made of air. They transmit what is then borne by speech. But in these air gestures, thought lives and weaves and moves, which is the abstract expression of the life of our souls.

But now we can give form to the soul's experiences in quite another way. Our nerve-sense system is, after all, only one pole of our human organism. Its opposite pole is our system of movement, with all that belongs to it. Obviously, by means of our ordinary gestures and posture, this pole of the movement system supports and reinforces those air gestures that we have found to be influenced by the nerve-sense system. But this primitive aid to our speech that our everyday gestures provide can be developed further. We can find gestures artistically formed, clearly articulated, that relate to the ordinary gestures in the same way that articulate, beautifully polished speech relates to the babbling of a child. We can say that the gestures we see in daily life are a kind of babbling compared to what will come about through eurythmy as a cultivated, highly developed language of gesture.

Just what will this accomplish? Well, here is what we will accomplish. As human beings descend from pre-earthly existence into earthly life, they become denizens of the Earth precisely by virtue of possessing the special equipment of a nervous system, which is oriented toward the development of the head. It is the head that we form first when we come to Earth and cloak ourselves in a body, after having lived a pre-natal life in which we are all soul and spirit. The various organs of the head, which are the first to form when we enter into earthly existence, are actually there so that the part of our nature that aspires to play a role in physical earthly life is able to insert itself into earthly life in the right way. The head sits above the rest of our physical organism so that gravity, the force coming from the earth, will be restricted in its influence. The head is not really subject to gravity; it wants to be an expression of the cosmos it resembles. Indeed, we can say that the human head shows by its form that it is born out of the cosmos, where there is no gravity, and inserts itself into the active force of gravity that is controlling the human body from birth to death.

The fact that human beings learn an earthly language and sing earthly words to their music means that to some degree we are subject to the force of gravity coming from the earth. Most of all, we are subject to gravity in our movement system. When we walk, when we move our hands and arms, gravity is continually active in these movements. We overcome its force to some extent since, with every step we take, the free, weightless part of our organism is fighting the gravity that weighs us down, and to which all human beings are subject during earthly life.

Now, one is privileged to see something quite beautiful when an action takes place that is fundamental to speech: that is, when the weightless, supra-earthly human being that had been summoned down into the realm of gravity emerges on the other side of that process, as it were. Our movement organism bears a heavy weight, and we liberate ourselves from that earthly force only in a weak form, in an entirely elementary way, with every step we take, with every gesture. But we also have a way of liberating ourselves completely from those earthly forces: we can lead song over into rhythmical, metrical movements by making use of our most expressive human movements, those of the arms and hands. In that way, we can transform gestures weighed down by gravity into free gestures. Now something of supreme importance comes into view. We watch as human beings, even as they are enmeshed within the sphere of gravity, continuously overcome the force of gravity through the power of their own souls.

Thus, while the ordinary speech we use as we stand within gravity has become an instrument for abstract expression, the endeavor of eurythmy to overcome gravity by living gestures of hands and arms becomes a new kind of speech that accomplishes the opposite. Our ordinary speech carries heaven down to Earth and integrates heaven into Earth, as it were. Eurythmy, on the other hand, arrives at its revelatory gestures through the meaningful overcoming of gravity within the movement system; it allows us to tear ourselves away from the earth and to express the life of our souls in such a way that with every gesture we seem to assert: I carry a heavenly human being within my earthly human being.

If we wanted to put it a bit more imaginatively, we could say that when we make the usual, decent gestures by which we reinforce our everyday earthly speech, there are angelic beings standing by and helping. But if these everyday gestures are then transformed into the articulate gestures of eurythmy, into a speech that flows from one being to another, then what we see is actually that which the archangels say to one another.[173]

Humanity raises itself up in this way from the heavy earth into the region where divine-spiritual beings are pouring out their messages in the special way that is characteristic of them. Movements within that region are such that the gravity component is not integrated into them. There the gravity component unbinds itself and wants to sweep through the whole periphery[174] in cosmic freedom; there we find no trace of any inclination toward the earth. That is how, with the help of eurythmy, our eternal self is unbound within our earthly existence. The divine spirit that dwells within us comes to expression through our temporal earthly existence. When the human soul engages with eurythmy, the soul appears as that which pours into the transient human form out of the eternal wellspring of human nature.

Something is created thereby which lends essential support to the art of recitation and declamation, for example. The poet had already struggled to overcome the earthly dimensions of language by grasping its musical, rhythmic elements. In recitation, it is above all the eurythmic qualities that must be sought, as Frau Dr. Steiner[175] has been endeavoring to do for years. It is not the abstract content of the poems that should be emphasized but the structure of the language—the musical, sculptural, artistic elements. Then, when music or recitation are accompanied by eurythmy—that is, by the agility of a human being in the process of overcoming gravity, taking leave of gravity by means of the spirited movements of our limbs—then an orchestral collaboration arises, an orchestral collaboration that is able to bring to expression the full, inner, artistic beauty of the poem, of the song, or of the music—indeed, of any other kind of artistic creativity—in a fundamental way that is otherwise impossible.

After all, there are tremendous depths to real art. Now, when I make such a remark, right away I have to beg you, dear friends, to be charitable! While we are setting ourselves distant goals, we realize that we are only at the beginning of the course. We are our own severest critics. But we know that eurythmy holds endless possibilities of development. It frees the higher human being from gravity so that we are able to reveal our divine-spiritual nature. We can hope, therefore, that eurythmy will develop further and further until it is finally accepted as a fully justified art form on a par with the other arts that have long since won recognition. This may take a long time, but there should be an ever-increasing interest in the early stages of our endeavor to create this new art form.

The Imaginative Revelation of Language
Two addresses on the occasion of the International Assembly of Delegates of the Anthroposophical Society

II. Dornach, July 22, 1923[176]

Before the eurythmy performance today, I would like to say a few words to illustrate how eurythmy proceeds from the spiritual perspective afforded by anthroposophy. Numerous anthroposophical friends are with us today, many of whom have come from afar. In light of that important fact, I would like to pursue in greater depth what I said yesterday regarding art in general. Please grant me leave to base my remarks this time on anthroposophical foundations, to say a few purely anthroposophical words about eurythmy.

Whatever proceeds from our human nature—be it thoughts or feelings or impulses of will, or speech or song, recitation or declamation—all this proceeds not from any one part of our constitution, but in every case from human nature as a whole. It is possible to see how human nature reveals itself in any single instance only if we observe the part that is played by the several members of our constitution in any such human manifestation.

The spiritual knowledge out of which we are speaking is no less exact than any branch of science in the intellectual life of today—if anything, it is far more exact. Speaking in the light of this knowledge, we have to anatomize the human constitution as follows. We have our physical body, then the first suprasensory member of our being—the so-called etheric body or body of formative forces—and then something that is already connected with the inner life of the soul: the astral body. Lastly, there is the whole I-formation. If we direct our inner eye toward these four systems, we get a preliminary overview of the whole of human nature.

According to their several basic forces and elements, these four members are involved in every manifestation of human nature. The only question is what part they play. Naturally, I can give only brief hints in what I am about to say. However, since this is a meeting of anthroposophists from all the world, I would like to speak about eurythmy, for once, in an entirely anthroposophical way. Popular explanations can accompany performances on other occasions.

Let me begin by reminding you of this fact: Every time we enter sleep, our I-formation and astral body are separated from the physical body and from the etheric body (or life body or body of formative forces). However, the I and astral body thereby assume a relationship to the things and processes of the earth of which we are not immediately conscious. In truth, with our real inner being—that is, with our I and astral body—we are not as intimately related to the outer world in waking life as we are during sleep. For in our waking condition, we can perceive the outer world only with the aid of the physical body and its organs, and with the aid of the etheric body and its organs. On the other hand, every time we are asleep throughout our earthly life, the I and astral body become associated intimately with the outer world. Hence, the relation of I and astral body to the outer world is very close and intimate (if I may use that term) and for that very reason they can mediate the revelations of human nature that enter unconsciously into consciousness.

Suppose, for example, that we speak. We speak in vowels and in consonants. To the way of thought which is almost exclusively recognized as valid in our time—that of the senses and of the intellect combining the sense impressions—speech is bound to the physical body; it arises from the forming of certain organs. It is quite true: what happens in the physical body when we speak can be described more or less exactly. But the other—suprasensory—members of our human constitution also play an all-important role in all our speaking.

Let us consider first of all what the etheric body, or body of formative forces, signifies within the human constitution. This suprasensory body stands nearest to the physical body, and in the night—in sleep—it does not separate from the physical. The etheric body or life body or body of formative forces is the bearer of the life of thought—the bearer of all those forces that shape human thought. It really is the case that we form our thoughts with the help of the physical and the etheric body. We are far away from thought in sleep; we only just encounter it, in our dreams, in falling asleep and on awakening, and even then only chaotically. That is because, in sleep, our own inwardness, our individual I and astral body, has also been separated from the part that is the bearer of thinking. Truly we think all through the night: it is just that we do not know it. Hence our activity of thinking lives within the etheric or life body. And that is also why the education that our physical bodies—and also our etheric or formative-forces bodies—undergo is a more important determinant of the way we think than most people imagine. If someone has received—pardon the word!—a slovenly training in the employment of his or her bodily instrument, then that will manifest itself in the form of sloppy thinking. These subtle structures, when they are inhabited by the body of formative forces, determine the quality of our thinking. And that which flows into language or even into singing springs from the physical body and from the etheric body, the body of formative forces. But language—let us focus principally on language—actually receives an influx of elements from the outer world. We must learn to recognize within our language what has entered into our speaking and into singing from the I and the astral body by way of respiration and the circulation of the blood. What enters into our speaking and singing by way of respiration and the circulation of the blood originates within the I and the astral body, which have ever-recurring opportunities to connect intimately with the inner world when they are severed from the outer world.

Say we undertake to investigate, for example, the characteristic shape that the human lips assume in forming certain consonants. Then we cannot restrict ourselves to human beings if we want to get to know this really quite mysterious shaping of the lips, tongue, etc. In this regard, our so-called "scientific age" today remains extraordinarily superficial.

As you may know, there are two schools of linguistics that have attracted quite a bit of interest. (Less so today than in the recent past.) One is called the "bim-bam theory," and the other is called the "bow-wow theory." Now, these theories have been set forth by scholars, and you can study these contributions in greater detail than I shall present today by reading the works of the Oxford professor Max Müller.[177] But the gist of the "bim-bam theory" is that when a bell tolls, something in the inner nature of that external object resonates, and hence it is by way of sensory perception—not just of hearing—that we as human beings are able to enter into external objects. Now that process is not as superficial as the "bim-bam theory" makes it out to be: rather, it arises by virtue of the inward, intimate communion of the I and astral body while severed from the outer world. Just as we have memory in ordinary life, so do the astral body and I resonate in us, so to speak; their effects persist. We are not conscious of these aftereffects of the astral body and the I. Yet, strange as it may sound, it is not for nothing that we sleep: that is when the relation established with the outer world echoes on within us. The I and astral body carry into us the intimate, inner qualities of outer things.

Nor do we adapt ourselves to animal sounds in the superficial way that the "bow-wow" theory of language assumes. Nevertheless, through our I and our astral body we do experience outer things. Nor can we understand the wondrous formation of lip and tongue and palate, and so on, down to the various speech organs, until we realize this fact: tongue, lip, palate, and so on are formed not only from within outward, as ordinary physiology may prove, but from the outer world *into* the human being. The things of the outer world are actually living in the forms of the organs that underlie our speech. If that were not so, human beings never could have attained the faculty of speech. Speech is not merely a revelation of what we experience within ourselves—inside our skins. Speech also contains all that is living in the secrets of the earthly things around us, of which we become aware because our I and astral body are separated from the physical and the etheric bodies. Speech is the very thing we learn in the outer world around us. Right into the vocal chords, everything that the I and astral body discover through their intimate acquaintance with the outer world in sleep is vibrating, oscillating, and echoing. Languages of the developed world have by now completely worn away this wondrous kinship, this intimate union of language with the outer world. We need a knowledge deeper than any that is founded upon materialistic physiology. With deeper knowledge of this kind, we can perceive a fact, the importance of which should not be underestimated. When, for example, we pronounce an *I* (*ee*) or an *E* (*a*) or an *U* (*oo*),[178] it is not a mere manifestation of human nature: it is something that our entire human constitution experiences in communion with the outer world around us. We need only consider the forms that are conjured up before the eye of the soul as living imaginations when we perceive the relation of an *I* or of an *U* to the things of the outer world. Anyone who can really feel an *I* knows well that in this vowel—when rightly felt and sensed—lies something which works from the outer world so as to lend us our own existence. Hence, all languages that have the *I*-sound in the word "I" [*Ich*] give speakers a sense of existence directly through the language itself. Languages that do not have the *I*-sound in the word "I" cannot give us this sense of existence. Again, how does the *U* appear to the soul? The *U* is as though two kinds of suprasensory elements in the outer world were coming into touch with one another, and human beings must become aware of their touching.

Thus, there are manifold pictures, musical or sculptural, that arise before the soul when we try to enter into the intimate qualities of speech. Only when we understand these pictures can we begin to gain insight into the wonderful union that exists between our life of soul—our life of mind and feeling—and our speech. Then we learn to recognize how everyday speech reaches up, on the one hand, into our thinking and, on the other hand, reaches down physically as far as the circulation of the blood. Needless to say, you cannot coarsely feel the pulse to tell how it changes when you speak *I* or *U*. Nevertheless, in a delicate way, the change is there. We can actually speak of a microscopic change of the pulse (figuratively speaking) when someone empathizes fully with the soul's experiences in the course of a word or a sentence—when the soul vividly enters into the intimacies of the spoken sounds or of the notes of song. It is the blood to which we have to look for those human movements which answer to ordinary speech or song and carry within them the thought—that is, the content—which is actually an inartistic element.

But when we pass from speech to imaginations (whether musical or sculptural or painted in color), we feel it is possible to express what lies inherent in speech—with the same inner law and principle as in speech itself—through visible spatial movements of individual limbs or of the entire body. Thus we obtain a truly visible speech, revealing directly what can be revealed in audible language only by the "how,"[179] by the treatment. If we are able, as we speak, to color one sound by another—if we are able to treat it poetically and artistically, rightly embodying in it rhythm, melody, and theme—then we are able to enter gradually into the mysteries of declamation and recitation. Frau Dr. Steiner[180] has sought to study these things for many years, seeking to get beyond the inartistic tendencies of our time, which only look for prosaic emphasis and pathos. Laying stress on the treatment of all that is shaped poetically and artistically within the life of speech, she has sought to attain the true art of recitation and declamation.

This secret eurythmy is already there, inherent in the very treatment of language. Every true poet has it. True poets, alas, are but a small percentage of those who are considered poets nowadays. Ninety-nine percent, we might say, of those who write poetry today are not genuinely poetic artists. The moment we enter thus into the "how," the "how" of the handling of language, we feel that it provides far greater possibilities to express the life of the soul than the mere prosaic content of the words. The prosaic meaning of the words conveys only the inartistic aspects. It is the *how*, not the *what*, through which the artistic life is expressed. By a kind of divination, we always have to first redeem the artistic element from the little that can be conveyed by the printed words of the poem.

The poet gains a feeling for the whole of our human nature by living right inside language itself. Again and again, I must recall [Schiller's] beautiful, poetic line: "When the soul *speaks*, alas, the *soul* already speaks no more!" This is entirely true of the kind of speech that principally aims to convey the prosaic meaning. How different is the speech that lives in the sculptural form and coloring that sound can give to sound—which the deployment of sounds itself can give! How different, again, is speech that lives in the musical element! When the soul speaks this kind of language, it is the soul, above all, which is trying to say what cannot be said through speech that has grown prosaic and inartistic. This is the very thing we can derive from speech and song through eurythmy, because the most expressive human members are brought into movement. Not like the dance, which moves the legs and feet—undoubtedly, the less expressive human members: eurythmy is not dance. Although it also moves the legs and feet, these are not the main movements which it brings about, and eurythmy has no essential kinship with the dance.

The forming of the arms and hands—those most expressive members of the human body—is the true visible speech corresponding to what I have just indicated. Out of such insight into human nature—I have only hinted at it here—we can discover the laws and principles of expression for every finger, for every movement of the arm, for every subtle change of the human organism in space, even as nature or the spirit of nature finds the same when in our childhood, out of unconscious human life, she lets us learn speech and song in our childlike way. In a similarly lawful way, we now can create a visible speech, which plays upon a different instrument, if I may put it in that way, the theme which song or declamation or recitation plays on the other side. Truly, we come to a kind of orchestral harmony between the eurythmy on the stage and the chords that are struck on the musical instruments, or the sounds that come forth in recitation and declamation through the human voice.

Thus we are able to derive from the very fountainhead I mentioned yesterday an art that humanity could not discover hitherto, for the simple reason that every art must first be created out of the special conditions of culture that the successive epochs in the life of humanity provide. In eurythmy we have a new kind of art, making use of our human constitution itself as an instrument—even more than mime does. And because we human beings contain within ourselves all the secrets of the universe, as microcosm in relation to the macrocosm, and because of the way in which we do this, the special way in which eurythmy employs human nature itself, which bears all the secrets of the macrocosm within itself as a microcosm, we may hope—keeping in mind that we are our own worst critics, that we stand today still at the very beginning—that in time eurythmy will become what it cannot yet be today: a fully justified younger art taking its rightful place beside the older, fully established arts.

Introductory Words for a Eurythmy Performance

August 8, 1923, August 14, 1923, September 4, 1923, and September 11, 1923, Ilkley, Penmaenmawr, and London[181]

Eurythmy is intended as an art whose means of expression are movements formed by the human organism in itself and in space, as well as by groups of performers moving together. It is not concerned, however, with the gestures of mime or with dance movements. Instead, it strives to become actual, visible speech or visible singing. When speaking or singing, the stream of air is formed in a certain way by the human organs of speech. If we study, by means of a vital, spiritual intuition, the formation of tones, vowels, consonants, syntax, prosody, and so forth, we can form definite concepts of the plastic forms that are produced by the corresponding revelations of speech and singing. These forms can be emulated by the human organism, especially by its most expressive organs, the arms and the hands. In doing so, we create the possibility of *seeing* what is *heard* in speaking and in singing.

Because the arms and hands are our most expressive organs, eurythmy consists primarily of consciously formed movements of these organs. These are then accompanied by movements of the rest of the body, even as ordinary speech is accompanied by facial expression and everyday gestures. The difference between eurythmy and dance can become especially clear when we see the eurythmic accompaniment of a musical composition. What appears to be dancing is actually only of secondary importance, whereas the visible song, which arises through the movements of the arms and the hands, is the most essential.

One should not believe that any eurythmy movement is ever arbitrary. At a given moment, a particular movement has to be brought forth as a musical or a poetic expression, just as in singing a specific tone is produced or in speaking a specific sound occurs. At that point, we are as bound by eurythmy's language of movement as we are bound by tones and sounds in singing or speaking. We are, however, just as free to shape the forms of movement beautifully and creatively as we are free in the forming of speech or song.

That makes it possible to represent eurythmically a piece of music that is being played, or poetry that is being recited, as visible song or visible speech. Moreover, since speech and music stem from the whole human being, their inner content becomes readily apparent only when the visible revelation is added to the audible. Actually, our whole human constitution is brought into movement by everything that is sung and spoken. It is just that in ordinary life, this latent tendency to move is restrained and localized in the organs of speech and song. Eurythmy *reveals* that an innate disposition to move is always present in these expressions of human life, even though it generally remains latent. When eurythmy is combined with the playing of instrumental music, or with recitation or declamation, the result is a kind of orchestral ensemble of the audible and the visible.

With regard to the recitation and declamation that are performed in conjunction with eurythmy, care must be taken that they be fashioned in accordance with a truly artistic shaping of language. Reciters or speakers who stress only the prose content of poetry cannot collaborate in eurythmy performances. Genuinely artistic poetry arises only through the imaginative or musical shaping of speech. The prose content is not the artistic element, but rather only the material basis upon which the pictorial element of the language, or the meter, the rhythm, the verse forms, and so forth, are revealed. All poetic language is already a kind of hidden eurythmy. The reciter or declaimer must employ the painterly,[182] sculptural, or musical elements of speech to bring forth all that the poet has put into words. Frau Dr. Steiner[183] has been developing this kind of recitation and declamation independently for many years. Only such an art of speech can be performed together with eurythmy, because only then can the reciter provide for the ear, in the shaping and forming of sound, what the eurythmist presents for the eye. Only through such a collaboration can what really lives in poetry be brought to the soul of the listener and spectator.

Eurythmy is not framed for any kind of mediated intellectual understanding; it is framed for direct perception. Eurythmists must learn visible speech, form by form, just as infants learn to speak. However, the effect of eurythmy, when accompanied by music or speech, can be directly experienced through observation alone. Like music, eurythmy is also able to affect those who have not learned the forms themselves, because eurythmy is a natural, elemental revelation of our own human nature, whereas ordinary speech always has a conventional quality.

Eurythmy has arisen in the present age, just as all the other arts arose in their respective epochs. These other arts sprang up when people sought to reveal something in their souls through corresponding artistic media. Whenever our forebears mastered a specific medium to such an extent that it became possible for them to reveal their souls' inner experiences through that medium within the world of the senses, a new art form arose. Eurythmy arises when we learn to employ the noblest of all artistic media, the human organism itself—this microcosm—as an instrument. In the art of mime, as well as in dance, this holds true only for certain parts of the human organism, whereas eurythmy makes use of the whole human being as a medium of expression. And yet I must again, as we do before all such performances, appeal to the kind forbearance of the audience. Every art form has had an infancy at some time in the past. So it is with eurythmy as well. Eurythmy stands at the beginning of its development. But since eurythmy employs the most perfect instrument imaginable, it must contain unlimited possibilities for further development. The human organism is that most perfect of instruments; it is truly the microcosm that embodies within itself in a concentrated form all the mysteries and laws of the cosmos. If we employ the movement-formations of eurythmy to reveal the comprehensive language latent within us—a language that enables the entire experience of the soul to manifest itself through the instrument of the physical body—then we should be able to express artistically the mysteries of the cosmos in a comprehensive way.

At present, eurythmy can only begin to offer what lies within it as potentiality along the lines I have indicated. Since eurythmy employs means of expression that can stand in such an intimate relationship to the being of the cosmos and our own human nature, we may hope that, in its further evolution, eurythmy will take its rightful place alongside the other arts.

Excerpt from a Lecture

Dornach, November 11, 1923[184]

[abridged]

I now have something to announce that will please you very much. A rehearsal of eurythmy that took place here a of couple days ago revealed a remarkable new development—namely, eurythmy by men! Mostly you have seen only women on the stage up to now. But now our security detail,[185] who have made so many great sacrifices in working with us, have learned eurythmy under the careful, exemplary guidance of Ms. Dziubanjuk.[186] But you see, one thing is still missing for this new development of male eurythmy to be complete. And that is—we have already thought about it—the undergarments, for example, and other pieces of clothing for the male eurythmists. Those need to be created. We have thought about it already, but there needs to be money for that purpose. One needs money for everything! And that is why Frau Dr. Steiner[187] took the initiative of organizing a performance next Sunday at 7 p.m. here. And so that this radical metamorphosis does not take place right away, the first part of the program will be performed by our tried-and-true ladies. Then, in the second half, the gentlemen of our security detail, who have devoted themselves so commendably to the study of eurythmy, will take the stage (but still in their old undergarments). So you will see a kind of division, first eurythmy by women, then after that eurythmy by men, and needless to say, you will work up the enthusiasm to attend this performance even if we cannot be there ourselves. Come, because the proceeds of this performance next Saturday (November 17, 1923) will provide the beginnings of a fund that will be used to buy undergarments and so forth—in short, the full costumes for the male eurythmists, so that we will have costumes for the men in the same way we have them for the ladies.

INTRODUCTION TO THE EURYTHMY PERFORMANCE

Dornach, December 23, 1923[188]

My dear friends!

Today our guests from further afield who have already arrived make up the majority of those present at this opening performance of eurythmy. There is no need for me to speak particularly about the nature of eurythmy, for our friends know about it from various writings that have appeared in print. But especially since we are gathering once more for an anthroposophical undertaking, I would like to introduce this performance with a few words.

First of all, eurythmy is the art that has grown entirely from the soil of anthroposophy. It has always been the case, of course, that every artistic activity which was to bring something new into civilization originated in suprasensory human striving. Whether you look at architecture, sculpture, painting, or the arts of music or poetry, you will always find that the impulses visible in the external course of human evolution are rooted in some way in esoteric, suprasensory ground, ground we may seek in connection with the Mysteries.[189] Art can flow into human evolution only if it contains within it forces and impulses of a suprasensory kind. But the present-day view of art is mainly an artifact of the entirely materialistic tendency in thinking that has seized hold of Europe and America since the fifteenth century. And though a certain kind of scientific knowledge can flourish in this materialism, genuine art cannot. True art can only come forth out of spiritual life.

Hence, we can view it as completely natural and understandable that a special art has arisen out of the spiritual life of the anthroposophical movement. We need to understand that art must be born out of the suprasensory realm through the mediation of human beings. Consider the descending scale stretching from the suprasensory realm down to externally perceptible phenomena: you find the faculty of intuition[190] at the top, at the point where—if I may put it like this—our human nature merges with the spirit. Inspiration has to do with our capacity to face the suprasensory on our own, hearing it and letting it reveal itself. And when we are able to integrate what we receive through inspiration so intensely into our own being that we become capable of molding it, then imagination emerges.

In speech we have something that appears in the form of an outer image—although it is an outer image that is extraordinarily similar to inspiration. We might say that what we bear within our soul when we speak resembles intuition; and what lies on our tongue, is shaped by our palate, comes out between our teeth, and settles on our lips when we speak is the sense-perceptible image of inspiration.

But where does this thing that we push outward from our inner soul life in speech originate? It originates in the mobile shape of our body, or shall we say in our bodily structure set in motion.

Our ability in childhood to move our legs as well as our arms and hands and fingers is what gives us our first opportunity to sense our relationship with the outside world. The first experience that can enter into the consciousness of our soul is our experience of the movement of arms, hands, and legs. Other movements are more connected with our own inner lives. But the limbs that we stretch out into the space around us are what give us a sense of the world. And when we stretch out our legs in a stride or a leap, or when we stretch out our arms to grasp something, or our fingers to feel something, then whatever we experience in doing this streams back to us. And as it streams back, it seizes hold of the tongue, palate, and larynx and becomes speech.

In this way our bodily constitution becomes through movement an expression of human nature as a whole. As soon as you begin to understand this, you begin to sense that what resembles inspiration in speech can descend into imagination. We can call back something that is a gift to our limbs, to our tongue, our larynx, our palate, and so on; we can retrieve it and let it stream back, asking: What kind of feelings, what kind of sensations stream outward from our bodies in order to create the sound *A*?[191] What we will always discover is that an *A* arises through something that expresses itself in one way or another in the air, through a particular movement of our organs of speech; or as an *E* in the crossing of the optic nerves,[192] and so on. Then we will be able to take what has streamed out in this way and become a sound or element of speech, and send it back into our whole being, into our human system of limbs. Instead of something that causes speech to resemble inspiration, we obtain something else, something that can be seen and shaped and hence resembles imagination.

. . . So, actually, eurythmy comes into existence when the unconscious processes that transform our capacity for movement into speech are subsequently retrieved from speech and turned back into a capacity for movement. Thus an element that belongs to inspiration becomes an element belonging to imagination.

Hence a full understanding of eurythmy would require that we discover through eurythmy how intuition, inspiration, and imagination are related. Of course, we can only show this in pictures, but the pictures speak clearly.

Consider, dear friends, how a poem can dwell purely within the soul. When you have entirely identified yourself inwardly with this poem, and have taken it into yourself to such an extent and so strongly that you no longer need any words but instead you have only feelings and can experience these feelings in your soul, then you are living in intuition. Then let us assume that you recite or declaim the poem. In the vowel sounds, in the harmonies, in the rhythm, in the movement of the consonants, in tempo, beat, and so on, you seek to capture in speech, through recitation or declamation, what lies in those feelings. What you experience when doing this is inspiration. The element of inspiration takes what lives entirely within the soul, where it is localized in the nervous system, and pushes it down into larynx, palate, and so on.

Finally, let this sink down into your human limbs, so that in your own creation of form through movement you convey what lives within speech; then, in the poem brought into eurythmy, you have the third element, imagination.

In the picture of the descent of cosmic evolution down to the human being, you have that scale which we have to reascend, from imagination through inspiration to intuition. In the poem transformed into eurythmy you have imagination; in the recitation and declamation you have inspiration as an image; and in the entirely inward experience of the poem, in which there is no need to open your mouth because your experience is totally inward and you are utterly identified with it and have become one with it—there you have intuition.

In a poem transformed into eurythmy, experienced inwardly, and recited, you have before you the three stages, albeit in an external picture. In eurythmy we have to do with an artistic element that inevitably emerged out of the anthroposophical movement. What you have to do is bring into consciousness what it means to achieve knowledge of the ascent from imagination to inspiration to intuition.[193]

✽

Three Addresses at the Christmas Conference for the Foundation of the General Anthroposophical Society

III. Eurythmy, the Language of the Whole Human Being

Dornach, December 30, 1923[194]

We have already had a series of eurythmy performances here during your visit. I took the occasion to speak a few introductory words regarding the place of eurythmy within the system of the arts. And I indicated in particular how it was that eurythmy simply had to arise out of a spiritual movement that is focused rigorously upon the signs of the times. For it is simply the case that, in the course of human evolution, every new artistic impulse, every new thrust within the realm of art has always come when new territory has been opened up to humanity spiritually, or when something that has already been opened up approaches humanity in a new way. Of course, it will be very easy to raise the objection against eurythmy that it wants to be a language, a language that reveals itself by way of gestures called forth out of the human constitution. Audiences do not understand these gestures at first, but that is not what matters. What matters is that what emerges as such a gesture satisfies the aesthetic sense, and that out of this satisfaction of the aesthetic sense, there arises a similar kind of sensibility for poetry—just as an understanding for poetry arises out of rightly oriented declamation and recitation.

Eurythmy as a whole is actually grounded in something of which modern science has discovered only a sliver. Scientists know that the region of the central nervous system, of the brain, that is principally associated with language lives within the left brain.[195] And they also know that the right brain, the left brain's symmetrical counterpart, is actually not configured in such a way that a speech center could arise there as well. But in the case of left-handers, the situation changes immediately. People who are born left-handed, hence people whose right hands remain relatively inactive when performing operations requiring intelligence—people who want to write with their left hand, sew with it, crochet with it—for such people, the speech center will arise within the right brain. From this, scientists have rightly concluded that a connection exists between the possibility of moving—the capacity for movement in the human arm and in the human hand—and language. They have deduced that language is the movement of the human limbs that has been fixated, as it were, within a certain system of organs; that it is a meaningful moving of the human limbs. Tactile exploration of the outer world, and the expression of this tactile experience by means of the organs of speech, are evidence that it is actually the human limb system that gives birth to language.

But that is the case in a much more comprehensive sense. It is just that people don't know much about these mysterious connections. For example, it is not known that the rounding, the hardening of certain consonants, especially the palatal consonants, are connected with the way that individuals walk upon their heels or upon the balls of their feet. In speech, we can find a clear expression of the entire range of human beings' capacity for movement in their limbs.[196] And anyone who has a sense for that will be able to see how it is that the way a person walks and grasps is actually able to explain fully how that person speaks. That is why scientists who connect the right hand with the speech center in the left brain are holding but a sliver of the truth.

Language is decidedly a product of the whole human being. That is why if you investigate the physical body while someone is speaking, you will see that certain parts, certain regions, are in motion. But if you observe someone's etheric body, then you see that whenever a certain sound is produced, the whole etheric body is caught up in a specifically configured movement. Everything that expresses itself verbally always proceeds from the whole of the human constitution. That is why it is possible to follow the path back from language into movement. The child explores his capacity for movement, projects onto his speech organs, as it were, all the tactile experiences of his limbs, everything discovered through outer movement. And then in his speech, the child makes a copy of these capacities for movement. We can turn around and delve again into the realm of potential movement, which corresponds both to the individual sound and to the combination of sounds, stressing of syllables, and so forth. We can translate the whole of language back into the moving human being, and in that way call forth the mobile sculpture of which I have already spoken.

As I said, it has always been my wish to open up a couple of new perspectives at the outset of our performances. I do this in order to illuminate everything from a variety of angles. That is easy to do because eurythmy is such a natural outgrowth of anthroposophy.

When you see our performance of *Olaf* Åsteson[197] in the second part today, after the intermission, it will become especially clear to you how natural it is for eurythmy to arise when poetry lifts us up into a higher, spiritual sphere. It really is quite straightforward to set something like *Olaf* Åsteson to eurythmy because the spirituality that lies within the movements of eurythmy really does correlate best with events in the spiritual world. *Olaf* Åsteson is a wonderful poem from medieval Norwegian literature that was discovered in Scandinavia. It reveals to us a kind of primitive folk art that is actually bound up with a kind of folk clairvoyance, with a kind of folk vision. As I said, *Olaf* Åsteson will be performed to eurythmy after the intermission; it will be an offering that is especially well suited to this Christmas season and to a Christmas conference.

The Importance of Cultivating the Arts within the Anthroposophical Movement

Dornach, presumably January 5, 1924

On the occasion of the Christmas Conference for the Foundation of the General Anthroposophical Society[198]

Within the circle of our friends—of whom an especially large number are present today—I have often spoken about the meaning of eurythmy. The heart of those talks has been published in our periodical, *Das Goetheanum*.[199] Therefore, I would like to preface today's eurythmy performance with just a few words that flow from the simple fact that, by its very nature, the art of eurythmy has arisen out of our broader anthroposophical striving. The question that presents itself quite naturally in this regard is the whole issue about the cultivation of art as such within the anthroposophical movement. What should art signify?

When the anthroposophical movement began under the aegis of the theosophical movement, it first had to strip away everything within the theosophical movement that was and has remained sectarian within that movement. Right from the very outset, the anthroposophical movement had no innate disposition whatsoever to that kind of sectarianism. Right from the beginning, anthroposophy has sought to grasp the spiritual life in its wholeness, and by its very nature, anthroposophy was able to establish connections with every realm of human, spiritual, and also practical activity. Hence anthroposophy did not just inherit the reflexive sectarianism of the theosophical movement, whose initial response was to feel that the cultivation of the arts was something alien. (To this day, the theosophical movement still regards the arts is something alien.) Nevertheless, it was possible, while still ensconced within the theosophical movement—for example, at the Munich Congress of 1907[200]—to take up artistic initiatives: we staged a performance of Schuré's *Mystery of Eleusis*. And once such things caught fire, as it were, gradually a consciousness for such things arose within our Society. We began to understand how natural it is that the arts should be cultivated within this Society, and that they should be cultivated on an ever-broader basis.

You see, in the past—I want to say twenty, eighteen, fifteen years ago—when artists came to us, they felt more or less out of place as artists among us. The anthroposophists who self-identified as theosophists looked to them like artistic Botocudos. I am just quoting here what people said to me many times. And whenever I set foot on the premises of certain branches[201] that had been formed and were still staffed—sorry, I can't put it any other way—staffed by people whose aesthetic sense was still informed by theosophy, places where I was able to exert less of an influence because certain views prevailed there, then a quite remarkable mood would come over me. I would see barbaric paintings on the walls, such as paintings of the Rose Cross, for example, or schematic depictions such as this: down below the physical world; then the astral world, the spiritual world; and then, going upward, ever-higher "higher worlds." The whole business had an endlessly inartistic quality, so bringing the artistic element into the anthroposophical movement was accomplished only with great difficulty. But we worked at it.

And then we also came to perform the *Mystery Dramas* in Munich. We started to plan the building of a Goetheanum, a process that brought us all kinds of good advice. I see many people sitting here in the audience today who were helping to think through the plans for the Goetheanum back then. Some people wanted to "secretly embed" the pentagram into the building; others wanted us to find the "midpoint" between—I cannot even remember it all anymore. And anyway, how is someone supposed to symbolize *midpoint*? Every kind of thing was jumbled together there—but *art* remained something alien! And I really did have a lot of trouble bringing in a purely aesthetic element. Now, it was right at the time we were planning the Goetheanum when the right conditions arose—conditions that I already described to you—conditions that made it possible to create this art of movement in space, eurythmy. And then it became possible to *really* create something fundamentally new. For once, we really could say to ourselves: now everything can be made new.

Of course, dance was already there, and today there are still people who form their opinion about eurythmy by saying to themselves: performers are moving in space, so what we have here must be a kind of dance. People do not even bother to look; they judge eurythmy as a kind of dance. But only after they have already formed the judgment that eurythmy is a kind of dance do they realize that the movement of the legs is the less important aspect here, that the legs are moved only in order to call forth spatial forms. They gradually realize that what is essential here is the manifestation of human nature that arises when it is principally the arms and hands that move. And in this way, they arrive at a bizarre final judgment. Then people say: "There is movement going on, so it must be dance, but they are waving their arms around, so it isn't really dance. Therefore, it is just bad." What people do not notice is precisely what is most essential: that we are working with a completely new material—namely, out of the inner forming, shaping, out of the possibilities for movement latent within our human constitution as a whole.

Now, everything that comes to expression in human speech that is entrusted to words, to the forming of words—everything that is entrusted to what is shaped out of the word is a localized capacity for movement within human nature as a whole. For the whole of our human constitution is present by way of the physical body in that it has fixed contours. And we are partly determined by everything that influences our etheric bodies—that would be everything within us that is of the nature of liquids, fluids, circulation. We are governed by an astral body, which sends its forces into everything that unfolds within us in the way of airy effects, such as breathing, including inner respiration, etc. And finally, as human beings we have an I-organization, which manifests itself in our warmth organism, in differentiations of warmth, in organic warmth differentiations. These warmth differentiations are generated by the gathering within our "airy" system—localized in the respiratory system and everything belonging to the respiratory system—when everything within our human constitution that actually wants to get out is gathered together there.

Everything that has been localized in that way within the rhythm of breathing—within the respiratory rhythm that has been thoroughly spiritualized and sculpted—can be drawn back up again into the movements of the human constitution as a whole. And our whole human constitution becomes an organ of speech thereby. As I have often put it: the whole organism becomes a visible larynx in its movements. By taking recourse to the movement potentials that are latent within our human nature as a whole, we gain an entirely new artistic medium. And by studying the imaginations in the light of their language, we arrive at the insight that when we make the sound *O*, then there actually is something that forms itself before us into something embracing, something circular. When we manifest the sound *E*,[202] something like a caduceus conjures itself up before us and so forth. That is how we need to take hold of such things—of the corresponding imaginations that dwell within language, but that merely pass over into movements of the air and call forth the tone when we speak. If we contemplate all that, then we gain not only a new artistic medium, but also at the same time a whole new way of importing artistic forms into this medium, which is human movement potential itself.

But everything that is revealed here can be intuited only by means of spiritual science. Hence only spiritual science was able to create eurythmy, for it is the suprasensory human being that is grasped, expressed through the sensory form of its movements. Only spiritual science can comprehend the suprasensory aspect of human nature.

That is why it became possible to call forth an art of our own, once the organism of the anthroposophical movement itself had actually evolved sufficiently, as it were, to cultivate an aesthetic sensibility. An art of our own that could arise only out of an artistic sensibility within the anthroposophical movement itself. And all of this led us to say to ourselves that the whole anthroposophical movement is predisposed—profoundly predisposed, actually—to support what it seeks upon spiritual paths by also seeking the paths of the arts. And I am even convinced that, if the artistic element were to pervade our ranks ever more deeply, then it would become increasingly possible for our friends to overcome the difficulties attendant on actual, spiritual-scientific clairvoyance. For the arts are a path leading to spiritual vision. That is simply the case. If you comprehend the suprasensory aspect of our human constitution in its pre-natal existence, for example, that aspect actually reveals itself in a way that eurythmy seeks to imitate. Hence eurythmy stimulates us to turn the eye of the soul toward the suprasensory aspect of our own human constitution.

But true art has ever been the appearance of the suprasensory within the sensory. Within the sensory we enjoy an immediate intuition of the suprasensory. No symbolizing, no allegorizing. That is all just wooden; that is not artistic. The upshot of all this is something dear to my heart: the wish that friends of the anthroposophical movement would take it to heart to pursue intensively the artistic strivings within our ranks. That would pour life into the whole anthroposophical movement. The arts will be an elixir of life for the whole anthroposophical movement. And when we are finally able to say to ourselves that the anthroposophical movement has become as strongly artistic as it was initially inartistic—as inartistic as could be!—then, precisely because it rose up from an inartistic foundation, something of great importance will have been accomplished not just for the arts within the anthroposophical movement, but for the whole momentum of the anthroposophical movement as such. And then it will no longer happen that when artists encounter the anthroposophical movement they say: "Those are just a bunch of artistic Botocudos." Instead, they will say: "We live in an age that is so often given to making barbaric gestures when it comes to art, but now, here is something that has a genuinely artistic sensibility again, true artistic enthusiasm." That is what we should want to happen, and it is something that can be attained through working up appropriate enthusiasm for the eurythmy movement in all its aspects.

That is what I wanted to say by way of introduction, a few words about the relationship of the anthroposophical movement to art.

❁

The Relationship between Speech Sounds and Movement

Dornach, February 2, 1924[203]

[abridged]

Eurythmy is striving to be a real language, a visible language, a language through which human movements in themselves come to expression, where they also come to expression by way of human movement within space. Spoken language consists after all of setting in motion the surrounding air, which then reaches the ears of another person; it is precisely because it is a movement of the air, which is also a kind of gesture—indeed, a gesture expressed in the air—that it is able to mediate the revelation of one human soul to another. Now, in our time, that process unfolds by way of a specific relationship between human movement and spoken language.

What I just described is, shall we say, a small part, a very small part of something that, if we come to know it thoroughly, can lead to the art of eurythmy.

It is held today that the speech organ lies within the left half of the brain. If this speech organ is damaged, then that person becomes incapable of carrying out sound gestures, which then become spoken language almost instantly.[204] With the great majority of people, it is the case that this speech organ is part of the left brain's third cerebral gyrus because they are right-handed. And the remarkable thing is that in the case of left-handers, the speech organ is on the right side.

That is the origin of the significant insight that the soul experiences, the soul impulses that children pour into the movements of their right arms (which always move more than the left arm) are closely related to what takes shape within the left brain. In normal development, the corresponding organ of the right brain also exhibits convolutions, but those remain unformed in the physical sense.

It follows that we can take any arbitrary speech sound—I, U, L, M, N—or we can take sounds and form them into words or sentences. Or, since a rhythmic or metrical shaping of sounds or words is a translated movement, it must be possible to transform all these back into movement again. Human beings do that when they accompany their speech with everyday gestures, when they become somewhat more demonstrative in speaking. But, compared to eurythmy, the gestures that arise as a support for spoken language in everyday life are like the babbling of a child in relation to fully articulated speech.

If you use what is presented here in Dornach as anthroposophy to look more deeply into the connection between human movement and language, then you find that everything in language has its counterpart in movement.

In language, you will find the strengthening of the sound, the accentuation of the sound. This emphasizing of the sound arises when, because of our own personality, because we consider something important, we give it a certain weight. We emphasize one word or one part of the sentence in particular. This kind of emphasis is expressed particularly in what the eurythmists do with their hands and feet. And through the way in which the feet are placed, through movement of the legs, it is possible to express what might be called a secret eurythmy that has been hidden within[205] language.

Through movement of the head, it is possible to express what ijs hidden within language in the form, shall we say, of irony, of laughing within speech, or also the seriousness of language.

That which lies deep within the soul, however—that comes to expression in the metrical or in the rhythmical movement.

✽

[Untitled]

Dornach, February 3, 1924[206]

May I say a few words to introduce our eurythmy performance? Certainly not to "explain" it! It would not be my idea to explain art, either in general or with regard to specific performances. But perhaps you will allow me to tell you about the artistic sources from which eurythmy has been created, which remain unfamiliar today, and about the medium that eurythmy uses.

You will see that a eurythmy performance consists of one or more individuals moving in space. At first glance, it may seem to be an art of gestures, but that is not what it is. Or it may look like a new kind of dance; but it is not that either. Eurythmy is actually visible speech raised to the level of art by virtue of its very special character. Speech itself, of course, must also be raised to the same level. Eurythmy can be called "visible singing" when it accompanies instrumental music.

When we speak as human beings, we are pouring into sounds what we experience in our soul; the sounds are forming into words, the words into sentences, and so on. Finally, a poet's artistic handling of all this creates something that has rhythm and beat with pictorial and sculptural qualities. One should realize that every single speech sound takes a definite shape and has its own particular form in the air that the speaker exhales. The form is brought about by the combined activity of the larynx, palate, tongue, lips, etc.

What issues forth from us in this way and reaches the others around us, what has been metamorphosed into speech and language had its origin in the human constitution as a whole. Today, except for one small detail, there is little knowledge of this fact. It is generally known that in most people the speech center—that is, the organ that generates the impulse to speak—is on the left side of the brain. But this isn't always the case. In a few people, it is on the right side. These are the "lefties." The fact that right-handed people, who always perform certain activities with their right hands, have their speech center on the left side of their brain naturally means nothing, of course, until we learn that left-handed people have their speech center on the right side. Then we are obliged to see a connection between speech and the movements of arms and hands.

Just think what this implies for the most expressive of our bodily organs, the arms and hands! Our soul stirs within us so strongly when we are especially moved that we feel impelled to accompany our words with gestures—that is, to pour out our feeling directly and at the same time into arm and hand movements. Often we find that we can understand people better through their gestures than through their language! In many people this speech of their hands and arms can be most expressive. Particularly in so-called "civilized" languages, there is such a conventional content, and also such detail of abstract knowledge, that Schiller's verse applies: "If the soul should *speak*, then—alas!—it is no longer the *soul* that is speaking." We adjust our speech to conventional or to intellectual constraints, but we disclose much more of our individuality when we make use of a gesture.

Just as with our arms, we can make gestures with other parts of our body, too. But all this kind of gesturing is as far removed from what eurythmy is intended to be as a child's babbling is removed from articulated, cultivated speech. For someone who sees deeply into human nature, what goes into speech, what eventually becomes the air gestures through which the speech sounds are conveyed, depends initially on what our whole human nature wants to convey through gestures. What we have here is a fragmentary knowledge of the connection that exists between definite inclinations to movement that are present in our human constitution and the final production of speech through the speech center in the brain. Anthroposophy understands this connection; it is anthroposophy, therefore, that can open up wider horizons.

When we have something to say, there is usually something about it that we want to stress. We stress one word particularly if we want to emphasize something, while stressing another word less strongly. So we proceed through all the levels from light to heavy emphasis. This is not connected so much with our impulse to make arm gestures as it is with the way we show our personality in our walking. Whoever has a sense for these things knows exactly from the way someone walks—whether more strongly, for instance, on the ball of the foot or on the heels—just how that person will stress this or that in speaking.

We can also observe someone's speech from the point of view of grammar. This has to do with the thought element, which is the most inartistic element of speech. If our intellect predominates in the forming of our speech, then what we want to express by gestures will be accomplished primarily through head movements. So if some boring know-it-all wants to show you that he takes great care in arriving at his judgments, he will make *this* gesture [demonstrated], or he will lay his finger on his nose, or take hold of his nose. That shows the dominance of the head.

But everything that lies between intellect and will (emphasis in speech comes from the will), what lies between in the realm of feeling, what the poet pours into rhythm and rhyme, into the choice of meters, and so forth—this is the really artistic element of speech. It can come to expression quite naturally through movements of the arms and hands, supported by a person's other movements. Dance emphasizes the will element, mime the intellectual; the real feeling element is expressed by eurythmy.

The poet felt quite rightly that the human soul is no longer to be found in speech. But speech can be recuperated into gestures. What a child actually wants to put into gestures is unconsciously concentrated in the organs of speech instead. And now if we give that back again to the impulses toward movement of the whole human body, then we have created a visible speech. The single movements relate to single speech sounds. A sequence of movements has the same significance as our customary sequences of sounds, sentence connections, and so forth in our everyday speech. In very truth, eurythmy is visible speech. It can also become visible singing.

As visible speech, eurythmy is accompanied here by recitation and declamation. Their collaboration shows at once that in its treatment of a poem, eurythmy is involved completely with artistic content. Today, in our inartistic age, there is no proper understanding for our attitude. People are only interested in emphasizing the prose content of a poem, but that has no value! People have to look to the poet's style, to something that is being expressed on a higher level than prose, something that works its way into the poem through the musical element or the pictorial, through the sculptural, the color elements of the poet's language. Recitation and declamation have to be brought back to what they were at the time when Goethe rehearsed his iambic dramas with his actors with a baton in hand like a choral conductor. He did that because he knew that the essential quality of language lies in its musical and imaginative elements. The feeling in a poem has quite a different power when, for instance, the reciter puts variety into the beat or rhythm of the recitation than it does when it is merely expressed in the prose content. That is why the "secret eurythmy" already hidden in the poet's language has to be of foremost interest when recitation and declamation accompany the eurythmy.

Unfamiliar as eurythmy is today, equally unfamiliar is this art of recitation and declamation that pays more attention to the style of the language than to the prose content. We hope that eurythmy will help to create an understanding for what the art should be. We can feel what eurythmy is intended to be when we see it as visible singing accompanying instrumental music. If a person were to sing and at the same time perform eurythmy gestures for the words or for the notes of the song, you would at once have the feeling that something is wrong there! Whoever would do this has not really understood the nature of eurythmy. It would be the same as if a person were singing a solo and someone else stood up to sing, too. You have to have the feeling that a eurythmist is not dancing to the music but singing to it, singing with her arms. Once you have felt this difference between dance and the tone eurythmy that is presented here, you have really grasped the nature of eurythmy. After all, such differences can be understood only through feeling.

But you will say: I suppose someone has to study eurythmy to find out what all those movements mean. But that is not necessary.

All that matters is that the movements and their sequences make an artistic impression. Eurythmy has to create its effect through immediate artistic perception, and it will truly have this effect. As you watch it accompanying the recitation of a poem, you will have the impression that this is the only way it could be done! There is no other way to perform eurythmy for that poem! Down to the smallest movement, there is nothing arbitrary, nothing personal. It is exactly as with speech: with speech you can't just use any random sound in place of another. If, for instance, you want to talk about "bread," you can't say "breed." Likewise, in eurythmy no other movement can be made than the one that corresponds to the speech sound the reciter is uttering.

So eurythmy becomes a moving sculpture. We have the feeling that our customary motionless sculpture portrays the silent human soul in all its stillness. A soul that is surging and struggling to speak can only be portrayed by bringing the living human form into movement. From this point of view, eurythmy is moving sculpture.

Dear friends, we know all too well that our eurythmy stands at its most rudimentary stage. We are our own severest critics! There will be more and more performances here, there, and everywhere with a rich variety of programs; we expect them to be criticized, especially by the professional critics. We believe that we know better than anyone else all the justified criticisms of this beginning we have made. We know it is far from perfect. Even so, we are confident that it has endless possibilities for development. Because eurythmy employs the most perfect medium one could have for an art, the human organism itself, all cosmic secrets and laws can be brought to expression. The human being is a small world, a microcosm that can disclose the secrets of the larger world, the macrocosm. Since eurythmy has a perfect instrument and will always have it, and since the secrets of the moving human being will be studied and artistically revealed more and more, eurythmy will undoubtedly make its way in the world. With eurythmy as with everything else, beginnings are difficult. But the artistic sources of eurythmy that today are still strange, and the artistic style that is also still strange, will gradually be understood.

PEDAGOGICAL EURYTHMY

Bern, April 14, 1924[207]

Recently, we were able to perform at the theater here in Bern samples of the art of eurythmy, which is under development at the Goetheanum. On that occasion our principal intent was to present eurythmy as an art form. Eurythmy is an art that works with techniques that are still unfamiliar today; it speaks in unaccustomed artistic forms. Perhaps it is necessary for that reason to begin with a few introductory words.

Human beings reveal what lives within their souls through music, song, and speech. Both musicality and speech proceed from our inner experiences. But they are concentrated, as it were, within a certain organ, a certain organic system: within the organs of speech and singing. So now we see how already in everyday life, when we speak, we so often feel the need to support what we express through language as much as possible by means of all kinds of gestures. And even if we do not always make it clear to ourselves, we believe that gesture is well suited to deliver the soul's engagement in what we are speaking more emphatically than we can do by merely saying it. So that is one thing we can glean from observation of everyday life. We shall see how it relates to eurythmy.

Another thing is a fragmentary understanding that contemporary science already has—something that could eventually lead to full comprehension. Today scientists know that the speech center, our ordinary human speech center, lies within the left hemisphere of the brain. They know there is a specific organ there, one that consists of cerebral convolutions, and that without it, we are incapable of speaking. Not because our organs of speech are incapacitated in any way; those can be entirely intact. Human beings cannot speak or sing if this cerebral organ is dysfunctional because they cannot invest these speech sounds with meaning. Now, the remarkable thing is that most people's speech center lies within the left brain.

The convolutions of the right hemisphere of the human brain do not usually exhibit this speech center. There the brain has convolutions that are different from those of the left hemisphere. Only the smaller number of left-handers exhibit the opposite: their brains have an unformed region on the left side and a formed speech center on the right. It is clear from this fact that the movements of the arms and hands have something to do with speaking. When children seek to express what wells up within their souls, they perform movements with their hands. Our hands are predisposed to perform expressive movements, to form expressive gestures. In the case of a person whose right hand and right arm are predisposed to become expressive, to become language, a mysterious inner system transfers this impulse of arm and hand to the left side of the head. And we can likewise assert that in the case of left-handers, it passes over to the right side of the head. It follows from all this that language must have something to do with latent tendencies of the arm and hand.

Scientists have only just begun to understand this matter, but anthroposophical spiritual science of the kind we are cultivating in Dornach is capable of expanding that knowledge. Ultimately, what we discover is that all of the human body's latent predispositions have something to do with the capacity for speech. Anyone who has an eye for it needs only to watch how a person walks, how he places one foot in front of the other when walking. With such an eye you can see whether this person has a language—even if he has never learned to speak. You can see very distinctly whether he stresses certain sounds or speaks in a monotone. Looking at the way someone moves his arms and legs, one can gain in intuition of the rhythm of his speech; the play of his facial expressions indicates the *melos* of his language, its melody. Over the course of our lives, we do not cultivate this further; otherwise, we would all be continuously making remarkable observations whenever we allowed our souls to reveal themselves through language. We suppress the attendant phenomena that our organism wants to manifest in favor of language itself. You can even see how the people of one nation do it more than the people of another nation. The English stick their hands into their pockets when they speak; the Italians underscore what they want to say, what they "have on their souls," with all kinds of gestures. If you have developed a rigorous intuitive faculty for perceiving such things, then you can trace every speech sound back to the movement of the human organism. Just as the movement that suppresses itself in everyday life transforms itself into language, so too can language be transformed back into movement. Then you get eurythmy. Eurythmy renders what we otherwise show when we accompany our speech with movements—movements that usually are not very expressive. The gestures accompanying everyday speech stand to eurythmy as the inarticulate babbling of an infant stands to cultivated adult language. The things we do to support our speech are a babbling in gestures. Here, in eurythmy, you see the fully cultivated language of movement, a visible language. But everything is more expressive; it is artistic because it is not subject to convention like ordinary language.

As for song, we can indeed say that it gives expression to what lives within us as musicality. Here the whole matter is much more interesting. Whenever we experience within ourselves what raises us up above the animals, we experience it as musicality. Hence, we find within nature models for all the other arts, because what is cultivated in the other art forms is there in the kingdoms of nature. Nature offers no model for music. If you want to compose music, you cannot just imitate nature. Anyone who is capable of viewing human beings in the light of musical intuition finds within them a living, continuously mobile musical instrument. You will find it in our experience of breathing, of the circulation of the blood, and then again in everything connected with respiration and the circulation of the blood that shapes us as human beings. Oh, it is so hopelessly pedantic and philistine when we try to characterize human nature solely in terms of conventional anatomy and physiology! This miraculous array of nerves that runs through the human constitution and is strung, as it were, upon the spinal cord and extends from there into the brain—taken together, this entire nervous system can actually be viewed as a wonderful gradation of musical effects. These effects pass over from respiration into the nervous system via the circulation of the blood; they deposit themselves within the nervous system as a most miraculous sort of music, living within us as human beings. That which is experienced musically is transposed once again into the *Gestalt* of the human organism. Just as the movements of the hands, the movements of the legs, the placing of the feet—just as that all lives within language, so also does our inner, human disposition to rhythm live within our musicality, within everything that we call forth in the way of song. Our brain makes itself into the speech center in accordance with our movements, and in the same way, another part of the brain makes itself into the center of something that manifests not outwardly in movement, but rather inwardly, in the circulation of the blood. We come to know our human inwardness by becoming aware of that movement which actually runs its course within our inner lives, and we come to know it as the musical movement of song, translated into outer gesture. That is what gives rise to tone eurythmy. Eurythmy is a representation of what stems from our rhythmical nature. That is the genesis of visible speech and visible singing, which are just as expressive as the spoken word and song themselves. So, all of that can be elaborated artistically, and it has been elaborated artistically, and now it takes its rightful place as an art beside the other, established art forms.

Now something else arises. At the Waldorf School in Stuttgart, we have introduced eurythmy as a required subject throughout the elementary grades and beyond, in addition to gymnastics. Eurythmy is a gymnastics for the human spirit and soul. Consider gymnastics, which is actually somewhat overvalued today: we see that it is an artifact of the age of materialism, a form of movement based on a view to our physical corporeality. There is a famous, widely known contemporary physiologist,[208] who happened to attend a performance of eurythmy, and heard me say that gymnastics is one-sided, and ought to be complemented with such a eurythmy for the spirit and soul. He replied from his standpoint as a physiologist—so it was he who said this, not I, and if I were to say his name, it would shock you—he said: "I say gymnastics is barbaric; there is nothing pedagogical about it." Anyway, I do not want to go that far myself.

But in the Waldorf School, we are introducing something that allows a speaking and a singing to unfold just as naturally out of our human constitution. We are introducing it as a spiritual play of movement, and that is the guise in which you will see it here, presented by the students in our eurythmy school at the Goetheanum in Dornach. I can add that eurythmy runs through all the grades, beginning with students aged six or seven. Eurythmy can be done at any age. People often ask me when they should stop doing eurythmy. And then I usually reply: Well, in any case not before age eighty. But actually, eurythmy should be done right up until you die. It is always something that rises up in such a harmonious way out of our own organism. Children take to eurythmy with the same inner satisfaction, with the same sense of inner comfort that they felt in taking up speech and song when they were much younger. That alone is enough evidence to show that eurythmy arises as a necessity out of our human constitution as a whole.

A third aspect of eurythmy we have developed is therapeutic eurythmy. Because it emerges from the healthy movement of the human organism, eurythmy is able to counteract the fundamental causes of illness and to supplement other medical treatments once its therapeutic potential has been developed. Please note: here, as in all things anthroposophical, we do not allow ourselves to become one-sided. We embrace the multifaceted complexity of life itself. Nobody who knows anything about anthroposophy would ever be tempted to view eurythmy as a panacea. But eurythmy will provide real support for many different healing processes, and that is why we have made eurythmy an essential component of [anthroposophical] therapy. Ever mindful of the qualifications I just mentioned, we introduced therapeutic eurythmy at the Therapeutic Clinic in Arlesheim, which is led by Dr. Ita Wegman[209] in conjunction with the Goetheanum. There the full significance of eurythmy is revealing itself. That work alone is sufficient to demonstrate that eurythmy arises out of the innate needs of a healthy human constitution. But eurythmy had to be modified somewhat for that purpose. What you shall see here today, and the art of eurythmy you saw in the theater, are not therapeutic eurythmy. Everything has to be modified in such a way that its influences upon those suffering illnesses are efficacious.

What we have undertaken to perform today is the aspect I mentioned second: pedagogical eurythmy. The value of pedagogical eurythmy lies in its ability to educate us in such a way that spirit, soul, and body hold equal sway. But all sorts of things arise in that process. Let me mention just one of them. The things that one discovers while educating and giving lessons as a Waldorf teacher often lie hidden within human development. One thing we see is that eurythmy counteracts certain children's untruthfulness. We have also experienced that children who are not entirely truthful are the only ones who do not love eurythmy. The other children take to it quite naturally. Speaking falsely is a learned behavior. But if we can reveal the mendacity through movement as well, then we can banish the lie from the child's soul again. Hence eurythmy is an outstanding medicine for the promotion of truthfulness.

Because we are our own worst critics, we all know that eurythmy still stands at the very beginning of its development. It will gradually integrate itself into the three areas I have discussed. Nevertheless, I believe I am justified in saying that we are conscious of having made a good beginning. And I think there is something charming about being able to witness the first steps of something that has a significant future. Surely eurythmy shall gradually work its way into the whole of culture over time. It shall find its place in every kind of art, pedagogy, and therapy; thereby it shall contribute both to the development of the individual child and to cultural evolution as a whole.

✽

Address for a Performance of Eurythmy

April 20, 1924, 11 a.m.[210]

We would like to give a eurythmy presentation that is meant to speak to the feelings and sensations you might well have brought to this first large event since the Christmas Conference here at the Goetheanum.

The essential thing about the inner unfolding of our anthroposophical movement has to be that in the future things really evolve, so that progress isn't repeatedly interrupted and we're not working piecemeal. That was too often the case in the past. As with all living things, the later has to evolve out of the earlier. But the members need to understand this. And with the eurythmy performance today we want to give something that might be called a continuation of that which the Christmas Conference inaugurated.

For that reason, these matinées had to be separated from the afternoon performances of eurythmy, which will be given in a public context on Easter Sunday and Easter Monday. Today's eurythmy performance is preeminently suited to the further development of the anthroposophical movement itself.

Consequently, the words of wisdom that accompanied our soul- and heart-imbued laying of the Foundation Stone for the Anthroposophical Society[211] shall be presented in eurythmy today for the first time.

Such things have to be understood in the right way. Up to now all things of this kind have been taken too theoretically—far too theoretically!—so that people did not see how significant it is that things such as the words of wisdom do not just exist, but rather they run through the anthroposophical movement as a living force, and actually drive it forward. For that to happen, however, you cannot look only at the content of these words; you have to look toward the real fact of the way such words flow through the anthroposophical movement.

Hence today is the second step in the progressive effect of these words, initially within the context of the Goetheanum.

That is what I wanted to say in advance about this eurythmy performance that has been specially inserted into our proceedings as a kind of greeting for the anthroposophical friends who have arrived today.

The Wisdom Words of the *Foundation Stone*

Dornach, April 22, 1924[212]

Today's eurythmy performance was conceived with the thought that substantive programs within our movement should be given a different stamp in the aftermath of the Christmas Conference[213] at the Goetheanum. And our work should be given an impulse that is not just transitory, but rather something that persists and continues to evolve. That is the only way we will progress within the anthroposophical movement. It cannot be the way it has been heretofore; we cannot keep beginning new initiatives over and over. What we have inaugurated now really has to find its proper continuation.

Thus you will see here what first revealed itself to you during the Christmas Conference. You shall hear the words that were meant to be laid down within our hearts during the Christmas Conference, so that they might become the foundation stone for the reconstituted Anthroposophical Society. Today you shall apprehend these words transposed into eurythmy, and thereby what was begun at Christmas shall be carried a step further.

That will be followed by eurythmy performances of poems that are extraordinarily well suited to a celebration of Easter. What we attempted to offer at the Christmas Conference was only a beginning then; today we mean to carry it further. And it is to be hoped that if an ever-greater consciousness of the meaning, of the ongoing meaning of the Christmas Conference would enter into the hearts of the dear friends of the Anthroposophical Society, we might be able to progress further along this path. Then our anthroposophical movement would indeed become more than a mere string of pearls, upon which pearls are lined up one after the other. It would become something that grows, sprouts, shoots up, and evolves further in the process of growing, sprouting, and shooting forth.

Movement as the Language of the Soul

Dornach, April 27, 1924[214]

We take the liberty of presenting another performance of eurythmy. Eurythmy begins with movement potentials latent within the human constitution itself, which are then carried over into movement by groups of performers, something that—to begin with—appears to be elaborated gestures. On the stage you will see in the movement of one performer or groups of performers something that seems at first to be gesture. But in eurythmy, gesture becomes an actual language. Now before a little child begins to express the life of his soul as he forms the sounds of speech, he babbles, and this babbling only later on becomes articulate speech. In ordinary life, we find that when we realize the need to impart more inner intensity to the sounds of speech, we try to accompany these sounds with gesture. This makes the sounds more personal and intimate in character, filled in greater measure with the quality of soul.

These gestures—which proceed purely from the realm of instinctive feeling—are thus a kind of "babbling expressed in movement," and they can be developed and elaborated. Just as the babbling of a little child is a gradual revelation of his soul, so can we elaborate to the point of actual speech the gestures made with varying degrees of emphasis by different individuals or communities according to whether they want to create a more personal or an impersonal effect. These gestures can then be elaborated further into an actual language.

The gestures cannot be elaborated in just any old way. We cannot simply take the content of certain words and then proceed to express this content in movement, for such movement could never be really expressive. It would be just as if we were to do exactly what we liked with speech and imagined that we could substitute the sound *I* [ee] for *A* [ah], according to the mood of the soul in the word. The movement must reveal the actual *experience* of the soul, just as each sound—whether it be vowel or a consonant—brings to expression an experience of the soul. In the languages of the so-called "civilized" world, however, speech has departed very far from its original source; and this is the very reason why we have so many languages. We can invariably recognize that the simple, primitive sounds are the expression of certain quite definite experiences of the soul.

"Ah!" or "ach!" have remained expressions of wonder, astonishment; the sound *E* [eh] remains an expression of disturbance, and so on. And just as the vowels—expressing inner experiences of the soul—reveal gradations of feeling and sensibility, so do the consonants imitate outer happenings, outer existence. In this respect, our speech is a continual interweaving of what, in the consonants, we imitate from without, with all that arises in our feeling and perception in relation to outer events—events which we meet with sympathy, antipathy, or the intermediate shades of feeling.

Now, just as in speech, a sound, a phrase, the turning of a phrase, a question, an exclamation, an ordinary declarative statement, or in poetry, rhythm, measure, rhyme correspond to experiences of the soul, so we can find, in exactly the same way, an expression of the human organism in movement. Moreover, this movement can be just as unequivocal as the sound itself. Here we have one kind of eurythmy, speech eurythmy.

We also have tone eurythmy, where movement potentials latent within the human organism become visible singing. In speech eurythmy, the movements corresponding to the sounds are carried out by one performer or a group and are accompanied by recitation or declamation. Tone eurythmy—visible singing—is accompanied by instrumental music. And just as every sound, every syllable, every syntactic structure and turn of phrase is, in speech eurythmy, an expression of the soul, so every tone, musical phrase, melody, rhythm, and harmony can be expressed as visible singing. Along these lines, we can actually develop an art of speaking in a definite language of forms, using our own human nature as an instrument. Moreover, we can do this in such a way that everything we receive as static form is brought into a movement that is consonant with those static forms.

Now if we study the ways in which static form can express itself, we are led to the art of sculpture. Any receptive sensibility will behold the silent soul in everything that is thus given plastic form in space. As a matter of fact, any sculpture that does not aim at expressing the permanent qualities of the soul—temperament, character, the whole range of the human soul's states—in short, that which has come to labile rest in the soul—ceases to be genuine sculpture when it attempts to give expression to a momentary movement of the soul. It is inconsistent for the art of sculpture to attempt to capture anything that is not the silent soul, the soul at rest in herself.

If, on the other hand, we would portray the inner speaking of the soul, we must use the human body itself as an instrument, realizing that all human form is striving perpetually to become movement.

Think about it: the form of the human hand at rest is really a self-contradiction. The very form of the human hand reveals in itself that it is meant to be moved. The outstretched hand already bears within itself, in a kind of embryonic state, the grasping hand, the pointing hand, the beckoning hand. The moment the hand at rest becomes the beckoning or grasping hand, our movement becomes an expression of the speaking soul—just as the forms of sculpture are an expression of the silent soul.

We as human beings actually contain the whole of the cosmos within ourselves. Our observation is extraordinarily impoverished if we have eyes only for earthly conditions. We look out into the world, and many things surround us. And then within us is the sum total of our thoughts and ideas to which our feelings cleave. We might conceivably hear someone say: Take someone who has a vast knowledge of the world, someone who has attentively observed his whole environment. I can also look at this environment; and, if I were somehow able to look into this man's soul, I would find a "soul-photograph" of the environment. In short, all that lives within human thought is a soul-photograph of our environment.

There is a great deal more to us as human beings than our thoughts, however, despite the seeming contradiction. Human nature is a complex system. We seem initially to be physical beings, but is not our physical nature really quite inessential? In our materialistic age, we think otherwise, but this is just the same as if I were to gaze at this colored picture [the Easter eurythmy program][215] and say to myself: I'm studying the violet patch here, and the brownish-purple patch there; I'm studying all the details. And then I proceed to describe how the blue lies above the violet, the yellow under the green and so forth. But that is not the essential thing at all; the essential thing is what is expressed in the picture. The material is not the essential thing.

The same holds true when we observe ourselves as physical beings. The way in which modern science looks at human nature is actually childishly naïve. Regarded as a picture, our human organization is an expression of the whole cosmos. But it is precisely our souls, our so-called life of the mind, that express the physical world. And if we could only regard it properly, we would see that what we bear within us physically is an expression of the cosmos. For humans are a microcosm. That is the form. And if we bring this microcosm into movement, if we capture everything that lives within form by allowing it to pass over into movement, then indeed it is the whole divine-spiritual cosmos that is speaking through the instrument of human beings. In relation to the great world, the macrocosm, the human being is a little world, a microcosm. Compared with the great work of Creation, art as an activity is creation in miniature. And this creation in miniature may be accomplished preeminently when its instrument is one that contains all cosmic mysteries, all cosmic laws: namely, the human being.

And so, when movement is released from the human form at rest, which expresses the silent soul; when we succeed in allowing form to pass over into movement in eurythmy—all cosmic secrets can be expressed. If a true poet desires to give expression to cosmic secrets, a kind of secret eurythmy is already there in his words.

When eurythmy is accompanied by declamation and recitation, one must avoid (as we do) stressing the prose content of the poem. Nor must the aim of the reciter be to pump feelings and emotions into recitation and declamation: that is not artistic, it is merely artificial. In an inherently inartistic time like ours, there is such a strong desire to pump feeling into the prose content of a poem when reciting or declaiming, or to pump enthusiasm into it. In true art, this is impossible. What we have to realize is that imaginations are actually expressed by the sounds used by the poet, and that musical or sculptural principles dwell within the poet's treatment of language. All this has to be expressed in recitation. Then a true, quick rhythm, for instance, will of itself convey all that is revealed by a definite feeling; a slow rhythm will express something different. When melody enters into language, the whole range of feelings will be introduced by the treatment of language rather than by an artificial infusion of emotion. A secret eurythmy is contained in the very way in which the poet handles language, and this secret eurythmy must also be expressed by the recitation and declamation. And so it is that eurythmy aims to bring a truly visible singing and a visible speech into being.

When we see tone eurythmy, which is accompanied by instrumental music, the difference between dancing and something that is *sung* in movement and not *danced* is quite apparent. If we recognize the difference between tone eurythmy and dancing, we shall at once realize the aim of tone eurythmy, and also begin to understand what speech eurythmy is striving to become.

It is, of course, obvious that in our day, when people are so opposed to and dismissive of anything new, there will not be much understanding of eurythmy's aims, nor of the new kind of declamation and recitation. We know and understand all this, but we also know that we have the beginning here of a definite impulse of development in art—a development that will only become fully apparent in the future.

On the other hand, we know that only a beginning has as yet been made. We ourselves are our severest critics and we realize all the objections that may justifiably arise. Moreover, we pay attention to them because we are striving to reach greater and greater perfection. Only a short time ago, a course of lectures on tone eurythmy[216] was given in the School with the object of bringing our work a step forward.

When people say glibly that all our aims are already contained in the other arts and that we can simply stick with speech as it is, remain at the beginning, this shows that they have no true feeling for art. Those who do have it inevitably feel a longing for an expansion of the domain of art.[217] And really it is just such a longing—a longing to draw from art's primal springs—that was the source of our efforts here to develop these nascent arts of tone and speech eurythmy. And that is why we are convinced that a greater and greater understanding of eurythmy will arise within the hearts of all who are possessed of true artistic feeling. For what genuine artists long have felt will surely come to pass. Anastasius Grün,[218] for example, once wrote these beautiful words: "When will the last poet be living? Even as the Earth herself is facing her end, for so long as there is life on Earth, so long will there be poetry." So long, too, will there be art, and artistic sensibility. And we are convinced of this: so long as there is an aesthetic sensibility, so long will there be delight in any expansion of art. Eurythmy indeed has come forth from this desire for and delight in an expansion of art. And thus we dare to hope that eurythmy, taking its place among the other arts, will play a real part in their development and growth.

Extending Artistic Media

Dornach, May 4, 1924[219]

[abridged]

If somebody really wants to understand art, there actually is no other way than by taking joy in art. And then that person takes joy in every kind of art. And then we must say, such people will understand when an attempt is made to extend art and artistic media.

Only someone who does not actually stand in the right artistic relationship to art will raise objections out of old artistic habits vis-à-vis a new art form. Someone who really observes how a genuinely artistic human sensibility response to art will not raise such objections. I always considered it to be an extraordinarily beautiful—well, what shall I call it, I don't want to say definition—a beautiful characterization of art when I read in the last essay on Raphael by Herman Grimm: "What is art?" to which Herman Grimm, who had a genuinely artistic nature, replied: "Art is what gives joy." When you get right down to it, this is actually the only true definition of art: Art is what gives joy. If we really take this up into our sensibilities—art is what gives joy—then since joy can be expanded, can become more comprehensive when a new artistic medium is found, then we will come to view eurythmy more and more as a justified art form. And that is where we have placed our hopes. We know very well that eurythmy today is still at its very beginnings. Only recently was I able to advance this matter somewhat by giving a course on tone eurythmy.[220] And it was only very recently that we were able to create lighting eurythmy,[221] and thereby complete the staging in a certain sense, so that what reveals itself in human movements can reveal itself further in the lighting effects. It was only recently, as I said, that this extension of eurythmy was accomplished.

[Untitled]

[Torquay,][222] *August, 1924*[223]

If eurythmy really is a work of art, then it cannot be introduced. Art has to speak for itself, and the wish to explain an artistic creation is inherently inartistic. However, our experiments with eurythmy are not dealing with the old, usual sources of art and the normal language of artistic forms. In both regards we are dealing with something new. For this reason, we have included a few words on this new artistic medium and this artistic language of form.

You will see on the stage individuals and ensembles moving. These movements express the contents of poems and of musical compositions. But this takes place neither through gestures of mime and pantomime, nor through dance-like gestures. Eurythmy should not be confused with its sister arts—against which absolutely nothing critical is directed.

Eurythmy really is a visible speech and a visible singing. It is created out of the lawfulness of the human organization, just like the musical sounds in singing and the word in speaking.

This has to take place through a painstaking study of what occurs within the human organism when speaking and singing. You cannot arrive at this through normal physiological observation, but only through "sensory-suprasensory beholding."

Such a way of beholding establishes that gestures, mime movements, are suppressed in human speaking. These gestures want to arise but do not. Instead, they are transmuted into formative forces by the structures of the brain. These formative forces are linked to the activity of the will organism, and they are transferred to the air through the larynx and its associated organs. In the study that has created eurythmy, the living gestures suppressed in speech and in singing are brought to light and transferred to the whole human being and to groups of eurythmists. That makes it possible to speak and sing through movement. Through this, one gets movements in space by the human being, compared to which the usual gestures of mime and dance are like babbling in language.

Eurythmy renders poem or a piece of music visible to the eye, just as it is heard by the ear in speaking or singing.

The whole stage can be set up for eurythmy. Thus we try to arrange the sequence of lighting effects, so that they become a visible, melodic expression of the poem or piece of music.

Recitation and declamation parallel the visible, eurythmical rendering of the poetry. Both have to be formed eurythmically when they appear together with the eurythmy. Creative speech underlies all truly artistic poetry. It is this rather than the prose content of poetry that is most important. The melodic element and the imaginative element are contained in the forming of the word. These musical and pictorial elements within language have to be brought out in declamation and recitation; not an emphasis on the prose content. In this way, the artistic element of poetry will be presented with recitation and declamation especially for eurythmy. Speech emphasizing the prosaic content is not used for eurythmy because in the eurythmical movements, image and melody are living, and not the logic of speech.

Alongside the artistic element of eurythmy which is presented in this performance, two further things are relevant: the aspects of health and therapy and that of education and instruction.

Because the movements which are carried out by the human being in eurythmy originate out of the healthy organism, they can also be so refashioned that an ill or weak organism receives healing and strength when this is carried out in the professional manner. That gives rise to therapeutic eurythmy. It is not the same thing as artistic eurythmy, but it has proceeded out of it. In the clinics and therapeutic institutions that are linked to the Goetheanum in Dornach and Stuttgart, this kind of eurythmy is cultivated as a therapy.

In the Waldorf School in Stuttgart and in the further training in Dornach, eurythmy is cultivated in its pedagogical aspect as a gymnastics of the soul and spirit. Many years of experience have shown that children live in the same way into this language of movement as they previously did into spoken language. And because the soul and spirit are involved, without disregarding the body, this eurythmy is taken as a beneficent supplement to gymnastics. In particular, it is the very thing for training of children's wills in the free mastery of their bodies.

At present eurythmy is still at the beginning of its development. Its creators are well aware of that fact. But they also know that it is capable of an unlimited perfection. For it uses as its tool the human organism itself. The human organism is, however, an expression of all the secrets of the world. It is a true microcosm. If the human soul speaks through it, it can render visible all the secrets of the world through revealing its own inner life. For this reason, we believe that one day eurythmy will be able to place itself as a fully justified younger art alongside the fully justified, older sister arts.

Part III: A New Aesthetics of Movement
Eurythmy and the Other Arts

Introductions, 1914 to 1924

On the Essence of Eurythmy

Dornach, October 7, 1914[224]

Do we not seek with everything that expresses itself in our building[225] a new form of the old beauty? Striving for beauty, for beauty means much more than what one usually associates with this idea, with this concept. If one wants to become aware of how significant it is that, in an epoch such as ours, new forms for the entire mood of the human soul must step forth, then we only have to make it clear to ourselves how varied human progress actually is.

. . . After all, Goethe, when he felt the longing to immerse himself in beauty, could do nothing but go to Rome in order to experience Greek beauty in his soul. Indeed, the whole nineteenth century could basically do nothing but travel to Rome as well. But the epoch has come when one does not merely go to Rome, or merely immerse oneself in Greek forms of beauty, but rather one enters into the spiritual worlds in order to find out of spiritual worlds new forms of beauty. . . .

We strove to give humanity something that already in its external form reveals evolution, the sense and the spirit of evolution. We could do that only by becoming clear that we live in the world; in immediate life we live also in the world of forms, and that progress means penetrating into the world of movement. The world of forms rules the physical body, but the world of movement rules the etheric body. Now the movements must be found that are innate in the etheric body. We need to be guided towards expressing what is natural for the etheric body in gestures and movements of the physical body.

That is sought in eurythmy. It will be revealed that human beings in their movements are truly an intermediate member between cosmic letters and what we employ in human sounds and letters in our poetry. A new art will arise in eurythmy. This art form is suitable for everyone. And one wishes very much that humanity will be seized by understanding for this art form. . . .

In many regards, I have already spoken about the relationship of the large cupola to the small, about the relationship between what stands under the large cupola and the small. Now someone could ask: How do the small forms proceed from the large in our building with its double cupolas? The answer is: Someone should attempt to allow the forms under the large cupola to dance according to the laws of eurythmy; then the forms under the small cupola will emerge. Imagine that someone could unite in eurythmic movements everything that comes to expression in the large cupola and that he danced into the smaller space and radiated out from there what he danced: then the twelvefoldness of the columns and the cupola would emerge on their own. Then I hope that something else will dance eurythmically in the building, invisibly: the *word*. That will yield a good acoustics.

In short, we can define eurythmy as the fulfillment of what the human etheric body demands of us according to its natural laws. Thus with eurythmy something has truly been given that belongs to our spiritual life and that has been conceived out of its wholeness.

On Eurythmy

Munich, February 19, 1918; Stuttgart, February 26, 1918[226]

When, a number of years ago, Mrs. Smits[227] suggested creating something along the lines of a spiritualized art of dance within our movement, the question was this: In what way could this particular art form be approached today? Is it not true that on such an occasion one has to consider that in our time there is much in the artistic field that, I would like to say, represents a very late product of something that leads back to times long past? One can say: In our time, there are such and such strivings of which one knows only later stages, nothing of the origin. But if our movement is to have greater significance, it must, among other things, also gain this by linking up in many respects to what was originally part of humanity. And so it is a matter of looking for the sources of this art form.

On one occasion or another, we have emphasized that art did not arise in isolation, but rather emerged from the same source from which other human cultural ideals developed. Knowledge—what one often calls science in ordinary life—religion, and art: all three came from the same source. And if you go into the ancient temples, you will find that there was not a separate art, a separate science, a separate religion, but that there was knowledge to be found that went directly to the formation, to the configuration of the universe, that viewed in ideas what they then tried to express in a religious cult, so that in this religious cult the relationship of humanity to what was scientifically, cognitively perceived was expressed. And art, on the other hand, was nothing other than a shaping, a forming in the human spirit of what was recognized to be religiously uplifting. In short, the three currents of culture—religion, science, and art—grew from a single source, from a single root.

But just as everything that has developed further in human life only comes about by separating it into isolated currents, so it has also happened with religion, science, and art. We now live in an age in which what had to be kept separate for millennia due to the necessities of development is striving to come together again. Richard Wagner[228] already dreamed of the total work of art [*Gesamtkunstwerk*], and also carried it out in a certain direction. But if such a striving for union is to take place, not only must individual branches of art take on a more inward character, a more spiritual character, so that they can find themselves again in the spiritual, but there must also be branches of art that are more or less uncultivated to add to the old ones. And one can say that the way we understand eurythmy is something that can only come about in our time.

The art of dance in solitude, in its isolation—the individual arts have also isolated themselves again—became more and more an expression of the subjective, the personal, the emotional. This is not a criticism but a characterization. Now it is a matter of finding something related to human nature in general, to the all-encompassing, universal human. So the first thing that happened was this experiment. What is offered as eurythmy is initially only an experiment, but over the years we have seen that the experiment has made progress, that there is more eurythmy among us today than a few years ago. Everything progresses, and the fact that we follow this law of progression is proof that there is something alive in eurythmy. It is about creating something alive, and we came up with the idea of transposing in a certain way what is already there in the human being.

The various artistic endeavors—we are convinced of this when we go back to the sources through esoteric science—actually arose (if I may express myself briefly) because we developed our being in a certain way; what initially is directly in us is exported outside us in a certain way and is imitated in the physical world. This is how all artistic endeavors came about. Experiences that take place in the subconscious are made visible in the outer world. This gave rise to the idea of observing what always dances regularly in the human etheric body—namely, the region of the human etheric body, or body of formative forces, which enclose the larynx in particular, and the organs of speech in general.

If you know the human being, you know that we are not just a complete system, a completely organic system, but rather consist of several systems. What we call the etheric body, or body of formative forces, is structured differently from the physical body. And one can say that in this respect the etheric or formative body underlies the organs of the human larynx and everything connected with them: palate, lips, and so on. This part of the human etheric body, which underlies the instruments of speech, actually dances in a certain way, performing expressive dances. We cannot speak unless that part of the etheric body which is associated with the larynx and appendages makes certain movements. These movements can now be transferred to the whole human being, can be carried out through the physical body, because by nature not only do the individual human systems merge into one another, as Goethe's theory of metamorphosis shows, but also the whole human being in a certain sense is a metamorphosed, single organ system. The whole human being can become a larynx.

And that is essentially the art of eurythmy, that what the etheric body of the larynx carries out invisibly when speaking or singing is carried out by the whole human being. It is, therefore, nothing that has been deduced or conceived in any way, but rather only the movement of the hand, head, arms, and legs—if one transfers what the part of the etheric body that forms the basis of the speech system carries out supersensibly without this—that translates it into the sensory: the eurythmy of the word, the supersensible eurythmy of the word.[229] So the movements that the etheric body of the larynx and the appendages carry out are converted into physical movements, into movements of the physical body.

There are other movements in addition that the etheric body of the larynx holds back in a certain way. It holds them back; they remain latent, if I may use a physical expression.

We do not speak only abstractly, indifferently, but rather we permeate our words and sentences with what swells from the heart, with feeling, perception, suppressed impulses of the will, and so on. All of this is so interwoven in the movements of the etheric body of the larynx that it is held back there, that it is not expressed, that it hardens into forms. In eurythmy, we dissolve what is transposed into forms from the world of feeling, from the world of sensations while speaking, by using the organism itself, either in itself by bending the head forwards and backward in space, allowing movements to be made, or in such a way that we carry out these movements through other personalities, that we transfer to group dances what is expressed in feeling or some other emotional formation of the materiality of the word. Even the pure rhythm and movement of the larynx of the etheric body, which is otherwise held back, is converted into movement. Thus, eurythmy, as far as we have developed it up to now, consists of two parts: translating natural movements of the etheric body of the larynx, and dissolving the movements of what is held back in this etheric part of the human being, which has been transformed from movement into form. So, you see, it is only the transference of what is already there to the whole human being and in relationship to human beings.

In this way, one goes back to the principles of the old temple dance, for everything that was originally authentic temple art had as its principle the penetration of human life with the power of the word. The word did not mean what we can understand by it, but rather the wisdom resounding through the world in the sounding of the spheres, which finds expression in the most diverse areas, which leaves a pure imprint in human language, and a somewhat more abstract expression in human singing, which has a materialization in instrumental music that can be redeemed if the whole human organism is shaped and moved in the manner described. That is actually the principle at issue. I believe that something has been inaugurated, even if it has not yet been accomplished, that is capable of much further development.

In a certain sense, this creates something that can be described as meeting the needs and longings of the present. You will have heard on several occasions how the present, while unable to develop certain future-sensing impulses, is striving for certain artistic phenomena by employing certain catchwords. Catchwords like Impressionism and Expressionism have, I would like to say, acquired a ring in our time that is both justified and unjustified. That ring is justified, however, because the striving for Impressionism and Expressionism conveys something that underlies all art and is fully justified. One can say: Expressionist art strives more for what one could call the sensory, the external sensory conversion of what in human beings constantly strives for a vision, but which must not become a vision in healthy people. For what constantly strives for visions must be suppressed in healthy life. If one places in the outer world what the vision actually wants but is not allowed to express inwardly in hallucinations, then one has Expressionist art. In this sense, eurythmy is an expressionistic art to a particular degree, an art that is genuinely and justifiably an art of expression, especially when everything arbitrary is avoided, everything that stems from the subjective human personality, all pantomime, all facial expressions, and so on. It is an expressionistic art if only the objective, which I have indicated as the implementation of the movements of the etheric body of the larynx, comes into consideration.

Over the years, we have learned something from doing eurythmy. At first, we thought of making it a mere art of expression. That was worrying because there actually cannot be such a thing. But eurythmy is protected from this, it has a life of its own. It is protected from being borrowed from reality—that is, from what cannot merely be an expression but can be permeated with inner, autonomous life.

In the beginning, we let the recitation take a back seat, and meant to present eurythmy directly as such. That can of course be the case, but in the course of time, it has become apparent that, precisely with the development of eurythmy, the cultivation of recitation can go hand in hand in an independent way as another artistic element. For if one can say that eurythmy is really expressionistic art to a high degree, then recitation, and also singing, is impressionistic art to the most express degree. And this combination, this harmonious sounding together of an expressionist and an impressionist element in art, is something that I believe can advance important artistic impulses in our time.

You see, one can really only look into what art is supposed to do from an anthroposophical-psychological point of view. It is a matter of looking into the soul for the right evaluation of the artistic, what actually happens in the soul of the person who enjoys art as well as the person who creates and practices art. That is not so easy. The artistic process of receiving as well as creating is an extraordinarily complicated one. There is never just one thing going on in the soul when we record something artistic or create something artistic; rather, something that remains subconscious and rhythmic takes place in the soul. And if one analyzes what is going on in the soul in artistic creation and reception, one has, like a chord striking in two directions, a striking of the soul mood in two directions. The only thing that prevents awareness of the matter is that one paralyzes the other. For it is precisely in the artistic field that certain impulses of the soul—I would like to say—rise upwards like waves in the life of the soul; but before they are expressed, they are blunted, just as if waves were rising up inside the sea but first had to be held back by something.

Namely, there are two emotional impulses that underlie all artistic feeling, all artistic creation. One is an impulse of sensation which, if fully developed, would lead to blushing. If you think of the emotional impulse that causes a person to blush—as in the case of shame, for example—working down in the soul before blushing occurs, then you have a rhythm that does not fully express itself.

The other thing that lives in art would, if lived out, lead to blanching. Everything that lives in fear must not lead to blanching. Now think of these two emotional impulses, one leading to blushing and the other to blanching, flowing into each other: then you have the life of the soul which actually underlies the artistic, which in a certain way remains in the subconscious. It must not come to an extreme; rather, these must interact.

Now, we have the possibility, if we allow recitation and eurythmy to work together, to let what would lead to blanching through eurythmy, and what would lead to blushing through recitation, to resonate with one another. So you really have something that meets the artistic needs, the artistic disposition of the human soul in a special way. You get a wonderful compensation when you let both things work together. The psychological process involved in the simplest things in life is a complicated one, and as little as one suspects, in real artistic life, souls are actually torn between fear and feelings of shame, between blushing and blanching. But the fact that the peculiarity of life in art presents itself to consciousness in a different way is based—just as in the sea, so also in the soul—on something which must be described in such a complicated way and which must be known to those who immerse themselves in art, as this was done in the times when one did not seek to create artistic forms arbitrary but out the depths of spiritual life itself.

I now believe that it might soon be time for those personalities in our society who have dealt extensively with eurythmy to present eurythmy to the public. However, this is associated with some difficulties because we have to be very clear, on the one hand, that—due to many recent efforts which seek to cultivate an emotional art of dance and have presented an art of dance to the public—prejudices against this kind of art have arisen. One has long since scoffed at those psychoses that have joined the other psychoses when one danced in the most varied of ways over the last few years. On the other hand, what is actually desired in eurythmy, namely, to give something that is in accordance with inner laws, is not what speaks from the outset about subjectivity. What is actually wanted in eurythmy will encounter resistance. Getting used to something that resists [discourages] some people from the outset.

Until now, I would like to say—but it is also at the tipping point—the art of music has been saved from the danger that those who understand nothing about it are actually the right judges, that one does not first have to build up an understanding. That, too, will be different in the near future. But with regard to the fine arts and all other arts, people have long been of the opinion that those who have not really worked their way into the laws of art, i.e., what art is supposed to be, have the right judgment. With eurythmy, it must be the case that one has to work one's way into it. Therefore—with respect—journalism, which sets the tone today, will complain terribly, and I have a slight reluctance when our ladies, who have naturally become somewhat sensitive through art and life, have to appear in front of the public and there be thoroughly scolded. That is inevitable, it goes without saying, because otherwise, their art would be worthless. If they were praised, the matter would be very suspicious. As I said, I am a little shy about it, but it has to be endured. We have to be prepared to prove our justification in this area too by enduring a thorough scolding of our performances. That should not discourage us in any way; rather, it should strengthen our backbone.

Those are the few words I wanted to say about eurythmy.

❁

THE ARCHETYPAL NATURE OF THE ARTISTIC

Berlin, June 28, 1918[230]

Eurythmy, like everything else in our movement, has been brought to us by karma. A couple of years ago, Mrs. Smits approached me to see if something could be found within our circle that could be a kind of dance art. Not an ordinary art of dance in the external sense but something more serious, more significant had to be thought of, if the idea was to be approached.

One must remember again and again that all cultural currents have emerged from a common source. Not only the individual arts but what we call religion and science also emerged from a common source. In the earliest culture of humanity, these were not so separate as today. In the mysteries,[231] all of these still had something in common. If it was presented so that the secrets of the world were shown to the soul in a sensory way, then it was art. If it was presented in such a way that the human soul should be seized within and find a bridge to the eternal mysteries of existence, then it was religion. And if one put it in such a way that the cognitive faculty was used, then one was in the realm of science. In the course of the evolution of humanity, in the course of the epochs, the common whole was then divided into science, religion, and art, and art was divided again into the individual arts. More details about the arts are contained in the booklet *The Being of the Arts*.[232]

Now it was necessary to fall back, so to speak, to the original character of the arts, since eurythmy wants to go back to the origin of art. Art takes up the relationship of the macrocosm to the microcosm. The universe expresses itself in the microcosm. Those who can see human beings in their totality as an image of the macrocosm penetrate also the individual arts. And every single art is connected to the universe and the microcosm insofar as what is related in the universe to the human being can come to light.

Eurythmy was not based on something invented but on something that is thoroughly a part of the human being.

The starting point was human language: How does what comes to representation in human beings actually live when one speaks? Artistic speech was laid down as the basis.

The human etheric body is divided in certain ways, and a partial division corresponds to the larynx and what is connected with it. The etheric body of the larynx and what belongs to it—tongue, palate and so on—engage in very specific movements when speaking, so that one sees this link of the etheric body in specific movements when we speak. Now everything that is expressed in one part can also be expressed by the whole person. Everything else can be held back, and the total force that the human being exerts when speaking can be expressed in a special way. In movements of the whole human being, one can express those movements which underlie this member of the etheric body. This was done in eurythmy.

What the eurythmists then do with their bodies and their hands when they are at rest is nothing other than when what is involved in speech apart from the immediate speech instruments is expressed. What is otherwise partially expressed in the larynx is represented by the whole human being in the individual movements. It is something that can be read from the whole human being. In addition to the laryngeal movements and so on, there are also the effects in the lungs and in the other organs. This has a fine effect, gives the timbre, keynote, emotional content of speech. These are restrained movements. This happens through the whole movement of the eurythmist, an individual or also a group, a chorus. In group movements, we dissolve what are otherwise restrained movements. This is the initial basis of eurythmy.

The art of eurythmy is very diverse, as is music. It can be connected with the musical element. What I have said about linguistic expression is valid as well for musical expression, only in a slightly different sense. What becomes art in language, in poetry, can be expressed in eurythmy, dissolved in group movements. Thus, what is already quite neglected in poetic art today can come out in eurythmy. Usually only the prosaic aspect of poetry is emphasized, what is actually non-artistic. The artistic, however, can be found again through the eurythmic element. The things are determined in the individual just as in the music. Individualities come into consideration just as when one plays a Beethoven sonata. What is recited does not have to take a back seat.

The different arts can also work together. Impressionist art, poetry, can work together with the other expressionist arts. Thus they can lift and carry each other. Only the artistic, poetic element can enter into eurythmy, only the *shaping* of thoughts. The *content* of the thoughts has not much to do with the art as such.

When looking at a eurythmic work of art, many secrets of the poetry emerge. Eurythmy will still become more and more perfect. And when we later appear in public with it, the eurythmists will be sufficiently armed to be able to stand up to the critics, who will certainly rant. But we can be sure that if it were only praised, it would be something superfluous and would not need to be cared for. The more it is scolded, the more perhaps it will have to say to people.

ON THE EVOLUTION OF LANGUAGE
QUESTIONS AND ANSWERS

Zürich, October 17, 1918[233]

Honored guests, it was suggested to me that in answering questions I might be able to say something about an individual phenomenon in recent historical development that lies very close to human life. It was suggested that I say something about the evolution of language.

Of course, one could give a whole lecture if one wanted to say anything at all exhaustive about this. But I would like to take up the suggestion because I actually would like to draw your attention to the fact that anthroposophy truly does not stand there as though it owed its existence to a sudden intuition, as though it has been shot out of a pistol, as though it consisted of individual aperçus strung together. No. If you acquaint yourself with the literature that has been put out here, you will see that anthroposophy draws what it has to say out of the whole breadth of observation, out of the whole breadth of worldly phenomena. Of course, when one has to summarize broad realms in an hour—and I always regret that this cannot be longer!—one inevitably makes the impression that one is wandering about in abstract realms. But nobody is supposed to be convinced, only stimulated to go further. And then one will already see that there really is in anthroposophy much more conscientious, methodical seeking than in any other scientific enterprise.

It is interesting to observe precisely what I characterized in general today in an individual phenomenon like the evolution of human language. But I want to discuss only one aspect of this evolution. When we speak as human beings today, we usually do not at all consider how speaking actually compels us at each moment to be imprecise. Fritz Mauthner wrote a three-volume work, and in addition a *Dictionary of Philosophy*, in order to bring to expression how everything that is produced in worldviews and science rests upon language, and that language is imprecise, so that actually we can never have a true science.

Well, vis-à-vis anthroposophy, that is a foolish assertion, even when presented in three volumes! Nevertheless, it is important to get to the bottom of the partial phenomenon underlying this. If one goes back in the evolution of human language, one finds, as opposed to external anthropological linguistics, which works with insufficient means, that human beings of earlier ages, the further back one goes, were more and more inwardly bound up in their souls, instinctively and unconsciously, with what came to expression in their language. Humanity loosens itself gradually also from what its own nature contains, just as it is loosened from external nature. Humanity also is loosened in its direct coalescence with language, and language becomes something external. A stark dualism arises between the inwardly experienced thought, which many already do not have because the thought remains in the sphere of language, and that which is spoken. And if one does not want to surrender to illusion at the evolutionary point of humanity at which we are now standing, the age of the consciousness soul,[234] one has to regard the way in which language has been separated from humanity. Actually, it is only proper names, which refer to an individual being, that actually refer directly to this being. As soon as we employ general names—whether they be adjectives or nouns or whatever—these express only imprecisely what they are supposed to express. They are abstract; they are like commonplaces. And one will properly understand language and its relationship to human life only when one views it as a gesture, only when one becomes conscious that just as I point immediately at something when I designate it with my finger, in the same way, through the production of my larynx and through the sound it makes, I point as in a gesture to what the sounds of language refer to. To grasp language as gesture—that is what we are dealing with.

Thus ancient times had an indefinite, instinctive premonition, lying in the unconscious, of how the life of the soul is connected in a gestural way with sound. It did not confuse the inner life of the soul with what comes to expression in language.

In order to develop the strivings that lie close to one realm of anthroposophy, we have sought to make the gestural nature of language visible again in what we call eurythmy. There we have sought to bring the whole human being into movement. Through the movements of the limbs, through the movements of the human form in space, through the movements of groups, through the relationships between people, we have sought to express as gesture what otherwise comes to expression through the human larynx and its neighboring organs, which are also expressed in gestures but are not noted as such. We term this art of movement, which must penetrate human evolution as something new, eurythmy.

And we wanted to connect this lecture with a presentation of eurythmy, which would have been announced here in Zürich. It had to be postponed because, although we received permission in this difficult time to give a lecture, we did not receive permission to give our presentation of eurythmy. It would have shown directly how in a sense the whole human being becomes a larynx. By becoming conscious of what language is, we hit upon something that is especially important, very fundamentally important for the life of the present and of the future as well. Today one often hears in human life someone expressing an opinion—for example, me here in spiritual science. Another comes and says, "I have read that somewhere," and then points to a passage that, at least in certain details, matches the wording completely. I could show you striking examples of this. I want to emphasize only one case, which to my mind was a particularly excellent example of this. Because I really do attempt to apply to life all of the things that anthroposophy requires me to elaborate, because I want to penetrate into real impulses of life, I have long occupied myself, for example, with the whole way of thinking, the whole complexion of thinking exhibited by Woodrow Wilson. It has been interesting for me to study the essays on historical method, on the consideration of history, and on the American historical life of Woodrow Wilson. He plays so great a role in the life of the present that one must get to know him; that is what one says who does not want to sleep through what is happening in the present, but rather wants to observe it with wakeful thinking.

I have learned to admire the magnificent way, really hitting the mark in an American sense, that Woodrow Wilson depicts the development of the American people: the progress from the American East to the American West in an entirely extraordinary way. The emergence of truly American life only when the West is penetrated from the East, while everything else that preceded this is depicted by Woodrow Wilson incisively as an appendage to European life. This rooting-out of nature, this conquest of nature, the development of agriculture by the newcomers to the American West, the extraordinary way of making history, which is similar to much that has transpired in the life of mankind and yet completely specific—all this comes to magnificent expression. Thus it is interesting to see how Woodrow Wilson arranges his historical method.

I have pursued the descriptions where he depicts his historical method itself. In those places something very peculiar emerges. Out of this thoroughly American man's prose, there flow sentences that conform almost literally with the sentences of another man who developed out of an entirely different condition of life and thought. One could take sentences from Woodrow Wilson's essay on "The Method of History," which bore such good fruit for him, and carry them over literally into essays by Herman Grimm, who stands within modern Goetheanism as a thoroughly central European, German spirit. One could say, one only needs to lift passages out of Herman Grimm's essays and transfer them to Wilson's essays—a completely different character!—and to lift passages out of Woodrow Wilson and transfer them into Herman Grimm: one would find no great divergence in the literal words. But one learns from such an experience something very significant that I would like to express, though with trivial words. One learns: When two people say the same thing, it is not the same, even if the literal words correspond.

What one has to learn thereby is that one has to enter not merely into the words that are given through language but into the whole human being. Then one will find the specific difference between Herman Grimm and Woodrow Wilson. Then one will find that with Grimm, every single sentence has been worked through in the experience of the consciousness soul, as for example the progress in the genial essay by Herman Grimm where he speaks of historical method and historical contemplation. Truly it is the case that one sees him proceed from one sentence to another in an inner struggle of soul, so that nothing remains unconscious, but rather everything is raised into consciousness. One sees the constant inward struggle of the soul to progress.

On the other hand, if one looks at the way the matter stands with Woodrow Wilson, then one sees how out of remarkable, unconscious depths of the soul, out of the man himself—as opposed to external influence—the sentences well up. I do not mean any disrespect thereby. But I would only like, if I might express myself paradoxically, to make visible that with Hermann Grimm I always feel the life of the soul progressing sentence by sentence in the region of entirely conscious psychic life. But with Woodrow Wilson I feel that he is possessed by something that lies in his own inwardness and strives upwards; he is possessed by his own truths in his own inwardness. As I said, I do not mean anything either sympathetic or antipathetic thereby; rather, it is something that I merely want to characterize. It influences him out of his own depths of soul.

There we shall truly recognize that even when the wording is the same, when two different people say the same thing, it is not the same! We only recognize what underlies the phenomena if we do not look at the wording but rather learn to grasp what emerges from the whole life of the personality.

Modern humanity has to learn to overcome what is conventional today when one is presented with a text. One judges it only by the content. One will have to learn that the content is not at all what is essential.

When I speak about anthroposophy, I am not concerned essentially with the formulation of the sentences, with the content. Rather, the essential thing is that there flows into what I am saying that which is truly produced out of the suprasensory world. One has to place a greater value on the "how" than the "what"; one has to learn that one can sense, one can feel, that things have been spoken out of the suprasensory world.

And thus one has to learn this at present in general with regard to everyday life. Some newspaper, some journal, may say something ever so beautiful—one can say frightfully beautiful things today, for such things lie in the streets, the beautiful ideals and such—it does not depend on the wording, but rather from what soul source they spring. One has to look through the sentences to symptoms, to the person. We have to penetrate language and the literal wording as though through a veil and approach the person again.

The modern evolution of language teaches us precisely this. In our inmost nature, in our consciousness soul, we have been separated from language. This teaches us the necessity of looking not just to the literal words, but also through the literal words at the human soul. We must pursue all possibilities for this on all sides.

Something has to be overcome if we are to make progress in this direction. For people today are accustomed to abstraction, to this bourgeois, philistine insistence on the immediate content. If someone expresses an ideal and formulates something, we must be clear that today people like it as much as they like blackberries, for the ideals have been settled. One can put forth every possible ideal for humanity: they have taken shape. What it depends upon is whence they come, whence in the inner life of the soul, in what region of the soul they arise. Life shall be tremendously fructified when we are able to look at life in this way.

Perhaps I may introduce something personal here. Many poetic productions of the present are given to me. How many people write poetry today! Among these poetic productions one finds some that are very perfect in form, that depict this or that wonderfully, and some that are apparently clumsy, that have difficulties with language, and some that are even bumbling and primitive.

Those who adopt a standpoint that is not yet modern will naturally take joy in the beautiful, formally perfect, especially in the language. They will not feel that Emmanuel Geibel[235] was right when he said of himself that he would find a public as long as there are teenagers. These poems are pretty, smooth, and they will find their audience. Among such people is the public that considers Wildenbruch[236] or similar people to be poets, and there are many such.

But another judgment is possible in this realm, and this is possible also with the other arts. But here I am speaking about language. Today there are poets over whose versus one can stumble, one can have difficulties, because they speak in a clumsy language, but there is a new impulse in them. One must seek out this impulse. One has to look through the veil of language in the case of the polished verses to see into the superficiality of the soul. The polished verses, beautiful, polished verses that are much more beautiful than Goethe's verses, are today is cheap as blackberries, for it is the language that makes the poetry. But new life of the soul, life that springs forth from the source of all life, that is what must be sought. That expresses itself often precisely through the fact that one has to engage in battle with language, that it is initially a kind of stuttering. But such stuttering can be preferable to that which is perfected and only aims at the superficiality of the soul.

Once I was given verses on an occasion when we needed such verses because we needed a translation from another language. Very beautiful verses. I became enraged at it, and made bad verses myself. I am conscious that as verses they are much worse, but I knew that on that occasion it was necessary for me to express in a perhaps awkward language what needed to be expressed if one was to draw from the source of life that corresponded. I did not overvalue at all what I had undertaken, but I also did not overvalue the perfected verses that were given to me.

Our seeking through language in the age of the consciousness soul is something that is yielded out of an actual consideration of linguistic life.

For that reason, today I have strenuously attempted not to speak every sentence as though I represented anthroposophy and constantly wanted to prove the supersensible. Rather, I have attempted to situate what I had to say in the "how" of historical consideration. And I believe that it is important not to say that a genuine researcher is someone who uses the word "spirit" and "spiritual world" in every fifth sentence, and who believes thereby he can suggest this to people, but rather someone who, through his way of looking at the world, even the most external world, through the "how"—how one presents things—shows that the inner guide from thought to thought, from viewpoint of viewpoint, from impulse to impulse, is the spirit. If this guide is the spirit, then one does not need to invoke it at every turn.

This was meant to show you how one can substantiate through language what I would have to present in a comprehensive lecture.

On the New Art of Recitation

Dornach, March 30, 1919[237]

If one enters into what this art wants in the way we have organized it, one can see, on the one hand, the human larynx embodied by the movements and formations of the whole human being and groups of people and, on the other hand, hear the poetry, the musical, so that both complement each other, both unite into a total work of art. And it should be understood that the recitation accompanying eurythmic art must now also be undertaken differently from what is usually understood by recitation today because it appears as a special artistic supplement to eurythmy. Today, recitation has already retreated from what is actually artistic. Recitation today is actually limited to accentuation of the poetic content. It is precisely the finding of an art form such as that on which eurythmy is based that will in turn lead to the return of recitation itself to what it once was, which the younger among us no longer even know. Those who are older still remember the reciters of the seventies and eighties [of the nineteenth century], who had perhaps already fallen into decadence but still offered an echo of what the art of recitation used to be. Today, few people know that Goethe rehearsed [his drama] *Iphigenia* for the stage in Weimar with a baton, like a musical work of art that one could hear through the rhythmic, the actually artistic element. This was the ambition of Goethe as well. This art of recitation has been lost. In a certain way, through eurythmy, it will make itself necessary again. Today, people do not even want to hear what is actually poetic, artistic. The poetic form is not something that can be expressed in accentuation of the content. Basically, the art of recitation today is nothing more than a particularly refined prose reading. And only by way of eurythmy will the art of recitation and declamation have to be found. Today, that is not understood.

Dornach, April 5, 1919[238]

An attempt has been made here to visibly represent the highest revelation of the world, the human being, this microcosm, as a great larynx. Of course, I am not trying to say anything other than how this art form came into being. Just as Nature creates in man something that can become art, in poetry and in musical songs, it is likewise possible for what lies in the whole human being to become art. But everything I have said is only meant to express the origin. The creative energy must be felt in direct perception, and we are convinced that it can indeed be felt.

Thus, we will endeavor, on the one hand, to make the tonal aspect audible through recitation, declamation, or music. And, on the other hand, we will make what can be heard visible through eurythmy.

Recitation also brings us into conflict with contemporary views. The younger people nowadays no longer know the old art of recitation, even in the decadent form that was still cultivated in the seventies and eighties [of the nineteenth century], the art of recitation that outwardly preserved the forms of recitation. One need only think of how Goethe rehearsed his *Iphigenia* in Weimar with a baton. Today, this recitation, which considers the formal, the artistic, and which has nothing to do with the content of the words, is often not appreciated. One appreciates much more declaimed prose, from which the content emerges and which expresses certain nuances. Here we must look to form the recitation, which is to come together with eurythmy to form a total work of art, in such a way that—just as our art of dance must in many cases go back to the sacramental dance of antiquity—we go back to older forms of recitation, which are less understood today but which can be understood again when something develops out of the declining artistic culture of the nineteenth century, which in turn has elementary spiritual, suprasensory things in it.

On the Nature of Eurythmy

Berlin, September 14, 1919[239]

The art of eurythmy is still in the early stages of its work. One could even call it the aim of an experiment. It will therefore be permissible to say a few words in advance of the presentation about the essence of this art.

Everything that is being attempted and that will surely be perfected in the future in relation to this eurythmic art is based on Goethe's conception of the world and life. This Goethean conception of the world and of life has a very special artistic attitude and left a special understanding of art in its wake. And it is precisely this that is peculiar to Goethe—that he knew how to build a bridge, a quite natural bridge, I would say, for his own outlook between an artistic attitude, artistic power and a general world-view. In this way, on the basis of Goetheanism, on which we stand with all of anthroposophy, an attempt could be made to create something in a very special field, in the field of the movement art of the human being himself, which would be entirely an expression of Goethe's artistic spirit. For this reason, I would ask you not to regard what we are able to present today as competition for any of the arts that are in the neighborhood of eurythmy. We do not want that at all. We know quite well that dance and similar arts, which could perhaps be confused with ours, are today at such a peak of perfection that we cannot compete at all. But we also do not want to do that at all; for us it is a question of introducing something essentially new into the general development of the arts for humanity. And without becoming theoretical, I would like to explain very briefly how this attempt of ours is connected with the greatness of Goethe's worldview.

The actually significant, the great and decisive aspect of Goethe's worldview has not yet been sufficiently appreciated. Goethe was able to orientate his world of ideas, his cognitive world of feeling in such a way that he could really make the ascent from the science of the inanimate—which still is basically all science today—to a certain knowledge of the living. It only looks theoretical when everything points to Goethe's great idea of the metamorphosis of organic beings and of a single organic entity. One need only imagine, in Goethe's sense, how a single plant becomes a living being, how it grows, perfects itself and reaches the summit of its becoming. For Goethe, each individual leaf of the plant—whether green leaf or colored flower petal—is basically a whole plant, only more simply formed than the whole plant, and again, for him, the whole plant is only a more complicated leaf.

This view, which is immensely significant, was valid for Goethe for everything that is a living being. Every living thing is formed in such a way that as a whole it is the more complicated formation of each of its individual members, and again each individual part reveals, only more simply formed, the whole living being. This view can now be transferred to the expressions, the activities of a living being and especially of the highest living being known to us within our world: man himself. And so, starting from Goethe, one can say: In that which is human speech, a part of the whole of human nature is also given. In what we express in speech out of the depths of our souls through the larynx and its neighboring organs, something is given which is a single, organic expression, a revelation of the human being. For he who is able to see what is actually predisposed in the human larynx in terms of forces, possibilities for activity, and movement in speech, especially in artistic speech, in the speaking of poetry as well as in singing—for he who can see this, who is not only limited to looking away from what the larynx performs in the way of movements, and who merely listens by hearing what is done in the way of movements, it is possible to transfer to the whole human being what is otherwise expressed in speech only in the individual organ—in the larynx and in its neighboring organs. It is possible to make the whole human being into a larynx, so that we move our limbs in the same way as the larynx is predisposed to move when the human being speaks or sings. One could also say that when one speaks, one has to do with the undulating motion of the air. What is sound is the movement of the air. But, of course, one does not see these movements of the air in ordinary life. Whoever sees this can therefore gain the possibilities of movement that he is able to transfer to the whole person—namely, to the limbs. Then a visible language comes into being, in that the arms and other human limbs move, that they move in a lawful way. And as the poetic and artistic aspect of language, of song, of music, is made manifest through this visible language, a completely new form of art is created. This is to be our eurythmy.

What you see represented here is nothing other than the artistically formed laryngeal movement of the human being transferred to the whole human being. Of course, that which is to be art, and which must make a corresponding aesthetic impression through direct contemplation if it is to have an artistic effect in what is directly seen, has arisen from the depth of human nature as its source. In this way, one can say that what is inherent in the human being simply by virtue of the fact that we are human organisms should be brought forth out of us. Thus there is nothing artificial in eurythmy. All gestures, all pantomime is avoided. Just as in music it is not a question of expressing something by means of an arbitrary tone, but of following a lawfulness in the succession of tones, so here, too, it is not a question, for example, of the hand or the like making an arbitrary movement, but of the human limbs making lawful eurythmic movements in succession. Therefore, everything arbitrary is avoided, and where something arbitrary still occurs, you can certainly regard it as something imperfect that is still present. If two people or two groups of people were to perform one and the same thing, they would only differ in their performances to the extent that the interpretation of a Beetoven sonata, for example, would differ between two different pianists.

Everything in eurythmy is modeled on the movements of the larynx and its neighboring organs. But human speech is infused with the warmth of the soul, with enthusiasm, with pleasure, with pain and suffering, with all kinds of inner crises. Everything that resounds through human speech as inner expressions of the soul, we express again in the relationships of the mutual forms, of the groups and through what the human being can reveal through movements in space. In this way, the inner mood of the soul—what penetrates the sound from the depths of the soul—is also expressed. You will therefore see, on the one hand, visible speech. We shall let it be accompanied either by music, which is only the other, the parallel expression of the same, or in the main by recitation, by poetry. In this regard, I must remark that, as eurythmic art is accompanied by poetry, it must be borne in mind that what is now the art of declamation, the art of recitation, is very much in decadence. If eurythmic art is to be accompanied by poetry, we must go back to the old, good forms of recitation, the art of recitation. It is not a question of the usual novelistic element, the content of a poem being expressed through emphasis. Apart from the purely novelistic element, from the content, what is actually artistic should be expressed through the recitation: the rhythm, the rhyme, the vibration of the artistic in a poem. We should express everything that is there beyond the content, in other words, the poetic-musical element. There is little understanding for this at present. But one only has to remember that Goethe conducted his *Iphigenia* with a conductor's baton, and one only has to bear in mind that Schiller, before he even brought the prosaic content of a poem to life in his poetry, had a general melody in his soul—that is, he started from the artistic in general. Today's emphasis on content in recitation is mischief, is decadence. We would not be able to accompany eurythmy with this art of recitation that looks only at the content. Therefore, we must return to an art of recitation that is little understood by our contemporaries. In this way, however, we believe that we can again emphasize a highly artistic element in the present through this eurythmic art, and thereby bring to life something of Goethe's attitude to art. Goethe says so beautifully: "When nature begins to reveal its secret, one feels an irresistible longing for its most worthy interpreter: art." He sees in art a revelation of secret laws of nature that would not be revealed without art.

This is particularly evident when we see how we ourselves express a visible, living language in our movement. Goethe says in another place: "Art consists in a kind of recognition, in that we grasp the essence of things in tangible and visible forms." And the highest part of external nature, the human being, becomes apparent to us when we can make visible what is in our movements and place it before our eyes. Therefore, we feel quite rightly according to Goethe's saying: By placing himself on the summit of nature, we see ourselves again as a whole of nature, which has to bring forth a summit in itself once more. To this end, we rise by permeating ourselves with all perfections and virtues, calling up choice, order, harmony, and meaning, and finally elevating ourselves to the production of the work of art.

We believe that through this eurythmic art, which is drawn from human nature itself, something is at the same time visibly placed before the human eye like an artistic revelation of the universal riddle which is expressed in the human being in the highest sense. So far, however, there is present only the beginnings of all this. We know this very well, and we ourselves are the most severe critics of the imperfections that still cling to this eurythmic artistic experiment of ours. In this sense, I would also ask you to accept today's presentation. If it is understood by our contemporaries, this will lead to its further perfection. For as much as we are convinced that it is still in its infancy today, we are, on the other hand, convinced that it has such principles in itself that it can be brought to such perfection either by ourselves or by others that, among other things, this eurythmic art will also be able to present itself as fully justified.

Essential Aspects of the Art of Recitation

Dornach, November 16, 1919[240]

Now, if that which lies in the individual sound of the word is expressed by the movement of the individual limbs, then what is warmth of soul, what is pleasure and sorrow, joy and enthusiasm, is expressed by the external movement in space or by the relations and the mutual movements of the eurythmists united in a group.

You will see the silent language of eurythmy accompanied, on the one hand, by the musical element, which basically expresses the same, and, on the other hand, by the art of recitation. And it is precisely in this recitation that it becomes apparent how through eurythmy the artistic element of poetry must be expressed.

Today, we are convinced that the most respected, the most well-liked art of recitation is going astray. Today, in recitation, one emphasizes the literal content—that is, actually, not the truly poetic, but the prosaic! In poetry, too, the truly poetic lies in the underlying musical elements, in the rhythm, in the meter, in the forms, in the rhyme, in everything that will be expressed through eurythmy parallel to the recitation.

One can convince oneself that this is so in the real art of poetry if one only goes back a little to that which in earlier times was regarded as the real art of recitation, and also as that which underlies the art of poetry. I need only remind you that Schiller, for example, in the best of his poems, did not first have the literal content in his soul, not at all; rather, he had in his soul a kind of melodious element, an indefinite melody or at least something melodious. And only then did he catch the literal element; only then did he clothe the literal element in it.

Goethe rehearsed his *Iphigenia*, which is an iambic drama, with the baton like a choir director with his actors! He placed value, the main value, not on the literal content but on what was in the poem in terms of verse art, in terms of form.

Everything lying at the basis of poetry must be called forth again. Precisely what is actually artistic is overlooked today in the art of recitation. Those who had the opportunity to experience the primitive recitation of simple folk poetry, as it was practiced in villages in Central Europe until the last decades of the nineteenth century—these opportunities are diminishing daily—could perceive, I would say, a primitive eurythmy originating from the primeval times of humanity. In those times, recitation was not done in such a way as today, that the prose content of the poetry was the focus of attention, but the street singer—pardon the harsh expression!—who always recited his ballad, walked up and down and gesticulated in quite regular movements. So that one can study from it the way in which from that deep element of the human soul, where eurythmy is sought—how from this the art of poetry has actually also emerged in the development of humanity.

This is the basis of a real Goethean psychology. When human beings speak, especially when we speak artistically, this can be studied. Then thoughts flow together in the language from one side. The thoughts pour out, so to speak—forgive me for expressing it so primitively, but it could also be expressed very, very learnedly, more scientifically—onto the laryngeal organs, and the will, from out of the whole human being, penetrates that which lies in the thoughts. Language is the summary of what lies in the human being as will and what emanates from the brain in the forms of thought. Both are combined by the human soul [*Gemüt*] in speech. The human soul [*Gemüt*] thereby sends its waves into this element of thought and will.

Here an attempt is made to leave out what can be conventional, what allows people to understand each other in everyday life, what therefore leads away from the artistic, and to make only that which comes out of the whole human being as the will element into a visible language.

Eurythmy, the Element of the Future in Our Culture

Dornach, January 25, 1920[241]

Allow me, ladies and gentlemen, to say a few words before our eurythmy performance today, since it cannot be assumed that all the honored listeners who are here today have already been present at some of the earlier events. I always speak a few words in advance because we are dealing here with the opening of a new source of art, not with the explanation of what is to be presented. Everything artistic should not require explanation but should have an effect in the immediate viewing, for the immediate impression.

Here, for the first time, the human being himself is used as an instrument, in contrast to certain neighboring art forms with which eurythmy can easily be confused, but should not be. We put ourselves at the service of the artistic as a means of expression. You will see on the stage the moving human being, movements of the individual human limbs as such, movement of the people arranged in groups in relation to each other, and so forth.

All these movements are not at all arbitrary; they are not even arbitrary to the extent that they are reproductions of gestures that the human being makes as an accompaniment to spoken language. All the movements you see here are really a silent language. They are drawn forth from the potentials for movement which are in the whole human organism, just as the tendencies to movement are in the human larynx and its neighboring organs.

With a certain sensory-suprasensory intuition, to use Goethe's expression, we sought to recognize which movement potentials underlie the spoken language. Then it was attempted to bring the same movement potentials to external revelation in this silent language of eurythmy.

This is entirely in keeping with the Goethean view and attitude to art. And compared to what can be achieved, for example, through poetic art with the help of customary speech, in this eurythmy something far more artistic can be achieved because in spoken language there is always interfering—otherwise it would not be the serviceable instrument of communication, which it must be—the intellectual, the ideal element. But the intellectual, the ideal element is the death of the artistic. Therefore, poetry that uses the ordinary spoken language is only artistic insofar as in the poetic language there are two elements: one which actually lies below the ordinary life of the soul—I would say, one layer lower than the ordinary life of the soul—and another element which lies one layer higher.

When poets form what they experience in the soul, first of all a musical element, and secondarily a formative, sculptural element is mixed into the usual language.

As poets, Schiller is more of a musical, Goethe more of a sculptural artist.

One can say that the less one listens to the literal content in the artistic perception of poetry and the more one attunes oneself to the musical—which carries and resounds through the language in rhythm, in beat, also in melody—the more one can attune oneself to what is actually artistic in poetry. For the literal content is not the content of poetry. The artistic content of poetry is the musical or sculptural shaping, which must accompany the verbal like a resonating element.

In eurythmy, everything that is connected with the development of the human will is taken out of the language, so that the whole human being becomes, in a certain sense, a larynx, and groups of people reveal themselves as organs of speech on the stage.

In this way, one achieves something that really can introduce itself as a new artistic element in our cultural development.

One can perhaps say that in our language there is something

whose origin is best pointed out by drawing attention to the time when language is learned. Just think: the spoken language is learned by the human being as a child, when he is not yet fully awakened to existence, is still dreaming his way into life. And, indeed, in the element of speech, there is something of a dreaming into life. While developing the meaning of speech sounds and their composition, we do not think about their connection with reality any more than we think about the connection with reality while we are dreaming. This dream element is one side of human soul life. It is, in a way, a subliminal element. The more we develop an egoistic feeling, the less we dream our way into ordinary life. And, in a way, it is not at all appropriate for today's tasks when one works towards this dreamlike element in the artistic. This dreamlike element is a discarded element of the artistic. In eurythmy, we strive for something that is a real future element of our culture.

If one can say that the more one develops in language the actual phonetic-thought element, the more one enters into the dreamlike element, the more consciousness is dimmed, then one must say: eurythmy contains the opposite of everything dreamlike. Eurythmy is precisely what is achieved by human beings waking up more than they have woken up in ordinary life. It is a more intensive waking, and a carrying out of deliberate movements in this more intensive waking, than what is present as a state of consciousness in ordinary life. Certainly, the eurythmic activity is the opposite of dreaming. Dreaming is a lulling of the human being; eurythmy activity is an awakening of human nature. In a dream, we do not move, if the dream is a healthy one; we lie still, and the movements that the human being makes in a dream are only appearance. In contrast, the pictorial element, the imaginative element in the dream is what prevails.

Here in eurythmy the opposite is the case. Everything dreamlike is suppressed: on the other hand, the element of will comes to the fore, which remains unconscious in ordinary life but which is brought out here. This, however, makes it possible for us to cast off all egotism and to perform such movements as, to a certain extent, harmoniously blend into the whole of enigmatic, cosmic lawfulness. And one can imagine in eurythmy that by looking at the moving human being with this silent, eurythmic language, one feels an inkling of the unraveling of nature's secrets, which cannot be revealed in any other way. Here we take into account Goethe's attitude towards art, which is already expressed in Goethe's words: When nature begins to reveal its open secret, we feel the deepest longing for its most worthy interpreter: art.

Now, if the whole of human nature is regarded as a mute, speaking element, in order to bring to expression through the movements to which we are disposed what underlies the whole world as lawfulness—for we humans are a compendium of the entire world, a microcosm—then one attains a highly artistic quality. Therefore, everything arbitrary, everything merely mime-like or pantominic is banished from eurythmy. What comes to life here is something universally human. The individual human being does not speak out of his everyday feeling as in the conventional language of gesture or art of dance. Rather, what is in nature itself expresses itself.

We are to achieve what Goethe already said in his book about Winckelmann,[242] where he expressed the high point at which art reveals itself: If healthy human nature acts as a whole, if we feel ourselves to be in the world as in a great, dignified, and valuable whole, then the universe should jump for joy at having reached its goal, and marvel at the culmination of its own being and becoming.

The universe itself can speak through the human being. Therefore, there is nothing arbitrary in the movements of eurythmy. Rather, they are drawn forth through sensory-suprasensory intuition from the potentials for movement of the entire human organism.

If, for example, two people or two groups of people in completely different places perform one and the same motif eurythmically, there is no more subjectivity or arbitrariness in it than if two pianists perform one and the same piece according to their own conception. If you still find pantomime in our pieces, it is because we are still in the early stages of eurythmy. This will be overcome with time.

Thus, you will see, for example, on the one hand, when motifs are represented eurythmically, these motifs are accompanied musically, for music and its unfolding lawfulness is only another expression of what is accomplished through the moving sculpture of eurythmy. But you will also see that this same motif, which is expressed through the silent language of eurythmy, can be accompanied in the recitation as a poetic motif. Thereby you will note that this very art of recitation, following eurythmy, must return to the good old forms of recitation.

That is why the art of recitation is trained here in this way. This very easily causes misunderstanding and misjudgment in the present. At the present time, recitation is considered to be inartistic because the essence of performance is thought to be the emphasis of the literal, and thus the delivery of the prose content of poetry. Here the recitation is completely different, because otherwise eurythmy could not be accompanied. The musical, the beat, the rhythm, the melody, precisely what is eurythmic in the treatment of language, in the most intensive permeation of language with the musical, becomes the most essential thing in the art of recitation. Therefore, just as eurythmy itself is still being challenged today, so too is our way of reciting. But it must be the way it is done here, if it is to accompany eurythmy.

This is our intention, and so we try to achieve by these representations exactly what can be attained in the unraveling of the secrets of the world only outside of thought. For the secrets of the world are ultimately revealed only through what we reveal out of ourselves. Goethe felt it keenly when he said: After all, what would all the millions of suns, of stars and planets be worth if a human soul did not finally take it all in and enjoy it?

If one can say that what weaves and works in the world can be represented through human shaping, then many of the cosmic secrets can be deciphered without taking the detour through thinking. And that is precisely what eurythmy is trying to do.

You will see that with many of the poems that would be presented today, certain ones already have a poetic tendency for eurythmy. Such poems readily yield eurythmic depictions. One example would be imaginations of nature, such as "The Rock Spring Wonder."[243]

I would like to say that our eurythmy has three aspects. Firstly, it should appear before the world as an artistic thing. Secondly, however, it also has a hygienic element, something therapeutic. If eurythmy gains interest in the widest circles, then it will be found that the situating of the human being within the whole cosmic lawfulness in a non-egotistical way, as is the case in eurythmy, can become a healthy influence. And thirdly, it has a pedagogical side. Conventional gymnastics should not at all be displaced, but rather complemented by eurythmy. Conventional gymnastics looks only to the body, but here in eurythmy, the whole human being is intuited. And what is expressed through body, soul, and spirit in movement is revealed through eurythmy: an ensouled and spiritualized gymnastics, besides what eurythmy is artistically. In this way, eurythmy really can be a fruitful element in the development of our time.

ON THE CHARACTER OF EURYTHMIC ART

Dornach, January 31, 1920[244]

Allow me to say a few words about the character of our eurythmical art today, as I always do before these presentations. This is certainly not done to give a kind of explanation about the art of eurythmy as such; that would, of course, be an inartistic beginning because everything artistic does not have to work through some theoretical view, but through the immediate impression and through what is immediately revealed in art.

However, eurythmy can very easily be confused with all kinds of neighboring arts. It would really be confusing if it were equated with the arts of dance, gesture, and the like because what you will be shown here as eurythmy is drawn from very specific new artistic sources. And just as everything that is being done here, which this building, the Goetheanum, is supposed to represent, is saturated with what one can call Goethe's worldview, so our eurythmical art is also saturated with Goethe's artistic sentiment and Goethe's conception of art. Of course, Goethe does not have to be taken as the Goethe scholars take him, as the personality who died in 1832 and whose life's work can be studied externally, but Goethe must be taken as a continuing cultural factor of humanity, who also now with each passing year becomes different. When we speak of Goetheanism, we are not talking about the Goetheanism of the year 1832 but of the twentieth century, beginning with the year 1920. And here it is a question of Goethe wanting to replace with a living one the dead view that still dominates our time. This lively view, especially of the work of living beings themselves up to the human being, as found in Goethe, is far from being appreciated enough, far from being understood in any way. It will have to become a turning point in the entire spiritual development of humanity. Those who believe today that they already understand something of the direction of Goetheanism misunderstand precisely what is most intimate, what is most important. What is offered here as eurythmical art is taken out of Goethe's sensory and suprasensory perception, out of the whole human being. Just as Goethe, according to his living conception of the world, saw in the whole plant only a more complicated leaf, so in fact not only in terms of form but also in terms of all the movements that we can make, we are only a more complicated development of one of our organs. In particular, we are a more complicated development of the most outstanding and most human organ: the larynx and its neighboring organs, which provide the tools for spoken language.

But now it is a question of bringing about eurythmy through sensory and suprasensory seeing, first of all putting oneself in a position to recognize what is a protracted labor of the soul and spirit to learn which movements, but especially which movement-potentials, lie at the basis of the larynx, the lungs, the palate, the tongue, and so on when they produce spoken language. This is based on a certain amount of air, which can be inferred from the fact that the entire mass of air in a room in which I am speaking is in motion. We do not pay attention to this movement when listening to sound while listening to spoken language. But this movement can be recognized separately. And then it can be transferred to movements of the whole human being. And so you will see how the whole human being in front of you here on the stage becomes a kind of larynx, and through this, a silent language arises in eurythmy, which is not to be interpreted in any arbitrary way, but which is just as lawfully drawn out of the organ systems of the human organism as is spoken language.

But because what otherwise remains invisible is made visible when speaking, partly through the moving human being, partly through the groups of people in their mutual movements and positions, through this one can express the artistic aspect of the self-revelation through speech especially well. For in our language, even if poetic art expresses itself through it, there is in fact only as much real art as there is music in it, on the one hand, and sculptural form, on the other. The literal content, to which one usually attaches the greatest importance when one looks at poetry in an inartistic way, actually does not belong to the real art of poetry at all. The works of real art are much rarer than one might think.

Before he visualized the literal content of a poem in his soul, Schiller always experienced a kind of wordless melodic element underlying it, a rhythmic, metered, melodic element, and only then did he attend to the actual words. Goethe, who was more of a sculptural poet, has something formative in his language. And this formative element can be discerned if one can really feel Goethe's poetry. So what actually underlies the poetry is itself already a hidden eurythmy. It is studied and applied to the movements of the whole human being. Then there is nothing arbitrary in these movements; then there is something in these movements that follows according to a law, as the melodic law or the law of harmony in the music itself is revealed. In this way, however, one achieves something particularly artistic in eurythmy, for much that is conventional and useful is involved in our spoken language. We have our language for human understanding. What clings to it from this side is precisely the inartistic element, so that what is artistic increasingly comes to the fore the more the unconscious element of language emerges.

One must not forget that language is actually born in the individual human being out of the unconscious, in a dreamlike fashion. The child has not yet awakened to full self-awareness while learning to speak. Just as the images of the dream enter human consciousness as something obscure, so the child's consciousness is still obscure when it learns spoken language. On the one hand, this indicates how spoken language contains something that wells up from the human unconscious. One must take account of this unconscious in all things linguistic.

I only ask you to consider one thing above all: grammar, i.e., the internally logical structure of language, which then becomes artistic when the language is treated artistically, is not more perfect or fully developed in civilized languages; rather, the more complicated grammar is usually present precisely in uncivilized languages. That which runs through language as its lawfulness does not come from what stems from civilized consciousness. This subconscious element is what is drawn out of the human being. In this way, however, eurythmy becomes the opposite of the dreamlike element. While the dream means a lowering of consciousness—above all, a lowering of the will—in eurythmy the will, as it arises in speech, which forms itself as an element, is brought out. Human self-revelation is brought about volitionally through mute language. In this way, however, we consciously descend into the human unconscious creative element, and we come to use the human being himself as an artistic instrument in all his organic formation and possibilities of movement. And if one considers that human beings are the most perfect beings, shall we say, that we know of in the physical world, then when one uses the human being as an artistic instrument, something like a perfection of the artistic expression must emerge. In eurythmy, everything is extracted so much from the laws of human nature that there is absolutely nothing arbitrary; there are no accidental gestures or the like. If two people or two groups of people were to present one and the same thing in eurythmy in two completely different places, the presentation would show no more difference than if one and the same sonata were performed by two pianists, each in his own way. There is always a regularity, as in music itself, in eurythmy. Therefore, through this mute language of eurythmy, which has been drawn from the same natural laws as spoken language, a deeper artistic element can be achieved, in that the thought element that otherwise works in language has been eliminated.

And so you will see how, on the one hand, poems are presented through the silent language of eurythmy. Parallel to this, you will then in some cases see musical things that only give a different way of expressing what eurythmical presentation is. On the other hand, you will hear poetry recited through spoken language, which is presented sculpturally on stage through eurythmy, accompanied by recitation. You will see that you are forced to deviate from today's poetry, which is based solely on emphasizing the content. Rather, what is important here in reciting is what is already eurythmical in the poetry itself. What underlies the actual poetry as sculptural form, rhythm, meter, music, what lives in the poetry as a moving element, metrical, rhythmic, what can be sensed behind the words in the form, must be present in the recitation which is to accompany this eurythmy. We will therefore return here to the form of the art of recitation that was practiced when one still had a feeling for the actual art of recitation. This is very rare today; one perceives more the prose content, what is actually the inartistic element in poetry, and then recites it.

Of course, eurythmy itself will still be misunderstood because it represents something entirely new, and so will the recitation that accompanies it. That alone is not important. Everything that wants to place itself as something fundamentally new in the development of human civilization is mostly viewed with skeptical eyes. Nevertheless, I would ask you to consider that we are our own harshest critics and we see what we cannot do yet today. We regard what we can already achieve as nothing more than a beginning that is in great need of further development and perfection. You will see that poems that are intended to be impressions, such as the "The Rock Spring Wonder," which already have something eurythmical in them, can, I would like to say, be transposed into eurythmy as a matter of course. But you will also see that where there is real inner mobility and plasticity in a poem, as in so many of Goethe's poems, eurythmy can in fact achieve a great deal. In the humoresques that we are going to present to you today, you will also see how these things can be achieved through eurythmical, musical, and spatial forms without using pantomime and facial expressions, which are only accidental gestures.

After the break, ladies and gentlemen, we will be able to show you a scene with gnomes and sylphs. The same attempts to bring to light the mysterious forces of nature that can reveal themselves in the coexistence of humans with nature, namely, that aspect of the sway of nature that cannot be understood by dealing with nature in purely abstract thinking or in so-called natural laws. Perhaps it will not be admitted for a long time that there is an activity and majesty in nature, a weaving and a life that cannot be attained through abstraction and through lawfulness, that can only be attained if our conception of nature is animated by really artistic forms. Nature tells us so much and so intensely that what it tells us must be said in more extensive and intense forms than can be done through abstract laws of nature. Attempts have been made to draw something out of the laws of nature that we experience when we properly relate the human being to what flows and weaves through nature. Thus something like that has been undertaken in this choir of gnomes and sylphs. And there, too, Goethe's artistic attitude underlies it, because Goethe brought art very much into an intimate relationship with knowledge, and he sees in art what at the same time conveys a higher knowledge of the riddle of the human being and of the world than mere knowledge of nature can. That is why Goethe also says: As soon as Nature has begun to unveil her open secret to us, we begin to feel an irresistible longing for her most worthy interpreter: art. And one will soon see, if even today this is seen as something amateurish or amateurish compared to so-called rigorous science, that what is in nature must be recognized by completely different means than this rigorous science can offer. What reigns as a secret is what nature reveals from within, if you only engage with it.

❀

The Search for the New Source of the Artistic

Dornach, February 14, 1920[245]

Whoever observes the development of the arts in our time will find that certain new goals for the development of art are being sought by a whole series of younger people striving in the arts. You know, of course, that these artistic strivings pop up under the most various slogans. When one does research into the deeper underpinnings of these often extraordinarily dubious strivings, one finds that artistic natures in all areas of art feel that the means of expression that the arts have made use of in various epochs are actually exhausted. They feel that a new artistic source has to be sought in various realms, that they must again appeal to elementary, primitive human artistic experience.

But when such a striving emerges, one must at least proceed from a very specific feeling in regard to the artistic.

Everything artistic, to the extent that it can be surveyed in human evolution, has essentially two sources. One is external observation. This external observation can deliver something to art that art can elaborate only when, as observation of nature, it does not proceed initially through concepts, ideas, and mental representations. In recent times, in the realm of various arts, one has tried to make something artistic according to the most immediate first impression that, for example, a landscape can make. One found that in this regard the old means of painting were exhausted as well, that one painted much too strongly according to ideas, according to already elaborated impressions of nature. Rather, one had in the moment to grasp what was revealed in nature through light and air and so forth before the process of contemplating. In short, there was a fundamental striving to put forth something as artistic that was the result of external observation, but of an observation that did not lead to comprehension in thought, because comprehension in thought is the antithesis of everything artistic; it is actually the death of everything artistic. Wherever there is symbolizing, brooding, hatching of ideas, ordering of forms, ordering of colors, and so forth, there art is deadened. Thus one tried to capture direct impressions. One named these impressions and strove for an impressionistic art.

But for painting and for sculpture, there we confront a considerable obstacle. We are hard-pressed to find at present—but here [at the Goetheanum] it has been attempted—to capture in sculpture and painting form and color according to the immediate impression in such a way that the purely artistic can have its effect, to the exclusion of everything ideal, to the exclusion of everything of the nature of thought. And when [the Goetheanum] will have been completed, it will be shown that here we did not seek to incorporate any kind of misguided, mystical ideas through forms of sculpture or painting—at least not in principle. We did not want to embody any kind of symbols here. Rather, we have sought to capture the impression in forms and colors immediately through going beyond anything related to representation, both in the architectural-sculptural and sculptural-painterly elements.

On the other hand, a second source of the artistic is inner experience that is raised up to inner intuition. And at present people have appealed to this source of the artistic as well from various sides. They have attempted to bring to expression what inwardly is merely felt or experienced. They have attempted to do this, for example, in the realm of painting. But we can say: In the circles of younger artists that have made efforts in this direction, until now only dubious forms have come to expression. This is simply because everything that is line, that is color, that is form opposes in a truly extraordinary way inner human experience when one wants to wield it technically.

Now there are two arts that want to express directly inner human experience: the arts of music and poetry. These arts as well show that the source that recent artistic feeling wants to open has essentially yet to be found in broad circles where one is seeking it.

Music is in its forms—in the harmonic, the melodic element—not immediately disposed to express itself immediately as the full inwardness that human beings experience. Thus music opposes itself extraordinarily strongly to Expressionism, to the visionary. Something unhealthy even enters into music when it gives itself over to visionary experience.

Poetry, on the other hand, is terribly dependent upon the evolution of human language. And here one must say that our civilized languages have already come so far that they have an extraordinary amount of the conventional element of thought in them. Thus poets are compelled today to express themselves literally, actually at the cost of original, elementary artistic feeling. But thereby they enter into the element of thought, which is from the outset the death of everything truly artistic. One can say that through a large part of the poetic that arises today, art is not promoted, but rather even suppressed and deadened. And one sees this particularly in what pleases people today by way of poetry. They often take poems as something prosaic that should work through literal content. The truly poetic, however, is only in the musical and the formal, sculptural elements.

If one really probes deeply into that from which our spiritual stream wishes to proceed, of which this Goetheanum building is the external representative, one arrives at the development of Goetheanism. With Goethe, something is striking in his whole artistic influence. I believe that I may say, because I worked for seven years in Weimar at the Goethe and Schiller Archives and participated in everything there, which, like the best of the present, remains unknown to the larger public. One can say that what was published from Weimar makes Goethe into an extraordinarily influential writer. Today one learns from many things that he did not accomplish. What made the greatest impression on me was what Goethe in the course of his life undertook, but did not bring to completion (unlike his dramatic works, *Iphigenie*, *Tasso*, *Faust*), but was lying incomplete, what came to a halt in its first beginnings. That shows precisely that in Goetheanism one does not have something that died together with Goethe. Rather, in Goetheanism we have something that is still influential in our time and can now become fruitful. Goethe simply bore such immense artistic intentions in himself that as a mortal human being he was no longer capable of bringing these things to something beyond the fragmentary. Thus in Goethe's works, the incomplete actually plays an immensely great role. Thus one always has the feeling that much, very much can be drawn forth out of Goetheanism. For one thing, this eurythmy has been drawn forth from it. Eurythmy makes use of the human being himself as a new artistic instrument that will open up a special new artistic source.

One can, namely, say that everything you will see here on the stage in the way of movements of human arms and the other human limbs, executed by groups of people, is not at all arbitrary. Those are not accidental gestures that have been invented to accompany some kind of poem or musical motif. Rather, they are something built up and composed in such a lawfulness as music itself, when it lives itself out in harmony or reveals itself in the course of time in the melodic element. Just as there is nothing arbitrary in music, but rather something inwardly lawful, so it is also with this visible but mute language of eurythmy, which permits us in particular to reveal something artistically, to reveal it through the most perfect artistic instrument, through the human being himself. Thus it is a mute language that you shall see here on stage, performed by movements of human limbs or by the movements of groups of people. And this mute language has arisen through—and here I shall use a Goethean expression—sensory-suprasensory intuition. It arises through a suprasensory observation of what actually happens when the spoken language, which underlies conventional poetry, is revealed and employed as a human mode of expression. Something very remarkable is revealed thereby. This spoken language is a confluence of what comes out of human thought and the will.

Now with the larynx and its associated organs, the situation is this: when the impulses to movement are carried out, they do not hit upon muscles, but rather they mix directly with the outer element of the air. It is the wonderful arrangement of our larynx that in its cartilaginous arrangement it is immediately adjacent to the outer element of the air. That gives the first possibility for what radiates forth from the human will into the larynx and its associated organs to be suffused with the impulses of the element of thought.

But thereby there arises in poetry, which must make use of language, something inartistic; the element of thought enters in. And yet, proceeding from the whole human being, the element of will is founded upon this element of thought. I would like to say: The thought swims in speaking upon the waves of the will.

Now, in the mute language of eurythmy, the element of thought is completely suppressed. Only what lives in poetic language as meter, as rhythm, as form—in short, the musical and sculptural element, is translated into movements. If one does not speak aloud, but rather only allows what is otherwise potentially present in the larynx and its neighboring organs to be performed by the whole human being or by groups of people in a lawful manner, then one has the element of will and, opposed to it, the human musculature. It makes a difference whether the potentials for movement of the larynx and its neighboring organs are translated to the air in picking up the element of thought, and there call forth the movements of the air corresponding to spoken language, or whether the human will, proceeding from the whole human being, strikes the musculature directly and brings the limbs into movement. Something entirely different is called forth thereby. The small vibrations, no longer perceived as movement, which underlie speech are no longer opposed by the muscular element in the larynx. But with the mute language of eurythmy, the will turns directly to the muscular element, to the entire human element of movement, to the muscular and skeletal systems, and the whole human being, who becomes a larynx in the mute language of eurythmy, makes that appear which otherwise only speaking makes appear. Thereby eurythmy will create a new artistic element, which consists of the rhythmical and the metrical, and especially of the poetic and musical.

Therefore, the element of recitation, often alternating with the musical, but principally accompanying what is presented as mute language, must be employed in a way different from that in which recitation is often employed today. And if what is actually desired by the eurythmic element is already misunderstood, the accompaniment by recitation will today be understood even less. It cannot go by the literal content—one would not be able to accompany eurythmy with recitation this way; rather, one has to go by what is actually artistic but is not felt at all in poetry in this inartistic time: by the rhythmic, the metrical, which underlies the literal content. The art of recitation itself must return to the good old forms of recitation, which are little understood today.

But you shall see that just when something is thought eurythmically as poetry, it can be brought to expression especially well with a linguistic form of the mute language of eurythmy. Today we will present eurythmically, besides some other things, a scene from my *Mystery Dramas*.[246] Cosmic lawfulness is expressed therein, and artistic means show what means one must employ in order to bring to expression what actually weaves and lives in nature. The human being stands there uncommonly much closer to nature in the world than with the merely abstract concepts of the so-called natural laws, which actually express only the outer side of nature.

But the arts also cannot find their footing in the present when they want to express inner experience. If we employ colors or forms, regardless of whether we wield the pen or the paintbrush, these means of expression resist inner experience with their extreme brittleness. That is why the Expressionist paintings of the younger painters looks so curious: it is because the means simply have not yet been found to express what is inwardly experienced. At the same time, they have not pushed it as far as the inner element, where it becomes thought, because this would be inartistic.

On the other hand, nature does not allow itself to be interpreted impressionistically. Nature itself makes it necessary in a sense, when we human beings confront it, for us not to exclude thought. Nature does not allow itself to be interpreted impressionistically; actual impressions of nature cannot be reproduced artistically. But if one takes the human being as a higher instrument, then one has the inner experience that does not rise to spoken language, nor to the element of thought. One takes human nature itself by bringing to appearance through human movements—that is, that which can be observed—inner experience excluding the element of thought. Expression in the immediate, impressionistic impression—that is what can very much be attained in eurythmy.

Now, I absolutely am not maintaining that eurythmy is the only art and that it should replace the other forms of art. But I assert that eurythmy can be a guiding light to those who today, out of good but imperfect, I want to say, childlike feeling, are seeking new sources of art.

The Sensory and Suprasensory in Art

Dornach, April 4, 1920[247]

Today, as always before these eurythmic presentations, allow me to say a few words in advance. What we allow ourselves to present to you as eurythmy in a rehearsal is an experiment in a new art form. You will see on the stage all kinds of movements which are carried out by the limbs, or which are carried out by people in space, by individual people in space, or also through alternating movements, alternating positions of groups of people. These movements, which are demonstrated here, are supposed to be the expression for poetic or also musical elements. At first, you might simply interpret these movements as gestures. But that is not what they are. For these eurythmic movements are not arbitrary gestures associated with anything poetic but are perfectly lawful expressions of what is experienced by the soul, like language itself.

We have sought to give an actual language in eurythmy, a language that consists in human movement. The way in which this is attempted is entirely in the spirit of Goethe's worldview. But you must not misunderstand the multiplicity of Goethe's worldview, and you must also understand how to develop it further. Eurythmy is what Goethe calls the form of expression of the sensory-suprasensory. This is because it is based on the study of the impulses and tendencies to movement that are located in the human larynx and all those organs that are set in motion for speech in connection with the larynx.

After all, spoken language serves as a means of poetic expression. You can say: The further any culture advances, the more the spoken language approaches the prosaic in its whole character as a means of expression. If one goes back to the poetry of earlier times, one can see that in earlier times it was definitely still seen in what actually lies behind the prosaic nature of language: in the rhythms, in the rhythmic movement of language, also in the sculptural imagery that is expressed through language. This song-like and sculptural character of language is more and more stripped away the more language is there for human understanding, for conversation. As a result, a non-artistic element flows more and more into the spoken language.

In this spoken language, however, one can seek out the actual artistry that underlies it. In it, two human revelations flow together from two quite different sides. On the one hand, there is the revelation of thoughts, everything that is representation and imagination, everything that flows from the human head into the larynx. This is the one element of spoken language. The other element is everything that comes from the whole human being. It is the will element in language. You can say: The lawfulness of the will, the inner life of the soul revealed in the will, flows together especially when the spoken language is artistically formed.

But just as every art becomes increasingly inartistic the more the ideal element flows into it intellectually, so also in what is presented poetically, the truly artistic element lessens when thinking, which is a prosaic element, flows into the artistic. The actual poetic quality is given by the will element, which expresses itself in rhythm and meter, in the whole forming, which also expresses itself in the images that underlie it.

Now, eurythmy is precisely about stripping away the element of thought. It then comes into its own in the recitation accompanying the eurythmy, which, however, must also be shaped in a special way for eurythmy, as I will mention in a moment. On the other hand, in the movements of eurythmy themselves, one strips away everything thought-like. The whole human being is made the subject of expression. Everything that takes place in movements, as silent speech, is the expression not of thoughts but of the will element, which expresses itself through the whole human being. It expresses itself particularly through all that is connected with and also integrates itself into the rhythmic system, into the circulatory system, and so on.

But in order to be able to do this, in order to really bring the will element to revelation through movements like a silent language, it is necessary to study the movement tendencies of the larynx and the other speech organs.

When we speak—that is obvious—our larynx and speech organs are in motion. One need only remember that while I am speaking here, the air comes into certain lawful movements, which are simply a continuation of what the larynx and its neighboring organs initiate in movements. But it is not so much these movements, which already—because in ordinary speech we turn our attention to what we hear—belong as unheard things to the sensory-suprasensory. It is not so much these movements that come into consideration for eurythmy. Now, according to Goethe's law of metamorphosis, according to which the whole organism is only a more complicated development of a single organ, one can bring the whole human being into such movement as the larynx actually wants to develop in the spoken language. This is the study which must underlie this silent language which comes to light in eurythmy.

In a sense, you see the whole human being become a moving larynx. The movements are different from those of spoken language only for the reason that in spoken language the cartilages of the larynx strike directly against the external air, while in eurythmy we let what pours out of the will element strike against the muscles, which offer a much stronger resistance to what comes forth through the will. Therefore, these movements appear in eurythmy in decelerated form. They appear as oscillating movements in speaking aloud, as it were, summing up the oscillating movements into a main form. And this is expressed through the whole of the human personality, through the whole of the muscular organization. This is this silent language of eurythmy.

Therefore, it is something that in the succession of movements represents something as necessarily lawful as music itself. In the succession of the melodic element, or in juxtaposition, it represents something as lawful as the harmonic element in music. And just as when one and the same sonata is played by two pianists independently of each other, nothing more than a certain degree of subjective conception enters into it, so it is in eurythmy. If one and the same thing, one and the same poem is presented by two personalities or by two groups, then what comes in through individuality is no more different than the individual interpretation of two pianists of one and the same Beethoven sonata.

Thus, there is nothing arbitrary in this art of eurythmy, but everything is just as internally lawful as in music itself. Thus, this eurythmic silent language—because it detaches the prosaic element, the element of thought from the poetry and translates what underlies the poetry, what is actually artistic, into visible movement—is also particularly suitable to serve precisely Goethe's demand to bring a sensory-suprasensory element into artistic representation. Sculpture in movement, one could also say, gesture that takes hold of the whole human being, understood as language, as real language, as unambiguous language: this is what should come to light in eurythmy.

Therefore, you will see that this silent language can be accompanied, on the one hand, by the musical element and, on the other hand, by the poetic element in recitation. This art of recitation must return again to the earlier, good forms of recitation, where one recited according to meter and rhythm, not according to the prose content of the poetry. The art of recitation today sees something perfect in this alignment with the prosaic.

How great poets have by no means considered this prosaic element, on which so much importance is attached today in our inartistic times, to be the main thing, is evident from the fact that Schiller, for example, never first had the literal content of a poem in his mind or soul, at least not in his great poems. He always had a vague melody in his soul, and only then did he attach the literal content to it. Goethe even rehearsed his *Iphigenia* with his actors with the baton like a choirmaster rehearses a piece of music, not seeing as essential the prosaic content of the recitation, but rather the artistic, rhythmic, metrical design. He focused on the sculptural, musical element in the poetic, which is what is actually the artistic element in poetry.

Then we will see how what is already eurythmically formed in the imagination, such as, for example, scenes from my *Mystery Dramas*, which will also be presented today, express the laws within human soul life itself, ways that this life of soul can pursue. What is already formed inwardly in feeling can also be eurythmically represented outwardly quite naturally. In such scenes, one will see how we must evolve toward a changed conception of the life of nature and the world as well. So that we no longer base ourselves on mere abstractions of the intellect if we really want to see through the life of nature and the world, but on imaginations, imaginations such as I have tried [to embody] in my *Mystery Dramas*, of which a sample is also given today.

For the fact that human development must go in this direction corresponds to a deep conviction that one gains if one looks at all into the mechanism of human and non-human nature. What is the use of philosophizing, for example, that real cognition, real knowledge, consists only in the intelligible, clearly analyzable, if nature does not yield its essence to the analyzable, to the discursive, to the intelligible alone, if nature works in images that reveal the inner essence of nature only as images! Then it is necessary that we also penetrate into the inner essence of world existence through images, through imaginations.

The fact that people wanted to understand nature only with the mind actually led them to say pusillanimously:

> Into nature's inwardness
> No created spirit penetrates,
> Fortunate the one to whom it only
> Shows its outer shell!

Out of his art and worldview, Goethe opposed these words of Haller[248] in advanced age, where he really thought about such things more clearly than many who philosophize intellectually:

"Into nature's inwardness" O Philistine! –
"No created spirit penetrates."
Do not remind me and my siblings
Of such a word!
We think: In one place after another
We are inside.
"Fortunate the one to whom it only
Shows its outer shell!"

I've heard that repeated for sixty years,
I swear at it, but stealthily;
Tell me a thousand thousand times:
Everything she gives abundantly and gladly;
Nature has neither kernel
Nor shell,
It is everything at once;
You ask yourself above all,
Whether you be core or shell![249]

So it is. Those who do not want to be shells themselves with their souls—that is, a bundle of intellectual ideas—must rise up to images. Then, however, cognition connects with art and one can say, say with understanding, what Goethe also demanded of veritable art: that art is a manifestation of secret laws of nature which could never come to revelation without it.

Then one understands what Goethe felt towards nature and art in another quote: When nature, he said, begins to reveal her open secret, one feels an irresistible longing for her most worthy interpreter: art. Such a worldview, such Goetheanism, is the basis of what we want to represent here eurythmically.

In the second part, after the intermission, you will see that in the performance of our children's eurythmy—the performance by children of eurythmical poems—eurythmy also has a very strong therapeutic and pedagogical side. Ordinary gymnastics, the one-sidedness of which is not yet recognized by the public, will have to be supplemented by eurythmy; for ordinary gymnastics takes into account only human physiology. And the animated art of movement, eurythmy, will make human beings really strong-willed, while the mere gymnastics of movement may make them strong in body but not at the same time in soul, especially not in their volitional initiative from within. The bringing out of the initiative of the will from within the human being will come about through eurythmy.

The Source of Artistic Activity in Human Nature

Dornach, April 11, 1920[250]

Allow me today, as is usual before these eurythmic performances, to say a few words about how an attempt is to be made, within this eurythmic art, first of all, to seek a kind of new artistic form, to seek means of expression, and then, in a certain way, to go back to the source of creative activity in human nature itself.

Here on the stage, you will see performed movements of human limbs, movements of the whole person in space, alternating movements, and alternating positions of people in groups. All this is supposed to be a kind of silent language, but not a silent language that would consist of random gestures, so that one would look for gestures to accompany the poetry that is recited at the same time, or to the singing, the music. Nor are random gestures sought here for what is to be expressed, as though the speech sound itself or the word is something that happens to be added on top of the meaning. Rather, it is something that connects the human organism itself with the meaning that the sound is supposed to express. To create such an art, one has to lay claim to what, following Goethe, we can call sensory-suprasensory perception.

If we follow the spoken language of the human being, then we turn our attention first to the vocal sound or the sound sequence. We do not become attentive to the fact—it lies in the whole organization of language—that our organs, which have something to do with the production of language, execute movements. These movements, to be sure, become rhythmically small movements, but they are based on potential movements. Those who can follow the language in a certain sense can see these tendencies for movement. They can get a picture of the tendencies for movement in the larynx and its neighboring organs while speech resounds for us.

Now one can transfer what one observes there, what a single organ or a system of organs carries out during speech, to the whole human organism. However, as I will show in a moment, one cannot accomplish this without further ado; rather, one must do this in a certain metamorphic transposition. Just as Goethe arrived at his view of metamorphosis as that which must underlie a genuine organicism, so must one also rise up to such a view of human functions as allows us to recognize how a single functional group—that is, what underlies the movement of speech—can be related to a corresponding movement of the whole human being, just as Goethe saw the entire plant only as a complicated, metamorphosed leaf or petal, or as complicated stamens.

This view, which Goethe applied only to the morphological, can be extended to the functional, can artistically penetrate the functional. However, in the same way, one can follow the central tendency of what happens when the larynx directly contacts the outer air during speech and translates itself into small rhythmic movements. Thus, another element comes more to the fore in this transfer of the sound movements to the whole human being than in the movement of sounds—namely, the element of the will, and also the element of willing feeling.

In our language, thought, ideation and will, feeling, willing feeling, and feeling will flow into each other. We do not need to distinguish these things because actually only ideation and will stand opposed. Moreover, in artistic perception, we always have to fight, I would say, against having too much of the ideational, the idea, flow into the work of art, into the immediate perception of the image. Not of the image as we otherwise perceive it in nature, but rather of the spiritualized image. This should be at work both in sensing art and in the creation of art.

However, when we look at nature in ordinary life or science, we transform the image through thought into a spiritualized image. Thereby, we lift it out of the sphere of the merely artistic. In art, the image should have a direct, spiritual effect. It should affect us as an image in the same way that otherwise thoughts affect us. However, as soon as the thought acts as thought, the artistic ceases, the artistic is paralyzed. In our language, there is actually all the less the possibility of artistic creation, in poetry as well, as language progresses with civilization. As spoken language, it becomes more and more conventional, and it becomes a form of expression for what we want to represent in an abstract, intellectualistic way. This actually impoverishes our poetry in terms of its means of expression. For poetry is genuinely artistic only to the extent that it contains music, on the one hand, or pictorial, sculptural elements, on the other.

Pictorial, sculptural elements are meant here such that, by listening to poetically formed language, one immediately perceives a kind of image in the sound. We get rid of everything that flows from the thought into poetry if we transfer to the whole human being what is otherwise carried out by the larynx and its neighboring organs. By carrying out this metamorphosis of the function of speech and [allowing it to be carried out] by the whole human being, it cannot, of course, come to expression in spoken sounds because we focus on the *macroscopic* movements, the tendencies of movement, instead of the *microscopic* ones. That which we get out of the spoken word is the will element that is bound to the whole human being. Therefore, if the human being appears as a whole, as it were—I may use the image here—like a larynx in living motion, we have given the form of expression through the human being himself. At the same time, however, we have the possibility of confronting what we encounter as an image in man himself, without brooding on it, initially in an ensouled and spiritualized way. The spiritualized image arises when human beings, who have spiritualized themselves, become this image in their movement. Therefore, we can have the ensouled image in immediate intuition. Through this ensouled image, which can become the means of expression of poetry in a mute language, we have actually achieved much of what art must strive for: to create the ensouled image without first having to take the detour through the intellect, through thinking, which has a deadening effect on art.

Of course, the recitation that accompanies the eurythmy must take care that precisely what is artistic, and not the prose content of the poetry, is brought to the fore. Today, because we live in an inartistic time, the main focus of attention in recitation is attached to the prose content, the literal. The artistic person does not feel what is essential in this emphasis on the literalness of the poetry, but focuses instead on the rhythmic, metrical, musical, or pictorial and sculptural shaping. Therefore, insofar as it is an accompaniment to eurythmy, recitation will again have to return to the suitable, older forms of recitation, to which Goethe, too, naturally felt drawn. Goethe, who felt artistically, rehearsed his *Iphigenia* with a baton like a choirmaster, emphasizing the form rather than the content with his troupe. Moreover, Schiller always had, before he had the literal content, at least in many of his poems, a vague melodious harmony in his soul that hummed in him, and to which he then added the literal content.

You will see that what is lawfully brought forth from the human being as a silent language is no more arbitrary than spoken language. You will find this eurythmy accompanied, on one side, by recitation, on the other side, by music. It is only another side of what appears in these two arts. Moreover, I believe that in eurythmy we can create what actually stands beside our older art forms as a new art form.

When we resort to the visual arts, we have to bring to rest, as it were, what is moved in the human being. The musical and the poetic, which are indeed moved, must simultaneously work with such a strong power of internalization that the outer sensory impression often recedes. Even in the case of the purely musical, the absolutely musical, the external sensory impression recedes in the face of a spiritualization, a "making inward." However, precisely because music, when it appears as pure music, can still speak to the refined senses, it preserves the purely artistic. On the other hand, we do not find in the traditional realms of art what I would like to call sculptural movement, artistically formed sculpture, which is not dependent on merely representing in stillness, in form, in the quiet realm of form, but sculpture, which can take account of human movement. At the same time, all by itself, this eurythmy reads the tendencies to movement out of the human speech organs and is transferred to the whole human being.

I have just made the attempt to represent what is spiritually underlying the world, which then is connected with the being of man. We can then perceive this poetically in such a way that one counts on more being present in reality than what is given by the mere abstract laws of nature, grasped in intellectual forms. This can most easily be represented eurythmically.

Here, as with the whole of eurythmy, we will probably still have to encounter misunderstandings and oppositions today because people today believe that what essentially underlies things must be grasped in intellectualistic form. However, nature creates in images, and therefore we can only get at nature in its actual creation and weaving of the world if we enter into images. Thus, we affirm what Goethe meant when he said: "As soon as nature has begun to unveil her open secret to us, we feel an irresistible longing for her most worthy interpreter: art."

To Goethe, art was something that, I would like to say, combined in continuous metamorphosis with merely scientific understanding. Perhaps one finds there, where the whole human being enters into movement, into lawful movement—which is at the same time expression, like spoken language itself—an affirmation of Goethe's saying: In the artistic, one has a kind of manifestation of secret laws of nature that would never be revealed without this artistic manifestation.

This is the one side, the side that is initially more important for the outside world, the artistic side.

However, it must be pointed out that beyond the artistic, there is also an essential therapeutic and pedagogical element in this eurythmy, that this is already given as a supplement to children, in the education of children, so that this inspired gymnastics is added to the gymnastics which is actually based only on the physiological view of the human being. When one judges a little more impartially, one will realize that gymnastics makes the muscles strong but does not at the same time help to bring out initiative from the soul and to form the will, but that the ensouled movement, the ensouled gymnastics, which can be brought to the children in eurythmy, can serve this very purpose. This is why eurythmy was introduced into the lesson plans of the Waldorf School in Stuttgart. It is based on crucial pedagogical principles. It has been found that through ensouled gymnastics the children can acquire an essential thing, a certain culture of the will, which is so important to cultivate at present, when they enter life after their first school years—an ensouled culture of will, a culture of will which is not only a child of the physiological view of the human being, but a child of the psychological view of the human being.

Therefore, after the break, we will show you something performed only by children, so we will also give a sample of children's eurythmy. Nevertheless, I ask you to regard this with indulgence. We are our own worst critics of these beginnings of ours, precisely because it is only a beginning! It is an initial attempt. But those in the audience who have been here before will see that we have made an effort to progress from month to month, and we will continue to make an effort to turn this beginning into something more perfect. Furthermore, one may be convinced that, although we are still at the sparest beginning of this eurythmic art, it is capable of perfection through which it will be able to place itself as a youthful art, but fully justified, next to the older art forms.

Introduction to a Eurythmy Performance

May 16, 1920

Today, as in the past, I would like to say a few introductory words before this performance of eurythmy. I do this not in order to explain what will be presented since, of course, what is artistic will need to have its effect through direct experience, and it would be inartistic to give some theoretical explanation before such a performance.

Nevertheless, I might say that the art of eurythmy is an attempt to reach down into a source of art that exists in human beings. That wellspring seeks expression in artistic forms that are particularly well suited to reveal the needs of all art—namely, to bring what is artistic into the realm of the sensory and suprasensory.

Goethe coined the expression "sensory-suprasensory intuition" out of the depths of his perspective on the world and his feeling for art. The form of eurythmy is completely based upon this sensory-suprasensory perception.

On the stage, you will see all kinds of movements performed by individuals and groups. At first, you might have the impression that eurythmy should be accompanied by poetic or musical performance, and that the eurythmy is simply another expression of that. You might have the impression that eurythmy consists simply of gestures invented to mimic what is presented through the poetry or music. That is not the case. Eurythmy is based upon movements exercised by the organs of speech themselves that have been revealed through a careful sensory-suprasensory study of human speech. In normal speech, the movements of the lips and gums and so forth directly affect the air. They are transformed into subtle vibrations that form the basis of what we hear. It is, of course, not these vibrations that are important in eurythmy; rather, what is important lies at the basis of an entire system of such vibrations. This has been studied and then transferred from the organs of speech to the entire human being according to the Goethean principle of metamorphosis, according to which, for instance, the entire plant is only a leaf that is more complicated in form.

What you will see on the stage are not simply random movements. Instead, they are movements that strictly follow certain laws. They follow the same laws and occur in the same order as do the movements of the organs of speech when producing sounds while speaking or tones while singing. Within these forms resides an inner necessity of the same sort as is created by music in forming a series of tones. What we are concerned with here is, in fact, a kind of visible speech that closely follows certain rules.

Modern culture will need to find its way into this visible speech, as modern culture contains something quite inartistic. Things that were quite common during the Romantic period are much less so today—for example, people intently listened to poems when they did not actually understand the words; they listened more to the rhythm and the inner form of the sounds. We will see this in the recitations that accompany eurythmy in much the same way as does music, that we could emphasize nothing other in this element of artistic eurythmy than the actual artistic element of the poetry itself. It is not the literal content of the poem that is important; rather, what is important is the form that the artist has created.

Thus, you will see that we attempt to present spatial forms created by groups. They are not simply mimicking the content of the poetry; rather something follows from the character of the poem into the words. Even when the presentation is concerned with something surreal, or something affected, such as we will attempt to present in the second part of the presentation today, you will see that it is concerned not with some imitative presentation of the content, but rather with forming connections of such a nature that the individual movements have little effect; the effect is formed through the harmonious forms acting together.

In general, we can say that through eurythmy we return to the sources of art because eurythmy is an art that should not affect us solely through our thoughts. When our concern is with science in the modern, materialistic sense, it is only thoughts that affect us, and for that reason, we can penetrate only into the sense-perceptible content of the world. In the art of eurythmy, our concern is more that the sensory-suprasensory character should be expressed than that the entire human being or groups of human beings are the means of expressing it. Thus we can say that the human being, the ensouled human being, the human being permeated by spirit, permeates each movement with soul and spirit—namely, with the soul and spirit that we can hear through the truths sounding from the poetry.

All this shows how the sense-perceptible, which we can see through the limbs of the human being, at the same time carries the spirit on its wings. It is, therefore, genuinely perceptible sensibly and supra-sensibly. Eurythmy thus expresses what Goethe demanded of all art when he said, "As soon as nature has begun to unveil her open secret to us, we feel an irresistible longing for her most worthy interpreter: art." For Goethe, art is a way of experiencing nature through feeling. How would it be possible to correspond to nature better than to bring to expression those capacities that enable human beings to move based upon their will, so that a kind of visible speech is expressed? Thinking, which in general ignores art, is thus shut out. It is only will that is expressed in the movements. Human personality is transferred to these movements in an impersonal way, so something that is highly artistic and represents something perceptible in a sensory-suprasensory way is expressed through these presentations.

Eurythmy also has a significant educational effect because it is at the same time a kind of ensouled gymnastics. If you think about these things objectively, then you will see that what has long been treasured as gymnastics and something which we certainly do not wish to eliminate is something that experiences a particular kind of growth when we place alongside it this ensouled form of gymnastics, as we have done for the children at the Waldorf School in Stuttgart. You will see some of this children's eurythmy during the second part of our presentation today. Normal gymnastics strengthens the body, of course, and for that reason we certainly do not want to go without it. However, ensouled gymnastics, which has an effect not simply upon the physical body but on the spirit and soul as well, is particularly effective in developing the will. Future generations, who will have an increasingly difficult life, will need stronger will energies.

Eurythmy also has an important hygienic side. The movements of eurythmy are those movements through which individuals can best place themselves into the rhythm and harmony of the world. All unhealthy things are essentially based upon people separating themselves from that rhythm. We are certainly not doing anything reactionary, and I would ask therefore that you do not consider me to be rejecting aspects of modern culture. There are many things today that are necessary, things we need, things we cannot eliminate. We also have to admit there are many reasons why modern human beings would want to separate themselves from the rhythm and harmony of the world. Each time we sit in a railroad car or an automobile, and when we do many other such things, we undertake actions that separate us from universal rhythms. This separation sneaks slowly into human health and undermines it in a way that is not even noticed. These things can be seen only by those who have an intimate understanding of the relationship between human beings and the universe. However, the universe seeks today to give something that will return human beings to health.

Where do people today seek health? I know that with the following I am saying something contrary to what is commonly held today, but in the future people will think more objectively about this. Prior to this terrible world catastrophe that crashed in upon us,[251] there was an attempt to achieve health through such things as the Olympic Games. That is a terrible thought that lies entirely outside of any genuine understanding. The Olympic Games were appropriate for the Greek body. When undertaking such things, people do not at all realize that each cultural period has its particular requirements.

That is something, however, that we attempt to do through the art of eurythmy. We do not attempt to provide humanity with something based upon some abstract theory or something from the past. Instead, we try to do what is necessary for modern civilization, something that we can find within human nature and which is appropriate for the structure of modern humanity. Such things certainly cannot be proven anatomically or physiologically, because we cannot dissect the ancient Greeks. Those who can look into cultural development through anthroposophy recognize that modern human beings in their physical forms and especially in their souls and spiritual structure require something else. Eurythmy represents a beginning toward finding those requirements placed upon us by our cultural period itself. Eurythmy attempts to correspond to our culture. As you know, what we will present here today is at its very beginnings and therefore remains simply an attempt. We are nevertheless convinced that because we are serious about working based upon the requirements of our cultural period, others will further develop what we can present here today, so that a mature art form will arise that is worthy of being placed alongside its older sisters.

On the Olympic Games

Dornach, July 4, 1920[252]

In many other regards, one will see that eurythmy can perhaps give to humanity in the current age what cannot come from anywhere else. People thought about everything under the sun before this war broke out in flames! People thought about reviving the Olympic Games. It is exactly as though people of a certain age wanted to become accustomed to what actually belongs to an earlier phase of growth. Today, one views everything only abstractly and intellectually, rather than how it is in reality. The Olympic Games were what the Greek temperament needed in the past. Today we need something completely different from the Olympic Games. We need something that also situates humanity in its spirit and soul within the whole cosmic context. And thus the Olympic Games and all of the thoughts that aim at something similar are nothing but a certain dilettantism vis-à-vis the human evolution of culture.

Musical, Pictorial, and Sculptural Elements in Poetic Form

Dornach, October 3, 1920[253]

What recitation must strive for here is to enter into the musical elements in poetry, and to see the sculptural element as well. For language becomes truly poetic only through the incorporation of the images, only through the incorporation of the musical element in poetry. Here it is a matter of the "how"; not what is expressed, but rather how it is shaped. Thus it is in this fashion that the recitation should accompany what is presented in eurythmy. And what is presented in eurythmy itself will be all the more perfect the less it approaches the prosaic content. Those honored guests who have been here often will have seen that we have attempted to progress over the course of time. More and more, originally imperfect elements of pantomime and mime have gradually been overcome. Just as it is in music, in the sequence of movements, in the inner harmony and disharmony, in the theme of the movements, we can reveal what the poet wants to bring to expression in forming language artistically. Thus we can present serious pieces in a corresponding eurythmic style, and also humorous pieces. I am also working at extending eurythmy gradually to drama. Up to now, we were able to depict only such dramatic moments as, for example, the entrance of the spirits in *Faust*, or various other figures conceived in a sensory-suprasensory way in *Faust*. We have been able to present only those scenes in which the dramatic rises up into the suprasensory. We have not yet finished what we are attempting to do in this realm, but we are seeking very earnestly to find a eurythmic form for pure drama. Such things require time, but they also require deepening through sensory-suprasensory intuition.

[Untitled]

Dornach, October 16, 1920[254]

[At the end of the presentation of eurythmy, it was Rudolf Steiner's express wish that the "Satirical Prelude" be performed. Rudolf Steiner had said that it would be necessary to perform this Prelude. (Note by H. Finck.)]

Rudolf Steiner: Most honored guests, just as we must turn to a real spiritual-scientific culture, art, and so on, we must just as strongly reject everything dishonest and untrue. We must reject what does not call forth upright sensations when they turn to the so-called spirit, because they are actually just playing at mysticism. And in order to show you what kinds of feelings we can have towards this false mysticism, this coquettish mysticism, this mysticism that is neither upright nor honest, we would like to perform a short bit of eurythmy.

Eurythmy as Ensouled Gymnastics

Freiburg, November 19, 1920[255]

What is achieved is that the soul experience, which the musicians, as well as the poets, want to represent, is revealed through other means of expression, just as the matter is not detached from the human being but is revealed through the human being himself. When we look at the musical element, we find that this musical element reveals soul experience. We can follow this soul experience especially in singing. But the means of expression are to a certain extent detached from the human being. In music, the tone carries the life of the soul on its wings, one could say, but it is detached from the human being. It releases itself in song. In spoken language, thought is inserted into the sound, the tone, as an inartistic element. In contrast, in eurythmy, the human movement itself is used as a visible language, to a certain extent also as visible music. As a result, the whole human being stands there as a physical expression of the soul. Because it is a physical expression of the soul, it can be observed in the artistic perception, and one immediately has something of a soul nature that is represented externally. What is all art really but the sensory representation of something suprasensory, something spiritual? When the human being himself becomes a tool, not a dead instrument, but a tool of art, then art comes to expression in the highest, most beautiful sense.

In particular, one will be able to notice how the musical element can again find its true expression through eurythmy. I just want to draw your attention to the fact that if you let the movements work on your senses more precisely in eurythmy, you will see what is expressed in a major mood and what is expressed in a minor mood when musical eurythmy is presented. Then we have to present eurythmic movements that flow directly from the human will. They are, so to speak, closely attached to the human being. Now, we can always see how in eurythmy we have to present everything that is in the major through movements that go out from the human being. Everything in a minor mood we express through movements that come toward the human being, that articulate themselves in a corresponding way. So that what is artistically revealed on the wings of tones in music can become visible precisely through what is expressed in the movements of the human limbs.

It is the same when what is presented in poetry through the spoken language is presented eurythmically through movements that are more detached from the human being, movements that are more connected to the pictorial. But all this is far removed from all mime, far removed from all dance, from all mere gesturing, both in the realm of the eurythmic representation of the musical and the eurythmic representation of the poetic. It is what is artistic. It is either a sculptural, moving sculptural effect, or a musical effect. Therefore, it is also necessary that the recitation, which occurs alongside eurythmy, which is just another expression for what one sees in eurythmy, is itself formed in eurythmy.

What is so often seen today as the pinnacle of recitation or declamation, the prosaic element that should resound in the recitation, is not what can accompany eurythmy. For in poetry there is only so much that is artistic as there is something sculptural or musical in it. Therefore, it must always be remembered how a real poet (Schiller, for example) worked. Before he had the prose content, an indefinite melody lived in his soul. What is rhythmic, what is meter, what is melodic behind the poetry, and not the prose content, the literal content, that is what is truly artistic about the poetry. And so, with this new means of expressing movement, you can create a visible language, visible music in people themselves, which we will allow ourselves to demonstrate in a few preliminary performances today.

But that is only one side of eurythmy. The other side will present itself particularly well today because we were able to bring several children from our Stuttgart Waldorf School here. At the Stuttgart Waldorf School, we introduced eurythmy as an obligatory subject. And for the children of this Free Waldorf School, which is formed out of anthroposophy, eurythmy is at the same time an ensouled gymnastics, and as such a wonderful educational means that the children love immensely. One must say that there is nothing wrong with gymnastics as such, but it is based only on physiological, physical laws. I certainly don't want to go as far as a famous modern man, Abderhalden,[256] who recently said that gymnastics is not a means of education, but rather barbarism. I want to acknowledge the importance of gymnastics for the physical improvement of youth. But it is something completely different when children approach this ensouled gymnastics, this eurythmy, which is at the same time an art. The child loves to accomplish that, to express what results artistically from the whole human organization. Through this, when one brings eurythmy to the children, something very special comes about, which, however, does not appear as much when older people are still practicing eurythmy.

The child, while translating the content of the soul into visible language, cannot fall into conventional phrases in any way. In our language, especially in the languages of more developed civilizations, conventional phrases play such a large role, and truth gently turns into lies. When the child is led back to the original, elementary expression of the soul's experience, to the movements of the limbs, he cannot lie and fall into phrases. This is why this eurythmic art of education is at the same time something that draws the children towards truthfulness, so that one has an important means of education in eurythmy. And it will be shown, at least as an experiment, how this ensouled gymnastics works through the child's organism.

EURYTHMY AND FACIAL EXPRESSIONS

The Hague, February 27, 1921[257]

Something else is still often misunderstood. Because people think that eurythmy has to do with mime and the like, they demand facial expressions but do not get them here. We intentionally do not give them in the usual form, but rather only in the form that every movement of the face and head must correspond to eurythmy. As little as one can accompany the movements of sound with one's face, which would be experienced as grimaces if they were exaggerated, so little can one accompany eurythmic speech with what, out of a misunderstanding, people demand as facial expressions. You will see how, exactly as is the case with the melodic theme in music, in doing eurythmy, the actual artistic element comes to expression in the lawful unfolding of movements. We attempt through ever more complicated forms, which have, however, an inner simplicity and harmony, to translate normal eurythmy into artistic eurythmy, which you shall note especially in several group movements.

In the second part, the humorous part, you will see how eurythmic style and eurythmic form is present also in this different style. On the one hand, we have the serious aspect; on the other, the picturesque. We attempt to do justice to both sides.

Archetypal Rhythm, Archetypal Song, and Arrhythmia in Their Relationship to Eurythmy

Dornach, April 9, 1921[258]

Honored guests, as usual I would like to permit myself a few introductory words before these experiments in eurythmy. I would like to speak about the particular artistic means, the formal language, in which this art of eurythmy moves. It is a matter of seeing on the stage a truly inaudible, but visible language—a language that is performed through movements of the individual, through movements of groups, and so forth. What is performed is then accompanied either by music or by the recitation of poetry. And what is presented as the movements of individuals or groups should be exactly the same revelation through a visible speech or through visible singing as, on the other hand, the same motifs come to revelation musically or poetically through recitation.

But what underlies today's performance is not any kind of mime or pantomime or any other kind of gestural art. It is also not the case that what is called dance in the usual sense underlies this. Rather, there has been developed an equally intrinsic language of human form and human movement as lives, only in another form, in speech and in song.

It has arisen, by means of sensory-suprasensory intuition, through uncovering in the human larynx and other speech organs the tendencies to movement that underlie the audible sound and the transitional movements that underlie the combinations of sounds, the formations of words, and the syntax of sentences. Thereby, something has arisen that is inwardly as lawful in the sequence of tones as music, for example, is lawful.

If one wants to penetrate what is really at issue in this art of eurythmy, one would do well to keep in mind something of human evolution. Although not distinctly visible in historical, but rather only in prehistoric times, human evolution proceeds such that with certain expressions of human life—let us say, for example, the human capacity for movement—the human capacity for language was formed. For our purposes, I would like to indicate one thing in particular.

There is an interesting fact, which is known today also to external, ordinary scholarship, and that points to an evolutionary element of the human race. It is the fact that in ancient, primitive languages, for the human movement that then became dance, for the rhythmic movements that later were translated, transformed into the movements that were executed during the dance—for these primal rhythmic movements and for song, there was a single designated word. They did not distinguish what they were persuaded belonged together inwardly: song and rhythmic human movement. Primitive people were caused, whenever it was at all possible for them, not to allow what was intoned for them to be accompanied by limbs at rest, but rather to always allow it to be accompanied by some kind of movement of their limbs. When possible, they accompanied the work that they were performing, which caused them to move their limbs, in such a way that their limbs could move in a certain rhythm. Thus they had for this movement of rhythm a definite lawfulness that was revealed to them instinctively. But they unfolded the same rhythm in allowing the sequence of a certain songlike sounding, so that there archetypal song and the archetypal rhythm of their movements flowed together. They were so unified that, as I said, they designated both things with a single word.

This, which was characteristic of the people of a very early age, later differentiated itself. As human beings progressed in civilization, the movements that proceeded from the will were separated out and obtained a certain autonomy. They were adapted more and more to external life. It was not the movements of the legs but only the movements of the arms that retained a certain freedom of movement. But what was possible in such movements, even if they did not serve mere utility, was still restrained in those movements of the limbs that were emancipating themselves from the tonal, songlike element. They were suppressed in a fashion, these movements, into the instinctual will in everything that man placed, as his own humanness, in the indefinite, unconscious will. Thereby, the movements that earlier had always been connected with song, differentiated themselves into ritual dances. And also, what was formerly called love dances were in a certain sense differentiated. But they were differentiated in such a way that the ritual dances were conducted in the nobler unconscious, whereas the love dances were conducted in the more instinctive, unconscious will. These movements had earlier been connected with the soul; movement was felt to be one with song and with the resounding word.

On the one hand, movement, which stems from the will, became differentiated and separated itself; on the other hand, what lay in sounds, in words was also differentiated. Movements passed over more and more into utility and games, even into rituals among certain peoples. The human being was differentiated according to the word. Thus, the word became the word of knowledge, became something into which the intellect pressed everything that can be expressed in the way of thoughts through the word. And while the lower movements differentiated themselves into utility, words differentiated themselves into the means of knowledge and into the outer, conventional means of understanding.

By progressing to a spiritualization of what is given for human knowledge, the word is once again permeated with spirit, which can in turn bind itself with the will. But if one wants to attain artistry, then one has to overcome the element of intellectual thought wherever possible. The element of intellectual thought lames art. But what lives as spirit in the element of intellectual thought can once again be united with movement.

Now, what was once a united human revelation in the art of song and movement, for which a single term existed, is intimately connected with the rhythm of human breathing. And it is extraordinary, one can say, to note what actually is at play as the most inward part of human nature when one looks at this mutual interplay of the soul-spiritual element, on the one hand, and the physical-bodily element, on the other. One sees how it expresses itself so finely in the rhythm of breathing, in the pulse, as that which is human rhythm as such. One can see how, on the one hand, what proceeds towards the head becomes the nature of intellectual understanding in the word. One can see that thereby a certain arrhythmia arises, arrhythmia in the human rhythmic system. And likewise, an arrhythmia sets in when human mobility is developed in the direction of utility.

If one strives to eavesdrop, through sensory-suprasensory intuition, on what it is that has differentiated itself as a singular group of organs in the activity of speaking, then one can survey particularly well how this speaking is connected to breathing. One can intuit the way that breathing is united with speaking, but when thought and understanding enters in, an arrhythmia arises. And we see this arrhythmia accompany speech that has developed too much in the direction of the intellect. But we also find arrhythmia arising through speech that tends to much towards the mere principle of utility.

Let us attempt to return to our inner humanity, to that part of our inner humanity that expresses itself in pure human rhythm, and, in the process, return also to the way in which the element of sound is suited to this human rhythm. Then we find that true poets arrange entirely unconsciously the treatment of language such that they give to the sequence of sounds in words, and the entirety of their syntax, a form that is united with the pure human rhythm of breathing. Or at least it stands in a very definite relationship to this pure human rhythm of breathing. But with the way that our civilization is today, if one initially were to proceed from the element of intellectual thought, a great deal of arrhythmia would enter into human nature. But when one proceeds today with a view to the soul-spiritual element, which develops from our full humanity in the will and then effects the movement of the limbs, particularly the movement of the arms, then the soul-spiritual element can be expressed, as it once was formed out of human nature.

Thereby one attains in the movements of the human limbs, particularly the arms, something that is entirely similar to what is present in the formation of the movements of air that are exhaled in the rhythmic process of breathing. Then one expresses the same thing in visible speech as what is formed in the air by the resounding word. And thereby one attains the possibility of taking what underlies singing musically, and what underlies formed speech, and leading it over into the visible. So that here one does not have the usual poetry, or an art of gesture, mime, or pantomime, but rather a genuine expression of the human soul and spirit in the physical-bodily nature. These harmonize most beautifully with those formations of speech that are not borrowed from the external principle of utility, but rather reveal themselves out of human nature itself.

Everything which is striven for in eurythmy actually reveals what underlies a poem or a song, on the one hand, from the musical, and, on the other hand, from the image, from the sculpturally formed side. And what lived in the poet as a full human being comes to outer, visible revelation. One also sees that, for example, all of the nonsense surrounding recitation and declamation that grows rank today in this inartistic time must be rejected. All of the importing especially of the content, of the prosaic, of the literal element into recitation and declamation must be translated into rhythm, beat, into what is musical or sculptural, image-like. Everything that is especially emphasized as prose in recitation and declamation cannot be used in the form of declamation and recitation that should accompany this visible speech that should be offered through eurythmy. For genuine and true artistry is drawn out of poetry, and that is not the literal, but rather what underlies speech as beat, as rhythm, which is expressed in the formation of speech. Thus many people who are shocked enough by the art of eurythmy itself will be particularly shocked that this special art of declamation and recitation is offered as an accompaniment that will promote eurythmy. That is something that is very much misunderstood today that is striven for by eurythmy, this visible language. Critiques emerge rather automatically. One could have predicted the complaint that our eurythmists show too little facial expression, that the face is the most expressive thing and so forth. For anyone who really enters into the connection between the human spirit and soul and the visible speech that is to be presented here, it is like asking us to accompany what is spoken with continual, unnatural grimaces. It is a matter of conveying what needs to come to expression here through a special language of forms, through a special language of movement, and not through accidental gestures or mimicry of the face that accompanies our usual speaking.

That is what I have to say about the one side of the art of eurythmy, the artistic side.

The Extension of Poetry and Music via Eurythmy

Dornach, July 10, 1921[259]

When poetry wants to express itself through language, one has to have movement, rhythm, and meter indirectly in what is heard. By bringing language into movement, into the forming of life and tone, what one is seeking to form indirectly, the musical that one calls forth from the cosmos, can be revealed. So that in fact through the moving human being the soul quality of a poem can be particularly expressed, just as one can add to music a singing through human movement. We can likewise express the musical through this visible language in the movements of eurythmy, just as through song we can express the musical, bring it to expression through tones. Thereby we are in a position in fact to suppress the thought element in poetry, which the poet has to use only in order to line up what is actually artistic in the poem.

And the other element that is contained in every poem is the element of will. That comes from the whole human being, and not merely from the human head. This is revealed all the more by the visible language of eurythmy.

Whoever really has an artistic sensibility will thus have no objection to such an expansion of the artistic as wants to happen in eurythmy. For that person will take joy in every expansion of art. And whoever says that one should not depict Goethe's poems in eurythmy—what would Goethe himself have to say about this?—such a person would miss the mark entirely. For precisely what is truly significant in poetry proceeds from the whole human being, and not from what someone can express in the literal content. And this fully human quality can be brought to expression precisely through eurythmy. So that much that lies in the deeper mysteries of poetry can be brought to the surface through this visible language of eurythmy. And on this intuition rests fundamentally everything that comprises the artistic impression in reality.

Dance, Pantomime, and Eurythmy

Dornach, August 14, 1921[260]

The aim is to create a visible language, a visible language which can be actually linked to tonal or spoken language, but which, on the other hand, has nothing to do with mime, pantomime, and so forth.

From a certain perspective, what the human being experiences within his own soul, and brings to outer expression in the most varied ways through the organization of his body, moves between two poles: between the spoken or tonal language that goes over into inartistic, prosaic speech and between that which the human being tries to develop, let us say, out of his organism's conditions and forms of equilibrium or balance. For both these poles, whether one leans towards spoken language or towards pantomime, the human being is on an inartistic path, or one that leads away from purely artistic goals.

What each person creates from his own psychic experience in the field of music or the linguistic-phonetic—if we feel it within our own being, that is—can be described as something that individuals have developed within themselves, so to speak, after they have separated it from the outside world, to then impose on the outside world. This imposition of our own nature on the outside world is most evident in prose. One might go so far as to say that in this spoken prose, in an aesthetic sense, lies the imposition of one's own human nature on the outside world. And in doing so, individuals proceed in such a way that they transform what they develop in themselves as a soul experience evermore into the expression of thoughts. These then either become a linguistic expression for inner spiritual experience or for conventional communication.

In both the case of conventional communication—towards which cultural languages in particular must develop—and the case of what is spiritually expressed as an inner experience of the soul, one could say that the aesthetic conscience is lost and replaced with logical reflection. To the extent that logical reflection intervenes in oral expression, aesthetic conscience is lost, that which is truly artistic is lost.

On the other hand, moving towards mime, the human being must behave in such a way that he either makes use of his organism such that he forms it—then he is dependent on the natural laws governing his body—or else he can set himself into motion in space, so that pantomime becomes dance-like. In this movement, which comprehends the soul within itself, the opposite occurs with the human being. He gives himself over in a certain sense to the external world. He becomes integrated into the external world. Thus, while he imposes himself in tonal language and also in the musical element, he transforms what he experiences within himself into air, thereby giving his inner experience over to outer objectivity.

Hence, on the one hand, while this is the case with language and with tonal expression in general, the human being integrates himself and selflessly submits to the laws of nature when he meaningfully moves his own organism.

But just as he loses himself in the spiritual when speaking or singing, so too does he lose himself in all that is natural when he falls into pantomime and into dance. Here, too, the aesthetic conscience ceases. And something finally happens when pantomime is developed and evermore brought towards a certain degree of perfection. Individuals may move as if they are being pulled by strings; they are integrated into an inhuman or extra-human system.

When man turns to dance, he comes close to ecstasy. Again, this becomes something inartistic.

Between these two extremes, balanced without leaning towards one side or the other, eurythmy aims to stand on its own as a visible language. It developed through careful study of the movement tendencies in which the human being lives, which are then, as it were, a part of the formation process within the larynx and other organs of speech before they are converted into movements of air. Just as Goethe saw the secrets of the whole plant embodied in a single green leaf in the most complex way, so too can one transfer into soul-filled movements of the arms and hands that which otherwise underlies language, and also song, but which only holds true when the human being speaks or sings, and this can, through the outer movements carried out by a person or a group of people, become as lawful as the lawfulness that lives in speech and song. In this sense, it is not an arbitrary pantomime or a simple coincidence of formations; it has real and coherent linguistic expression of the experiences of the human soul.

When an actual visible language is formed in this way, it brings to life the expression of our musical experiences, and, on the other hand, what we wish to transmit to the world around us about ourselves, about our own being, as well as our linguistic experience. This can be translated into movements through which the human being is integrated, so to speak, into the outside world, into the pictorial nature of this outside world.

This is why the truly artistic elements in poetry, elements which are also contained in music but are accessible to a pictorial nature, come to visibility particularly through this moving sculptural art, eurythmy.

In the case of poetic art, if it is true art, the poet is actually fighting a battle. Language naturally tends toward prose—that is, toward the place where logic shines through, where aesthetic conscience is suppressed. A poet is seized by this aesthetic conscience when he wants to express himself in language. He pushes back against what is at work in prosaic language. Through rhythm, measure, rhyme, and through thematic motifs, he pushes it back in *creative speech*,[261] so what once flowed out of the spirit via prose is led back into the soul.

Therefore, precisely those possibilities that the poet strives for, once expressed in creative speech, which expresses what is truly artistic, can be evoked through this visible language of eurythmy, through what was conceived eurythmically from the very beginning in creative speech.

Since it is coming in the program, I would like to draw your attention to the fairy tale "The Rock Spring Wonder." Here it is obvious how the fairy tale flows out into the outer, eurythmic sculptural movement.

Therefore, on the one hand, one can find eurythmy accompanied by music, since one can sing in this visible language, in this visible tonal fabric of eurythmy, as I like to call it, just as one can sing through tone. On the other hand, what is performed eurythmically on the stage will be accompanied by a corresponding poetic, verbal yet still artistic, expression of soul experiences.

In doing so, however, it becomes apparent that, in a certain way, eurythmy must return to the original source of art.

❁

FERCHER VON STEINWAND'S COSMIC POEMS

Dornach, May 27, 1922[262]

In the first part, we will present for you today a longer poem, a poem by an Austrian. Unfortunately, if one considers his truly great significance, he is someone who remains too little known: Fercher von Steinwand.[263] Besides many extraordinarily interesting dramatic, lyric, and epic poems—which are equally great in terms of their artistic charm, their depth of thought, and their deeply felt, enthusiastic energy—Fercher von Steinwand also created what I would like to call his cosmic poems. They are poems that lose themselves in the archetypes of the formation of worlds. He develops thoughts which want to follow into the most remote primordial times the course of the world as in dreams or in imaginations.

But thereby there arise such thoughts as can stand before us in noble imagery. Often—and I beg you to consider this in listening and watching today— they are not immediately graspable on a first hearing, but everywhere they reveal broad perspectives and a deep sympathy with the cosmic happenings in the world. And because they reach so far into the cosmic as thoughts, feelings, and sensations, and because what is depicted by the moving human being—because the human being is truly a microcosm that can bring most nobly to expression the macrocosmic movements of the cosmos that are imitated—Fercher von Steinwand's poems are thus most excellently suited to eurhythmic presentation. One can bring especially to expression these wonderful nuances of thought and feeling, with which he follows cosmic phenomena, precisely with this mobile language, if one draws upon the aid of the human being.

To be sure, we shall only understand it properly when we can enter into the nuances of movement. These actually always stand in connection with what the macrocosm speaks to the human soul when this human soul is able to open itself up to what underlies the wide world.

An older art form, which was similar to eurythmy but not the same, an art of temple dance in ancient times, sought in particular to bring to revelation in human dance and mimetic movements the motions of the stars, as these were understood in ancient times. That is something which, to be sure, cannot be presented today in a direct way, but can indeed be depicted in another form that is appropriate for today.

ON "THE DYING MEDUSA" BY C. F. MEYER

Dornach, July 2, 1922[264]

Here on the stage, you will see various things depicted in eurythmic forms. You will see poetry and music. I would like to emphasize that one can depict particularly what is of a more spiritual nature through eurythmy.

In this regard, I point you to the final number of the first part before the intermission, where we present Perseus confronting the dying Medusa ("The Dying Medusa" by C. F. Meyer). The dying Medusa is something with which you will be familiar from Greek mythology. It presents everything that humanity once had in ancient times as a world of ideas, whereby humanity was subject to many errors. And in Perseus we see depicted a strong personality who liberated human beings from the old, fantastic ways of thinking that burdened them like a mountain. This struggle of Perseus against old, erroneous, nebulous ideas that are as dangerous to humans as snakes—thus Medusa's head filled with snakes—will be presented in the last piece before the intermission. Then an intermission will happen, and finally, many different kinds of pieces will be presented, including humorous ones.

❁

Lighting for Eurythmy

Dornach, July 23, 1922[265]

Just as little as one can ask what a tone signifies in music, for in music the impression is achieved through simultaneous or successive tones in their relationship, it is the same with the movements here, the significance of which should not be seen in an abstract and intellectualistic way. Rather, they must be immediately grasped from outside. And then the succession of shaped movements—it is in this that the artistic must dwell.

Gradually we are attempting to come ever further and further with these things. Thus, for example, we add to the scene in general, so that poems or music that otherwise are revealed by tone or sound are also revealed by individuals in motion or through groups in motion as this visible eurythmic speech. To this scene that arises thereby, we are adding more and more things that belong to it. Thus I have sought particularly in recent weeks to add in the corresponding way the lighting, which should also be established according to eurythmic principles.

Thereby one should not look at the individual lighting effects, interpreting whether at one particular moment green or yellow is there. Rather, one has to be clear again that everything needs to be judged like music, how the one nuance of color follows upon the other or vice versa. Thus you have to do here with a visible language; but when we arrive at the performance of eurythmy, you have to do with the artistic formation of this eurythmic language.

Thereby, honored guests, we achieve something that is an autonomous art. It is not pantomime, nor an art of dance, but rather an autonomous art form that presents itself in addition to the arts of poetry and music.

❀

Dornach, July 30, 1922[266]

We can see in particular how gradually, eurythmy is given form, in that we must consider how it is not a matter of individual movements, but rather of the sequence of movements. Thus I have also attempted recently to give form to the lighting also in the spirit of eurythmy. This lighting is very much a part of eurythmy, but it could also be foregone. Thus you will also see in the lighting a visible language that is in harmony with the mood that the sequence of lighting brings to expression.

Dornach, September 30, 1922[267]

With eurythmy, one has to do with an actual visible language that can be artistically shaped, only now for the eye and not for the ear as in music or poetry. Then, we seek to adapt the whole stage to our presentation with our eurythmy. And those of the honored guests who saw eurythmy some time ago will note how now, for a considerable period of time, the attempt has been made to shape the lighting effects in the spirit of eurythmy—both the lighting effects that flood space and also the harmony of the lighting effects with the color of the dresses and veils of those performing eurythmy. So that one has in a sense a moved or self-moving flood of light, which also actually represents a visible language.

Dornach, February 4, 1923[268]

Recently, we have, for example, added to the movement of people that is visible on the stage a kind of eurythmic art of lighting, so that the stage has not only moving people and moving groups, but there is also, working harmoniously with this, the sequence of lighting effects, a kind of eurythmy through the lighting.

And, in this regard, something will immediately strike you. While in normal stage settings, when there is something dramatic or mimetic to be depicted, one chooses the lighting so that it is strongly adapted, so to speak, to whatever is happening in the moment. Let us say, for example, whenever a scene is played in the morning, one uses lighting that suggests the morning, and so forth. Here, however, we use no naturalistic effects in the lighting. Rather, the sequences of lighting must be tuned rather like the tones in a musical melody. It is a matter of the sequence of lighting effects. And this sequence of lighting effects must harmonize with what one sees as movements.

The Artistic Treatment of Language

Dornach, February 11, 1923[269]

Eurythmy should not be mime, a mere art of gestures, nor should it be a dance-like art. You will see moving people or moving groups of people on stage accompanied by recitation and declamation and accompanied by music. But what is carried out by the individual person in eurythmy, especially through the movement of the most expressive organs, the arms and hands, or through groups of people, is something to which the usual gestures, which one also makes in ordinary speech, start to seem like a child's babbling when compared to trained, articulate, human language.

If we observe somewhat livelier people speaking, we find that, unless they have lost it through a particular educational convention, they accompany their verbal revelation with all sorts of gestures. We see gestures applied to affirmation, and we see gestures applied to negation. We see gestures employed when this or that feeling arising from the content of language wants to show that feeling in a way even more expressive than the nuances of the language itself.

Through these ordinary gestures, which are also used in the art of mime, one actually only indicates what pervades the linguistic element in the form of emotional or volitional impulses. But if one applies what Goethe calls sensory-suprasensory seeing, I would like to say, this babbling of gestures can then be developed into what now appears as eurythmy. Human beings accompany inwardly with their whole souls, indeed with their whole bodies, when expressing in language—both when listening to what is spoken and when speaking—what they experience through the soul, which they basically experience in their entire bodies, if they can give it the attention it deserves.

But one can also study, as I said, through sensory-suprasensory intuition, how in the human being these inner movements of the soul shoot into those movements which the throat and head transform into movements of air, which then become audible. One can, so to speak, follow what comes out of the human being in speaking or in singing into the human organism itself. Then one arrives at a developed, visible language, not just at that babble of gestures that is present in the art of mime.

One comes to recognize that just as a certain tone that sounds is the expression of something that the soul feels but of which it is no longer aware, that a movement of the human organism can also express the same thing—what is felt, for example, when the person feels compelled to express something by the "I" or "A" sound. Or, again, one can find certain forms of movement that can parallel the sensation, the feelings when speaking the consonants. In this way, one can consciously develop visible speaking and visible singing, as we do in eurythmy, just as the small child unconsciously develops articulate speech and singing through imitation.

In the same artistic and human sense in which tonal and phonetic elements in song or language signify the inner life of the soul—not in an abstract, intellectual way, but in a human, artistic way—any movement signifies exactly what is experienced in the "I," in the "A," and so forth. One sees how the tone or the sound signifies that. The result is a really visible speech or a really visible singing.

When something musical resounds and eurythmy is performed to it, one does not have a dancing, but rather a visible singing. And it is precisely with this visible singing that one can see the difference between eurythmy and the mere art of dance. The art of dance exudes the emotion, the passion in a human movement, even if this is no longer known in the case of this or that dance, which is already formed in a more noble way. But the eurythmy that appears in the movement—parallel to a musical element—is a visible singing. These are movements that also express meter, rhythm, melodiousness, indeed the individual interval, the individual tone, like the song itself.

And it is the same when what appears as eurythmy gestures, as visible speech on the stage through the individual or through groups of people, is paralleled by declamation and recitation. Actually, however, eurythmy is already contained in the artistic treatment of speech by the real poet. In the artistic treatment of language by the real poet, the prosaic aspect of the poem's content has receded entirely. It is not at all important that someone as a poet only reveals prose that has been put into verse to a certain extent; it is important how poets express themselves in the treatment of language imaginatively, i.e., pictorially, or also, I would like to say, musically in meter, in rhythm, in the melodious theme of the language, how they express in the treatment of language what they want to express.

If we take a simple poem, for example:

Über allen Gipfeln
Ist Ruh,
In allen Wipfeln
Spürest du
Kaum einen Hauch;
Die Vögelein schweigen im Walde.
Warte nur, balde
Ruhest du auch.

Above all the peaks
Is peace,
In all the treetops
You feel
Barely a breath;
The birds hush in the forest.
Just wait, soon
You will rest too.[270]

It does not matter that the prosaic content "above all the peaks is peace," and so on, is expressed, but rather that in the treatment of the sounds—for, with Goethe, the treatment of language is always imaginative—there undulates and weaves what is outside in nature. For example, in a poem like this, the poem itself weaves and lives. It is not important that I express the peace in the peaks; rather, it is important that the syllables flow and weave with the same peace as what lives outside in nature:

> Über allen Gipfeln
> Ist Ruh,
> In allen Wipfeln
> Spürest du
> Kaum einen Hauch...
>
> Above all the peaks
> Is peace,
> In all the treetops
> You feel
> Barely a breath...

One would like to say that the same peaceful atmosphere that resounds from the forest also resounds from the succession and intermingling of the syllables, painting into one another and coloring into one another. This is already entirely inherent in the poet's actual treatment of language.

But this eurythmy is hidden. The reciter, the declaimer, must bring out this eurythmy. What lies hidden in the poem as eurythmy can only be brought to light through the treatment of language. Then, whatever is possible, the phonetic coloring of the individual through the whole, of one through the other, in which this visible language of eurythmy is developed, will also be able to appear visibly before people. This is then artistic work through the visible speech or through the visible singing of eurythmy.

In fact, through eurythmy, what lies in a poem, in a piece of music, can be expressed to a certain extent just as it can be expressed through singing and spoken language. Except that in singing and in spoken language, we have the interference of the thought element. And, actually, poets always fight against the inartistic nature of thought, since they have to make use of the words that come about in the sound, in the tone. The thought element is always something inartistic. This inartistic quality remains absent in the visible speech and the visible singing of eurythmy. Eurythmy prefers what in a poem is experienced through feeling or as a result of volitional impulses, hence what is actually artistic.

Schopenhauer[271] saw what is actually artistic in the human will. He expressed it abstractly. I would like to say that eurythmy gives the *praxis* of it. While in poetry one still has to struggle so that the thought does not come too much into its own, but rather the linguistic formation of the thought, eurythmy actually gives everything that the poet would like to give, that he carries within himself, as long as the poem that does not yet exist spills over into spoken language. One might like to say that through eurythmy one can particularly feel what Schiller meant when he said: "When the soul *speaks*, alas! the *soul* is speaking no longer." The soul has something much more inward; it is much more inwardly connected to the entire physical body, and recitation and declamation, if it feels this inner element, can certainly bring the hidden eurythmy into nuanced speech. But this hidden element of eurythmy can also be integrated into the movements of individuals or groups of people. And then something arises in a conscious way that is quite similar to what arises in an unconscious way during childhood in spoken language and in singing.

Well, today, as always, I would like to ask the honored viewers for indulgence, because we know very well that the art of eurythmy is still in the early stages of its development. But it uses the human being as its own instrument. Just compare eurythmy with what is comparable, with the art of sculpture. There you have an outer material. One can represent the resting human being, only the silent human being, in his inner life. In eurythmy, the inwardly moved human being is represented by the moved human being. The inner movement of the soul comes to light in the outer bodily movement. Since human beings are microcosms containing all the mysteries of the world, one may hope that this most perfect instrument, which is nowhere else used as such an artistic instrument as in eurythmy, enables the art of eurythmy to become more and more perfect. Finally, it will be able to present itself as an art that is really to be recognized alongside the other sister arts that are already fully recognized today.

That this is not the case today, we know, but we also know the immeasurably great possibilities of development that lie within eurythmy. Thus we believe that this will be the case again in the future.

We have three parts in the program. After the Beethoven minuet, there will be a short break of about five minutes; then comes "Fate" by Fercher von Steinwand.

THE LIFE OF THE SOUL AS EXPRESSED IN SPEECH AND SONG OR IN MOVEMENT AND POSTURE
CONSONANT, VOWEL—NERVE, BLOOD

Dornach, February 18, 1923[272]

As I have often said in these introductions to our performances, eurythmy should be a visible speech or visible singing. What is expressed through tone and song, what is expressed by sound in language, stands in the middle of that human experience which we develop completely quietly, in the middle of the soul life we develop when we confront the world by thinking about, by contemplating things, but with inner participation and inner interest in the world. There we develop our ideation. But this ideation is always permeated, vivified, woven through with our impulses of will and feeling.

Whoever gains clarity about the life of soul will be able to know that even when we confront the world with our whole body at complete rest, contemplating, when we allow the images that are presented to us in perception to pass through the soul, that there are also expressions of will and feeling that shoot into the life of ideation, coloring and lending it nuance in the most various ways.

We experience the one idea with a gentle joy, the other with a gentle anxiety, fear, and yet another with a certain reverence. We then experience entirely in the background of our soul being how the will arises: you want to have that, you want to grasp that, you want to perform that.

That is the life of soul in which human beings in a sense withdraw completely from their bodily expression and experience inwardly within themselves, quietly, what in the world has many forms and is variously mobile; we allow it to become an inner revelation.

Speaking and singing are then an outward intensification of this whole inner, resting life. While during the mere contemplative observation of the world in thought, nerves play the main role in human beings, and the blood plays its role only to the extent that in very fine streams it is the bearer of the will nature, weaving through and vivifying the nerves, with speaking and singing the activity of the blood and the activity of the nerves are equal participants, achieving an inward equilibrium. This expresses itself by influencing the process of breathing and bringing the air into movement with the help of the organs of speech and song. The blood expresses itself by participating as a still undifferentiated vital expression of the body in this whole setting-into-motion of the air by the organs of speech and song. There, nerves and blood participate equally. There, what we received from outside is imitated in the consonants. When the will and the soul stir within, the vocalic element permeates what is imitated. In a sense, it adds the human element to what we take up through the world by bringing consonants to expression in speech and song. Thus in speech and song, ideation and will meet in feeling in the soul.

Now, a third language can exist, and this third language is the one that arises when we claim our whole organism and place into it what is completely at rest in the mere observation of the world. What transitions in speech and song from a stirring rest into an inwardly resting movement is now transformed in eurythmy entirely into posture and movement.

What lives in consonantal speaking as an imitation of the outer world comes to expression in eurythmic forms and movements through the whole human being. What lives in the vocalic, coming from the blood, as willfulness comes to expression in the human posture, the posture that is integral to movement.

Thus when one sees moving individuals or groups of people on the stage in eurythmy, one always sees them in a certain movement, and in this movement in turn in a certain posture. When one sees movement, then the consonantal element of the imitation of the outer world is within it. When one sees a posture, which in eurythmy is particularly the expression of the vowels, then what comes from the life of human blood is present. But eurythmy is the complete antithesis of what we develop inwardly, quietly, in merely contemplating the world. There, nerves are the main thing, and the blood only comes into consideration as the expression of the will in fine streams to the extent that they pour into the life of the nerves. But here, in doing eurythmy, the main thing is what the body brings about as movement and posture by executing all of that with the will anchored in the blood. Thus it is that in eurythmy it is principally the blood that is active, and the nerve only insofar as it actually serves the circulation of blood, which is to say the inner rhythm, the inmost human rhythm.

And thus, one can allow the inner rhythm of the human organization, which has transitioned into movement and posture proceeding from the element of the will, to have its effect. At the same time, one can regard something that lies somewhat higher, approaching the contemplative human being: speech and song.

When recitation accompanies movement in eurythmy, one cannot recite in the way that is so beloved today, by merely accentuating the prose content of the poem. Rather, one has to bring what is a secret eurythmy into the formation of the sound, into the rhythm of the sound, into beat, also into what is melodious and harmonic, into the harmony of the formation of sounds.

When one sees and hears eurythmy and declamation orchestrally, then one really ought to gain a consciousness of what we always experience when we sense with our souls. Because the soul is bound inwardly to the body, what we experience inwardly in our souls is imitated in our bodies. Down to the tips of our fingers and toes, the soul lives in the human organism, and it can imitate spatially and bodily everything that lives within it. In speaking and singing, it takes what could otherwise express itself, movement and posture, back only as far as the organism of the chest. And because the chest organization has definite organs in order to express what would otherwise be the movement and posture of the whole human being, in speech and in song there arises something that is also posture and movement, but then passes over into the formation of the air imperceptible as movement, while in human beings proper, it is only revealed soul-spiritually in tone and sound. And, actually, in the presentation that you see here as eurythmy, only the contemplative side of our nature is suppressed. While we are outwardly revealed in our souls, for which the organs of the chest serve, and in our whole formation, for which the organs of will and movement serve, on the stage in declamation and recitation the contemplative human being is initially absent.

This contemplative person is then the viewer and the listener. But this contemplative person confronts what is offered on the stage and through declamation. The individual takes it up, which is to say, the individual lives into that most perfect instrument which eurythmy employs: into the whole human organism. He sees and contemplates the human being insofar as the human being is someone that reveals himself outwardly. And thus through eurythmy, what the human being is for the world becomes in contemplation entirely an inner world.

Whereas one has to do in the other arts with external instruments, and we only make use of them, in eurythmy we are ourselves an instrument. Thus, in eurythmy, the microcosm, this little world, steps forth, and the contemplative observer can say that what is inward cannot become the content of art, but rather only what wants to reveal itself outwardly, for art must be viewed from the outside.

But everything human that can unfold outwardly is offered in eurythmy to the inner life of the audience. Of course, we have to ask the indulgence of the audience every time a eurythmic performance is offered because everything is still in its beginnings. Nevertheless, eurythmy has a future, for it will place itself within the finest stirrings in the finest revelations of everything that works outwardly from the spirit and soul.

Thereby it will call forth soul and spirit in the fullest concentration for the intuition of the audience. And that is, after all, the fundamental and highest ideal of all art. Thus we can hope that precisely this art can serve as a complement to all the others: of the poetic, the rhythmic, the musical, the sculptural, and the architectural. As a synthesis of all this, it shall one day take its place as a fully justified, younger art beside the other arts. One can hope for this when one considers the means of expression that eurythmy employs: human beings revealing themselves outwardly. We appeal to that in the human being which has the fullest, total interest in all of humanity, insofar as this is an expression in microcosm, a revelation of the great world, the macrocosm.

EURYTHMY, DANCE, MIME

Stuttgart, March 28, 1923[273]

One has to say that, for example, when accompanying music, eurythmy does not become a dance, but rather a visible singing. One has to gradually enter into this special kind of intuition of eurythmic movements. Then one will find that, to be sure, eurythmy can transition, on the one hand, into something dance-like; in certain movements approximating pure eurythmy, we gain full reflection within our organism, and the result is something dance-like. But it must associate itself decently, shall we say, intimately, so that at most eurythmy flows into dance only on the one side. That will be particularly the case when in the progression of a poem something passionate arises, for the dance-like is a kind of inability to hold back, as one does in eurythmy; in the dance-like, human consciousness escapes into unconsciousness. One can characterize it as follows. In eurythmy, the soul has the body in its power in every individual movement, in every individual vibration, but in dance, the soul continually experiences a loss of control of the body. Thus it should enter with eurythmy only at those places where what should be revealed passes over into abuse, into argument, into anger and similar human expressions. That is the one pole to which eurythmy should not extend for fear of eurythmy becoming too much like dance. Dance has its justification, but it is something completely different. As eurythmy, it has a brutal effect.

However, there is another danger on the other side. When eurythmy has to express something that, shall we say, is a smirk, a smile, a put-down in the course of the speech, then it can slip over into the other pole, into mime. And yet, however justified the art of mime is in itself, if eurythmy transitions too strongly into mime—where there is not a particular occasion for the smirk, for the smile, and so forth—it becomes like someone who is continually grinned while speaking, or, let us say, instead of saying something unsympathetic, they stick out their tongue. It has something of a transition from language into a mischievous element in human life when eurythmy passes over into mime.

These things must be felt very keenly. Then one will see that what can be extraordinarily justified in mime is unjustified in the art of eurythmy.

LIGHTING FOR EURYTHMY

Dornach, April 2, 1923[274]

Recently, we have introduced the element of light and color into eurythmy. I would like to say: What appears on the stage in the way of movements of people and groups of people proceeds from the human soul and the human spirit. But the human soul is always connected with the elemental aspect of the external world. And what happens on the stage in the formation of human movements can be harmonized, can be extended harmoniously in what floods the stage as effects of color and light. These should be coordinated, on the one hand, with the costumes of the eurythmists and, on the other hand, their sequence should itself yield a musical element that is itself born out of the sound. So that the element of lighting on the stage can also be treated eurythmically. This stage setting of eurythmy is, to be sure, still present in an incomplete state, but it will perfect itself ever more and more.

Dornach, April 7, 1923[275]

Today, we have already tried to make the stage scenery with its lighting effects also appear in accordance with eurythmy. One can see how a kind of light-eurythmy can be developed, how the stage setting is in a sense framed by light, by the melodious element, and so forth. With lighting effects, it is not a matter of bringing an individual content that is there at a certain moment in a symbolic connection with the poem, but rather the sequence, just as one has a succession of tones in music. The sequence of lighting effects is what really matters.

[UNTITLED]

Dornach, June 9, 1923[276]

Goethe speaks of sensory-suprasensory perception as enabling one to grasp something artistically. If we try to grasp artistically human speech and the system of song, to grasp it in its broadest aspect, we discover something that lies behind speech and behind song: we find something that has to do with the whole human being, even though speech and song as such have only to do with a single, small group of physical organs. Who does not feel that whenever they give themselves over to speech or song, their whole soul is participating—indeed, so much so that they feel their soul weaving and pulsing through their whole organism? We can even say, at least when our speech is not merely serving to impart some conventional information or purely logical sequence of thought, but rather is shaped artistically, that then the entire human being wants to be expressed, and this expression, this revelation of the whole human being is merely concentrated in a limited group of speech organs.

We could ask what movement has to take place within us when we sing something or say something. Then we discover certain movements that are actually transformed by the speech organs, the larynx and its adjoining organs, into air movements and are in this way thrown out, as it were, to the outside world. We discover that these movements can also be traced back to where they originate in the human being. Ordinarily, we find that they have been suppressed. We respond to everything we hear said to us by these inner movements, or we suppress them; we then find them replaced by the sympathy we feel toward the world and our fellows as we listen to what is spoken.

Similarly, when we ourselves speak, there is an unconscious desire to accompany what we say by these movements, these gestures, but we suppress them because what we want to say finds its expression through the sounds of speech.

But everyone knows that in song, and also in speech that is formed artistically, there is something we call style, that language is shaped in a certain way, given a certain style by poets. They bring in a rhythmic element; they make use of certain meters; they introduce linguistic motifs like melodies into their language; they respond to a certain fantasy in their use of speech sounds.

All this is something that lies at the foundation of speech but does not enter permanently into it. People who have an intimate feeling for human life can sense that when they give over to their larynx what is in their soul, they actually externalize it. I would like to say that we give it over to the objective, spiritual sphere of life.

Now, what the soul experiences more inwardly can be brought to expression through "stylized" gestures, and it is eurythmy that brings this to expression, so that there comes about an actual visible speech and an actual visible song. The entire content of eurythmy, all the gestures of individual eurythmists or groups of eurythmists, are taken from the human organism as precisely, as properly as are the speech sounds themselves—that is, the vowels, consonants, sentence structure, and so forth.

The visible speech and visible singing that arise in this way can be quite correctly understood if we follow how the recitation and declamation, and also the musical pieces, are accomplished here by eurythmy movements. At first, people are inclined to regard tone eurythmy as dance, but eurythmy is not dance. It is really singing-in-movement, in which the singing is not done by tone but by movement. We begin to understand eurythmy properly when we are able to regard it not as dance but as moving singing, singing-in-movement.

In the same way, eurythmic movements accompany what is being expressed by speech sounds. In the speech of civilized peoples today, there lives a spiritual element, an objective element, that becomes more and more separated from the individuals themselves. We feel, and quite rightly, an unpleasant quality in the more sophisticated modern languages when a subjective element enters the speech, when something is over-emphasized, or when the prosaic content is stressed, and the like. We feel it is almost lewd when too much of a subjective element is imported. Speech should spiritualize the soul element and thereby detach it more or less from the speaker. We can take what comes to expression in "stylized" speech and put it back into human movement. Then the soul element is revealed in moving human beings; their movements—especially those of the most expressive part of their bodies, their hands and arms—become a visible speech.

When we give voice to consonants, the happenings in the outside world are expressed by them rather objectively. When we speak the vowels, feelings live in them that we entertain toward these happenings, but separated from us, spiritualized. I would like to say that with the visible speech of eurythmy—if, for instance, a poem is presented—one lives in it entirely as soul. What lives in our spirit is ensouled by eurythmy.

Eurythmy is able to translate the vocalic sounds as well as the consonantal sounds into movements. When the vowels are formed into eurythmy movements, they reveal what the soul experiences in its deepest inwardness. With the consonants, it is our lively relation to all things that the eurythmy brings to expression.

While our ordinary speech tends more and more to spiritualize our soul experiences, eurythmy, by its very nature, stresses the soul quality of our inner experiences. Indeed, every movement made here on the stage is a visible expression of the most intimate soul experience. When, therefore, we accompany eurythmy by recitation and declamation, the "hidden eurythmy" that poets weave invisibly into their poems must also be given expression. We cannot recite and declaim as is usually done, where the really artistic elements of language are not considered at all, but only the prose content is emphasized.

Here we want to recite and declaim in such a way that the artistic elements of the language will be brought into prominence. The tone structure and tone quality of the recitation must coincide with the eurythmy movements. When the recitation or declamation is intoned and the eurythmy movements are made simultaneously, as if together they were an orchestral ensemble, then it is as if the speech sounds themselves were part of the style that the poet is creating, and as if they were able to make the style more human. The style of a poem is the element that raises it to a suprasensory level, while the speech sounds themselves bring the suprasensory realm down to our human level of experience.

When we are watching eurythmy and listening to the recitation and declamation, the eurythmy continually raises the recitation and declamation to "style" before our eyes. One has the feeling, therefore, that in performing eurythmy we must enter as far as possible into the poet's style. It must parallel our endeavor to bring recitation and declamation back to those earlier times when Goethe rehearsed his iambic dramas with the actors with a baton in his hand like a choral director, showing that he valued an artistic treatment of his language far more than emphasis of the prose content. We, too, must return to the secrets of imaginative and musical speech formation if we would raise recitation and declamation to an art. At the same time, we will be developing a truly artistic support for eurythmy.

But there is also the need to support the style of our eurythmy in other areas. Those of you, dear friends, who have come often to the eurythmy performances here will have noticed our efforts lately to add new lighting effects to the stage scene. These are not intended to apply to single gestures in a naturalistic way, but just as in music a melody is only to be found in a series of tones, so here in the eurythmy lighting what we are trying to achieve should be looked for in the lighting sequences. We want to place the moving eurythmy picture within sequences of lighting that relate and belong to it, sequences that then are themselves a kind of "light eurythmy."

Today, as always before our programs, I must ask you to remember that we are only at the beginning of this art of eurythmy. We know our imperfections better than anyone else. What eurythmy intends will only be fully realized in the future. Eurythmy makes much more perfect use of human beings in motion than does the art of mime, for instance. Mime uses the moving human being for accompaniment. Eurythmy requires that everything within us shall be, I would like to say, brought out so that we are like a living, visibly active larynx. It tries in its movements to present artistically everything that lies hidden within the human form.

If we think of human beings as microcosms that contain a whole world within themselves, then we can say that eurythmy has a future, because it is through eurythmy that the most important, the most profound world secrets will come to be revealed artistically. If we are a microcosm and contain all the cosmic secrets within ourselves, these will become manifest to the eye. Then one can use the entire human being as a medium of expression. That is what eurythmy wants to do. So one may allow oneself to hope that although eurythmy is a young art, it will nevertheless gradually develop to such perfection that it will finally be able to take its place in full recognition beside the older accepted arts.

✽

[Untitled]

Dornach July 9, 1923[277]

To grasp the full significance of eurythmy, we must realize that it is an attempt to create an actual visible speech and an actual visible singing, so that the music that is being played or the poetry that is being recited can be presented at the same time on the stage in visible form.

First of all, we have to realize that every human manifestation in the physical world comes out of the totality of our human nature. Yet in complete waking consciousness, we really have nothing more than our ideas, our concepts. We do not experience our feelings with the same degree of wakefulness as we do our ideas. Our feelings are only at the level of dream consciousness. Only to the extent that we have transformed them into ideas have they become awake. Our life of will is completely submerged in sleep—indeed, in dreamless sleep. It is pushed down to the level of total unconsciousness. Of our will impulses, we only experience whatever thought element may be contained in them. We get an idea to make some movement; the idea disappears into our organism and we know nothing of it until we move. The intention that starts our willing, and then the action that we perform, are present as ideas in our waking consciousness. What goes on within us in order to bring the will impulse into action is as completely enveloped in sleep as our entire soul life is enveloped in sleep between the moment of falling asleep and awakening.

But now, when we express ourselves in speaking or singing, we are creating something out of our whole human nature. Let us consider speech first. When we speak a sentence, our whole being is revealed in it. Our feeling, which normally we experience as dreamy, is now the thread weaving through the words, through the sounds. Likewise, our impulse of will works its way into the words, into the sounds. But, leaving aside such abnormal phenomena as talking in our sleep, we have to be fully awake when we speak. Thus, even so, there is an unconscious element arising from the depth of our being that shows itself in the way our words are uttered, by the sounds coming out strong or weak, and so forth.

As we speak in normal daily life, we adjust ourselves to every kind of circumstance, and we let thought predominate in our words. But thought is an inartistic element. An artistic quality can only begin to be present in speech when thought is no longer active—and I mean not only the thought exercised in imparting knowledge but even the thought that is communicated between us in everyday, conventional life. Thought activity as such is inartistic.

A poet has to deal with thoughts because—well, for the simple reason that language must provide a place where thoughts can live! But the poet's chief task is to take what he hears sounding from the unconscious levels of his being and to weave this into his language, making that language imaginative and musical. From a poet's point of view, language only has an artistic quality if it is pliant so that it can be molded, if the speech sounds are given imaginative color, if the phrases are given a musical quality, if rhythms and meter are delicately worked out. Thus, poets must give their thoughts a form by working unconscious elements into it. We cannot have them stream into our normal thinking, because thinking is something alien to both elements. But poets can let them stream through their work as they mold their language.

When I say, "The tree is becoming green" [*der Baum grünt*], I have first of all expressed a thought, and my language is dry and abstract. But the moment I depart from conventional usage and say, "The greening tree" [*der grünende Baum*], I have already infused a nuance of feeling into my language. I can increase this by accelerating the beat, changing the rhythm, and so forth. By varying the stress, I can give more play to the will element that is also streaming into my language.

So a poet's language has eurythmy hidden within that originates in his feeling and will. This is what speech artists must work particularly to reveal. Otherwise, they are only giving a prose reading, not a real recitation or declamation such as [Marie] Steiner[278] has for years been developing here. Only if the speech artists give their recitations or declamations a truly eurythmic character can true eurythmy be performed by the eurythmist.

It is possible with spiritual-scientific perception to observe what flows from the unconscious into speech and song. We can observe, for instance, what the feeling element is in any spoken phrase, and also what the will element is. When people speak, this is all pushed up to their heads and their thoughts are colored or given a musical quality. We can trace back and discover how feeling and will colored their thought, affected its shape, and made it musical. It came about through their systems of movement. We can therefore represent it by movements and gestures that will themselves be made by a human being, that will themselves come from the human movement system. As a person makes these movements, there is first of all a spatial element to be found in them: it is, if you look for it in human speech, the imaginative activity that goes into the shaping of each sound. There is also the time element—that is, the way one movement follows another, the way they are coordinated and harmonized, the way they make a kind of melody. The time element can even be made into melodic themes. It is precisely the musical element in language that shows us how language is grounded in the human movement system. You can make a melody out of the way someone walks, or you can tap out a rhythm; you can even hum a so-called "musical embellishment" from the way he moves! In other words, everything that declamation should be concerned with is obtained from our observation of the unconscious impulses in human movement; it is certainly not to be found in human thoughts. All this is to be seen in specific eurythmy gestures and spatial eurythmy movements.

So an art form has been created that is neither dance nor mere gesture. Everyday gestures are really a kind of eurythmic baby-talk that helps us out when we are unable to express something in words of abstract thought.

So it should become clear to us that the speech we learn as children and use until the end of our life is only something for our earthly life. It is foolish to believe, as spiritualism does, that departed souls use ordinary human speech. They no longer have a national language; they have worked their way beyond it. When they died, they ceased being English, French, Italian, and so forth. They have simply entered another sphere. Therefore, it makes no sense to believe that the dead can accomplish some immediate materialization in a specific language. What they say must first be translated into human speech.

Speech is a product of earthly life, and it is fitted to earthly conditions. If people long in the depths of their souls to make their speech less earthly, they have recourse to gestures. The reverse is also true: people who like to stand as stiff as a poker and talk as stiff as a poker are always, if not in their world outlook, then surely in their feelings, materialistic, earthy. Those who speak more out of the spiritual world are always impelled to accompany their conversation with gestures, because what is expressed by our ordinary gestures has meaning in the spiritual sphere immediately adjoining our world. There our gestures are experienced as speech. It is as if beings from the angelic world, the world of the Angeloi, were always encouraging us to strengthen our earthly speech with help from suprasensory realms.

But now, if we consider eurythmy, if we examine the gestures in the visible speech of eurythmy, we find that they place us in the realm of the archangels—of course, in a certain sense, unconsciously, and more so or less so; when one undertakes to create eurythmy, for instance, it must be done out of an absolutely clear consciousness. We find that our eurythmy movements are speech in the realm of the archangels. So we are providing a significant, supra-earthly element as accompaniment for the poet's creations, which he, for his part, has worked to raise to a supra-earthly level by rejecting its prose character and, instead, infusing into it color, form, and music.

Of course, it may sound rather fantastic when one says that eurythmy is the earthly image of the speech of the archangels. But, however it may sound, for someone whose thoughts are not materialistic, it is actually true! When [Schiller] says, "When the soul *speaks*, alas! the *soul* is speaking no longer," he is right, because he feels that something deserving to be given artistic form is in every instance degraded when it is thrown into prosaic language. It must first be lifted up by the art of recitation and declamation, which restores poetic qualities to the art of poetry. What the poet experiences, what does not belong to the sense world, can be expressed precisely through these movements in eurythmic language.

Every art, in fact, raises what is earthly to a view of heaven; this is known to everyone who has lived in a really artistic atmosphere. It remained for this present epoch of materialism no longer to feel joy when it looks at Raphael's paintings. I experienced this with many artists I knew at the turn of the century. His pictures were too unearthly for them. They preferred to paint the warts on someone's face so as to have as much earthiness in their pictures as possible. One of them even told me—it was someone whose painting in earlier years had been especially valued by the theosophists—he was the first artist to have the courage to put hair on his nudes wherever a person normally has hair. While the other artists were willing to ignore such complete earthiness, he considered it especially clever. Michelangelo? Such people said, "Well, today he is still accepted since he at least tried to come down to earth." But Raphael? For many of them, he was impossible to swallow!

But every art wants to enhance the things of earth with a supra-earthly sheen. Actually, art only has its true justification if it does so.

So one may say that eurythmy, developing a new art form from the smallest beginning, is opening up a new path. Such paths have always been opened up when genuine art forms have arisen in the evolution of humanity. We may therefore wish this new art a full life because it does not disavow its true spiritual origin—the origin of every fine art. This makes its future unquestionably assured.

✽

On the Essence of Gesture

Dornach, July 15, 1923[279]

If eurythmy consists in being a cultivated revelation of human nature, it must be distinguished from the art of mime, on the one hand, and from the art of dance, on the other. Eurythmy does not want to be either. Eurythmy really wants to be the same thing in the movement of the individual human limbs or of the whole human being in space as what speech is through the air formed by the human organism. And eurythmy has really come into being in such a way that the same impulses which the human organism otherwise pours into the formed air as a mediator of the linguistic or vocal element as a revelation of the soul, that everything which lies in these impulses is poured into impulses of movement.

Therefore, eurythmy must not be interpreted in an intellectual way, but each individual movement and gesture must be felt in its artistic form. And the more one approaches what is given in eurythmy with an artistic feeling and not with an intellectual interpretation, the more will one come to understand eurythmy. For just as human language, albeit in an unconscious way, is extracted by the small child from the essence of the human being, eurythmy is extracted as a visible speech or a visible singing—although with consciousness, therefore not less elementary, therefore not less inwardly lawful—from this same human organism.

Basically, what is formed when we speak or sing is also a gesture, only a gesture that is formed within the exhaled air stream, through the varied formations of the air stream. Let us take the "A,"[280] for example, going back to the element of speech. In essence, what is revealed in the "A" as an element of the soul, if one wants to grasp it, expresses itself as a kind of wonder or astonishment. But when the "A" appears in the context of language, this pleasant astonishment is quite attenuated; it melts, so to speak, into the context of the word, into the context of language. We do not even think about it anymore, let alone feel anything of what originally flowed out of the emotional element, the common element of our being into the air. This "A" is formed as air by the fact that a full stream of air pours outward, becomes in a certain sense shell-shaped outward, so that it retreats in the outflow before the density of air already present outside.

When a person speaks "E,"[281] it is as if a kind of congestion were created in front of his speech organs. The exhaled air stream initially pours out into the outside world with full force, but is then stopped, dammed up by the outer air density and retreats.

When we speak the "I,"[282] we essentially let it originate very much in front; thus we give it a pointed force. And we eject the "I" in such a way that a sharper, arrow-like stream of air is energized into the density of the outer air, splitting the outer air, as it were, with a sword.

When we speak the "O," it is as if we were to hold back the mass of air that we ourselves give to the outside world, in a certain sense, by expelling it; so that we ourselves work the air that is outside us with the air that is pushed out, and thereby form something like a direction into the outside air.

With the "U," it is so that we split the outer air and feel the "U" again in the joining of two air streams of split outer air. And so, if we go into the formation that the air makes by bringing forth the sound, we can follow the air gesture.

What is present in the vowels, as I have just indicated, can also be seen in the consonants, can then be seen in the way in which man expresses his spiritual nature in the verbal, in the combination of sentences of the elements of speech or the elements of song.

If all this is then inwardly artistically felt and transferred to human movement, in particular to the most expressive possibility of movement by human arms or hands, then a visible speech or visible singing arises. And we then get a quite definite relation of what then reveals itself to the eye as speech, to that which reveals itself to the ear in hearing in the usual speech or in song. Human beings are organized in such a way that in speaking and singing they leave the rest of the organism unused in a certain sense, and use only a part of the rhythmic, respiratory, and cardiac organism as a foundation that sends its forces into the head organism. The head organism is then the main impulse generator of what lives in the word or in the voice of the song. And everything that comes out of the human heart must, in singing and in spoken language, flow into what we reveal in such a way that only the reflection, the echo of the experience of the heart and thus of the experience of the spirit flows into speech and song. This must be so because finally the whole human organism as a head organism is organized so that what is expressed through the head adapts to earthly life. Human beings, who are actually children of the cosmos at the same time, tear themselves out of the cosmos in that their head organisms are completely adapted to the earthly. But since the organism of the head lives on in speech and song—and receives in a certain sense its impulses only from below by what proceeds from the rhythmic element—human beings, in expressing themselves linguistically or vocally, are essentially the earthly beings which they are between birth and death.

Therefore, in poetry or in composition for song, everything that human beings are by breaking away from earthly, gravitational life must be placed, in a certain sense, between the phonetic and even the tonal. If we take language into consideration, poets, in the way they paint in sounds, in the way they brighten or dull one sound through another, must bring the heart to speak in the way they make the musical rhythm or beat or even the musical theme live, not in what lives in prose sounds but in what lives musically in the succession of sounds. So that one could say: the heart does not live in the sounds; the heart lives in the relationship of the individual sounds, in the movement of the stream of sound. What the poet can achieve in the whole treatment of the sentence or perhaps in the treatment of the stanza, can be situated by eurythmy in the visible language already in the shaping of the individual gesture for the sound itself.

And, furthermore, through this language of eurythmy, which occurs in forms of movement, what is to be expressed is again pushed back into the human soul. Every time, for example, when we pronounce a word that has the sound "A," that is, when we pronounce, let us say, the word *Blatt* [leaf],[283] the fully experienced sensation of this word *Blatt* is based on astonishment or amazement, which in turn is formed in a different way by the other sounds. Every time we vocalize, there is actually such a revelation of the soul as astonishment, as something lovingly rounded, or the like.

But what is ground away in the already conventional language that has become the expression of thought, one might say, in inartistic times, what lives of the soul, of feeling in language—language itself has become strongly prosaic—all this is fully awakened again, when in full articulation the visible possibilities of expression of the human being, which otherwise appear only in the very first rudiments, come to revelation in the articulated gesture and soulfulness of eurythmy. Therefore, simply that which, for example, comes to light in poetry and eurythmy, which can be given in recitation and declamation, can be accompanied by another instrument than the human larynx or other speech organs. If, then, recitation and declamation are accompanied at the same time by eurythmy, it is like the orchestral harmonizing of two different instruments, which in their different revelation can only bring to light the whole rich content of a truly artistic creation.

Basically, when eurythmy is performed and recited at the same time, it is something that can be felt artistically in the soul through the interaction of both. One can therefore also accompany eurythmy through recitation and declamation in such a way that really declamation and recitation are in turn treated artistically as in more artistic epochs than the present one is. Because today one lacks artistic feeling, it is mostly only the prosaic content that is accentuated in recitation and declamation. This is basically an inartistic thing compared to the poetry. Something artistic arises only when the hidden eurythmy already lies in the recitation and declamation itself, when in the artful recitation and declamation of the sounds, in the movements that lie in the sequence of sounds, when everything is awakened that is inner soul movement, elevation or depression of the soul, and so on, when all that occurs, what is considered in the treatment of speech is what lies between the sounds and in the movement of the sounds, not the emphasis of speech.

The difference between the art of dance and eurythmy can be seen if one follows how a musical piece is played on an instrument, in an orchestra, and is accompanied eurythmically. Here we are not dealing with a dance, we are really dealing with a song, which, however, occurs in movements, not in tones. The difference between eurythmy accompanied by music and dance is precisely that in eurythmy everything is pushed back into those impulses of human movement which are embraced with full consciousness, so that in eurythmy the soul actually moves in its limbs, whereas in dance the soul first gives itself to the limbs and the limbs then place themselves in the necessary spatial form. Therefore, in dancing, human beings lose themselves in the movement, whereas in eurythmy, when it accompanies music, they reveal just what holds human beings together soul-spiritually. Therefore, eurythmy is really suggestive in comparison with mime, which also accompanies speech. It is also, in comparison with dance, that which, of all the forms of movement, best grasps the innermost part of the human being. Thus, if we allow the eurythmic to have a correct artistic effect on us, we must still say: In ordinary language, even if it reproduces the poetic, it is so that actually only the heart speaks in a reflection through the head. Eurythmy calls upon the heart to speak through the whole human being and to suppress what is only thinking in the use of language as something unknowable.

One could say: Into the movements which are otherwise concentrated only in the heart, into the movements of the human life-element, the blood, one looks in, and sees what is going on in the total movement, in the total surging and weaving of the blood when speaking. And what we first take into the physical organ of the heart is transmitted from there to the soul as an excitation, so that it flows into the word, and then flows immediately into the movement of the human being, so that one could actually say: if one would follow that which undulates and weaves in the movements of the air when man speaks artistically, if one would follow that up to the heart, so that the heart would appear everywhere in its movements, its sounds, as an echo of the soul.

If one were to follow this directly and, on the other hand, if one were to follow what now attempts to lead outward instead of inward to the heart, if one were to follow this in the forms of the movements of the arms, or in the forms of the whole human being in space, then one would actually find in the vibrations of these eurythmic movements the heart pouring out from the human being into the space of the world in artistic feeling. It is, so to speak, the heart devoted to the world that lives in eurythmy.

All these things clearly still belong to the beginning of the experiment, but there are so many possibilities of development in the shaping of the movements, which will then be revealed as they develop further, that one may really hope that the art of eurythmy will one day, when it is fully developed, be a revelation of the human being, which will itself be an instrument of this art. Eurythmy will one day be able to place itself as a fully entitled younger art alongside the fully entitled older arts. Therefore, today one must still ask the audience for indulgence, but the interest can already be aroused, as it can and could always happen with the emergence of new art forms.

The Imaginative Revelation of Language

Dornach, July 21, 1923[284]

Address at the International Assembly of Delegates of the Anthroposophical Society

The fact that eurythmy originated within the anthroposophical movement is not the least bit arbitrary, even if the immediate occasion for its development seems almost like chance. Eurythmy developed in such a way that it was only in the course of years that its essential character was revealed. The whole process of the development of eurythmy has been such that it could only have emanated from the anthroposophical movement, this movement which is suited to the needs of modern times and which is in keeping with the conditions of the present and near future.

Eurythmy must be looked upon as a quite particular art, an art which arises when an expression of human nature, a revelation of our being, is carried out through movements of the limbs by a single human being or a group of human beings, either standing still or moving in space, in an artistic sense.

I have often called this revelation of the human being "visible speech." It is visible speech insofar as the content of a poem or piece of music may, by means of it, be brought to expression through human gesture based on laws not less exact than those which would be present if the same poem or piece of music were to be expressed through speech or song. Everything that may truly be termed art springs from fundamental sources that must be looked for in the spiritual world. It must be recognized, for instance, that architecture originated from quite definite conceptions of a suprasensory nature. One may call to mind the external fact that the further we look back in time, the more certainly do we find that monuments were erected over burial places. And when we call to mind such thoughts as are bound up with the erection of the tomb, these thoughts would take some such form as this.

We must say to ourselves: We human beings, when regarded in our entirety, do not achieve the goal of our existence by earthly life alone. We forsake the physical body with our actual being when we pass through the gate of death. Our existence is continued beyond the boundary of our life on Earth. The question arises: In what way will we be received by the cosmos when we forsake our physical body? And anyone who is able to perceive as imagination this mystery of the human being, anyone able to solve this riddle imaginatively, will discover that the answer is contained in the forms of the memorial monument or tomb.

A monumental structure erected over a grave is molded in forms that seem to conceal in themselves those lines and directions along which the soul, when released from the body, will wing its way into the wide spaces of the cosmos. The tomb answers for us the question: What is the direction taken by the soul when it forsakes the physical body?

This, of course, is a very radical conception of architecture. The conception of architecture may quite justifiably be widened out so as to include certain buildings necessary for life on Earth. We can then put the question to ourselves in another form, albeit this is more prosaic: If the human being, while on the earth, is obliged to have the protection of some quite definite shelter for the vehicle of his soul during earthly life, what architectural surroundings suited to what he has to do on Earth must he have for his physical body? I can only touch on these things, but I wish to point out by their means how architecture, for instance, has emanated from a suprasensory origin, from a spiritual vision.

And again, when examining sculptural art, one will find that the origin of sculpture lies in the answer to the question: What was the work of the gods on the human form, and what does the human being himself make out of this form during his life on Earth? What in this human form is the gift of the gods? How does the human life of soul influence this divine gift? What the human soul adds to this divine gift is left out of account by the sculptor as not belonging to art. What in the human form is the gift of the gods is what was originally made manifest through sculpture.

It was during an age in which people pondered the question, What are the directions taken by the soul after death? that monumental architecture came into existence. This may still be seen from those Catholic churches in which the altar is a tomb or memorial, and even from the Gothic churches, for these are erected over a tomb. Just as architectural conceptions were originally born out of suprasensory vision, so the conceptions of sculpture arose in an age when people were considering the question: In what way is the human body a gift of the gods?

In the case of each individual art form, it is possible to point out how in the corresponding epoch of time the origin of a particular art form arose out of the raising of human consciousness into suprasensory worlds. And all naturalistic tendencies in art, everything which is not a spiritual inheritance, must be looked upon as signs of decadence, as signals of the downfall of art. From this one can see that the origin of any art can only be traced back to the supra-sensory worlds.

When we examine the special character of our present age, it speaks to us on all sides of the way in which the forces of the subconscious and of the unconscious are weaving and working in human soul-spiritual life. Most people today, however, allow their unconscious life to remain unconscious. Formerly, when people showed a certain tendency in their souls, they simply expressed their trust in the goodness of God, which meant that they were not going to bother any more about it. And today also it must be said of most people who talk about "the unconscious" that they also allow unconscious life to remain unconscious; they are not really troubled about it. On the other hand, it is the task of anthroposophical spiritual knowledge to raise up this unconscious life and unite it with a super-consciousness, to grasp what lives directly in the human being as soul and spirit in its connection with higher spirituality.

In this respect, however, we find that, as a means of human expression, speech can be said to reveal the human being only partially. Speech is, above all, the vehicle of thought; and the way in which thought has developed in our modern civilization has led to the loss of poetry through too much thinking about it. This shows itself most clearly in the fact—in spite of a healthy reaction in this direction—that it is no longer possible to recite or declaim in a way that is really artistic. It is only with years of work and great pains that [Marie] Steiner has succeeded in leading declamation and recitation back to their true form.

A true art of recitation and declamation reveals the essential nature of poetry. For the nature of poetry can only be discovered by those who can echo the words of [Schiller] with full, inner understanding: "When the soul *speaks*, alas! the *soul* is speaking no longer." When the soul comes to the lips, finding expression in words that have long lost their connection with the realities of the universe, then we have prose; we no longer have poetry. We only rediscover poetry when we return to a manner of speech in which the words wing their way in greater or lesser curves, in undulating waves, or lines, sharp and angular, thus forming themselves into the stanza or verse. Such pictures of the imagination as are sought by the true poet must be led over into the rhythms of the iambic or trochaic, into pulse or beat, into the melodic phrase that can transform speech into music. Then we reach something that lies beyond words; whereas most people today emphasize the prosaic element in recitation and declamation—even if, as I have said, a reaction has already set in. Speaking in a broad sense, however, we must hold to the fact that a poem can only be fully understood when the following is borne in mind.

The reciter or declaimer has no means at his disposal other than the utterance of words. All the possibilities of his art lie in the way the words are spoken. Anyone who understands how to listen to recitation or declamation with the ear of an artist feels conjured up within him an impression either imaginative or musical, a picture arising out of the actual sounds of speech, or out of the musical element in speech—both of which are on a far higher level than thought.

Thought is a reflection of sense impressions. We ascend to the suprasensory. When we express thought by means of speech, then, because thought lives in the breath, it calls upon what unites itself with the breath. And with the breath is connected the pulsation of the blood.

The pulsation of the blood, even in its slightest variations, expresses the experiences and perceptions of the soul. It is the expression of the soul's life. Anyone able to enter into these things with true insight is aware that, if we speak, for instance, such a word as *Klingen*,the blood-pulsation during the first syllable, *Kling-*, where there is the *i*-sound, differs from that during the second syllable, where the sound is "*e*." When, with the help of the breath, thought is allowed to stream into words, the pulsation of the blood, the inner movement of the human being, is stimulated. This process continues as long as we remain in the sphere of thought.

If thought clothes itself in pictures, as it can do by means of words, then we are presented with a task that is different from the mere stimulation of the activity of the blood. Nowadays, when anyone speaks the sound "*i*,"[285] it is spoken with the greatest indifference. It is an "*i*" merely, a sound which occurs in so and so many words. But this was not the case when the "*i*" originally appeared in human life, when it was literally wrested out of human nature.

People who were really able to experience the "*i*" would feel the way in which this sound is permeated by the breath, and would also realize the intimate connection of the breath with the pulsation of the blood. They would know that with the utterance of the sound "*i*," the speaker places his own being, as it were, in space. With the sound "*e*,"[286] on the other hand, we feel an inner spiritual experience. When we utter the sound "*o*," we must have the feeling: the spiritual reveals itself to us. For anyone who can feel and experience language, each individual sound transforms itself into a picture, taking on quite definite contours.

Language is rich in feeling, and this manifests itself in the transition from one sound to another. In the course of civilization, we have lost that inner jubilation that should be experienced in the case of certain words. Soberness and indifference have prevailed, and the human life of soul has become sour and morose. That is why, when modern civilization speaks, one frequently feels that words are produced by tongues coated with a mixture of salt and vinegar. In this civilized manner of speaking, articulation has become such that all sounds tend towards a kind of hissing dental sound; they have the effect of a mixture of salt and vinegar on the tongue. But the primal language of humanity was a liquid honey. Language is essentially sweet in its nature, and it is the means by which the human being reveals himself in sound. Poetry today is fettered when it struggles to embody feeling in words; we have lost from language the feeling which it once possessed.

If this feeling is to be reawakened, language as such must be raised to a higher level. We must realize that human speech in all its aspects is, as it were, overshadowed by a heavenly world, wherein the whole content of the human life of soul is expressed in a mighty panorama.

When one gains the possibility of perceiving that archetype of which speech is the shadow, one becomes aware of an imaginative language in which imaginations can be expressed through the microcosm, a little world, through human beings, who are enabled by their form as spatial beings to bring all mysteries to expression.

When one has come to know those imaginations that reveal themselves in their relationship to all the separate forms of speech, one can then pass over to the separate forms of singing. When these are translated into sphere of human movement, we get the art of eurythmy. There is an imaginative revelation of language.

Language today has become intellectualistic. If we go back to the imaginative origin of language—and we must do this, for in each sphere we have to find our way back to what is spiritual—then we shall feel how necessary it is to import imagination into language once more. This can be accomplished by making use, as the most significant means of artistic expression, of the possibilities of human movement in space, of the actual movements in space of human beings themselves. When we wish to give expression to the deeper elements underlying language, we must do more than merely influence the circulation of the blood, which we do in speech owing to the connection between breathing and the blood. We have to enter a realm which soars, as it were, above the head, above thoughts, above abstract language; we must enter the realm of imaginative language. For this we need, not the circulation of the blood merely, which is influenced when we speak even when we are standing still; but we must pass over from the circulation of the blood into the visible movements of the human being himself. Then the gestures in the air which are produced by speech—for we unconsciously impress the imagination into air-gestures—are transformed into *visible gestures*. And these visible gestures are eurythmy.

Eurythmy has arisen out of the very nature of our age, and out of its fundamental needs. Just as one can show how an architectural style had to arise out of one particular epoch, and how sculpture, painting, and music arose in their corresponding epochs, so one day people will understand that eurythmy, this art of human movement, was bound to arise out of our present age.

Thus, even though one emphasizes again and again that eurythmy is only in its beginnings, it must nevertheless be said:

Whoever knows the origin, the source of eurythmy, knows that it is capable of immeasurable perfection. One day it will be included in the series of arts, such arts as painting, sculpture, music, declamation, and so forth—I even count the art of clothing, which has been so terribly mistreated in our time, among the arts—one day eurythmy will be included in the series of arts as a fully justified, younger member among the more established.

Introductory Words to a Presentation of Eurythmy

September 23, 1923

Eurythmy strives to become an art whose means of expression are shaped forms of movement by the human organism in itself and in space, as well as moving groups of performers. However, it is not about mime gestures, and also not about dance movements. Rather, it has to do with an actual, visible speech or visible singing. In speaking and singing, the stream of breath is shaped in a certain way by the human organs. If one studies, through spiritually living intuition, the formation of tones, of vowels, of consonants, of syntax, of verse forms, and so forth, then one can form very specific representations which give rise to sculptural forms accompanying the corresponding revelations of speech or song. These allow themselves to be imitated by the human organism, especially the most expressive organs, through the arms and hands. Thereby, one creates the possibility that what is *heard* in singing or speaking can be *seen*.

Because arms and hands are the most expressive organs, eurythmy consists above all in the shaped movements of these organs. The forms of movement of the other organs then play a supportive role, just as the play of the countenance and regular gesture do in ordinary speech. We can make the difference between eurythmy and dance especially clear if we watch the eurythmic accompaniment of a piece of music. There, what appears as dance is only a secondary matter. The main point is the visible singing that arises through arms and hands.

One should not believe that even a single form of movement in eurythmy is arbitrary. In a specific moment, a definite form of movement must be called forth as the expression of music or poetry, just as in singing a definite tone must be called forth, or in speaking, a definite sound. We are bound every bit as much in the language of movement of eurythmy as we are bound in singing or speaking to tone and sound. But we are just as free in the beautiful, artistic sculpting of eurythmic forms of movement as we are in speech or song.

We are thereby in a position to transform a performed piece of music eurythmically into visible singing, or a recited or declaimed poem into visible speech. And since speech and music stem from the whole human being, their inner content really appears only when the audible or visible revelation is added. For, actually, everything sung and spoken moves the whole of our human nature; in normal life, the tendency to movement is only restrained and localized in the organs of speech and song. Eurythmy only brings to revelation what is always potentially present as the tendency to movement in these human expressions of life, but remains hidden as a mere potential. In a performance of eurythmy to instrumental music and to recitation or declamation, we receive a kind of orchestral harmony of the audible in the visible.

For recitation and declamation that are presented in conjunction with eurythmy, one should note that these should appear in a truly artistic presentation of speech. Reciters or declaimers who only accentuate the prose content of poetry cannot be allowed to collaborate in any eurythmy performance. Truly artistic poetry arises only through the imaginative or musical shaping of speech. The prose content is not what is artistic; rather, only the material upon which the figurative power of speech, or also meter, rhythm, and the structure of verse and so forth should be revealed. Every kind of poetic language is already a hidden eurythmy. The reciter and declaimer must draw forth from poetry out of the pictorial or sculptural elements, out of the musicality of the language what the poet has placed within it. This art of recitation and declamation has been worked upon for years by [Marie] Steiner. Only such an art of speech can appear together with eurythmy, because only then does the reciter offer the ear in the shaping and sculpting of tone what the eurythmist offers to the eye. Only through such a collaboration can what truly lives in poetry be brought before the audience.

Eurythmy is not disposed to the mediated understanding of the intellect, but rather to direct perception. Eurythmists have to learn the visible language form by form, just as we have to learn to speak. But the effect of eurythmy accompanied by music or speech is such as can be immediately felt through mere intuition. It acts like music upon us if we have not actually learned the forms ourselves. For it is a natural, elementary revelation of human nature, whereas language always has something conventional about it.

Eurythmy arose at present just like all the other arts have arisen in their corresponding epochs. The other arts arose when one brought a soul content to revelation through the respective artistic means. When one finally accomplished mastery of certain media so that what the soul experienced could be brought to sensory revelation, then there arose an art form. Eurythmy is now coming into being in that we are learning to master as an instrument the noblest of media—namely, the human organism itself, this microcosm. This happens both in mime and in dance only with reference to parts of the human organism. Eurythmy, however, makes use of the whole human being as its means of expression.

However, I still must appeal to the indulgence of the audience before such a presentation. Every art has had some time to progress through a beginning stage. Eurythmy must do this as well. It is in the beginning of its development. But because it makes use of the most perfect instrument imaginable, it must bear boundless potential for development. The human organism is this most perfect instrument, and it is in truth a microcosm that contains in concentrated form all the laws and mysteries of the cosmos. If we reveal as a language, through the shaping of movement, what our being contains as a comprehensive potential, then we must thereby be capable of bringing the mysteries of the cosmos to artistic presentation.

What eurythmy can already offer at the moment is only a beginning of the possibilities that lie in this direction. But because it makes use of the means of expression that can have such a relationship to the world and human beings, we can hope that in its further development, eurythmy will take its place as a fully justified art form beside the others.

The Position of Eurythmy among the Arts

Dornach, December 28, 1923[287]

At our last eurythmy performance the day before yesterday, I made a few remarks concerning the relation of what one might call this moving sculpture, eurythmy, to our conventional, resting sculpture. Eurythmy is an art that has to do with the moving human being; it uses the dispositions to movement that have been found within the human organism and brought out as meaningful speech. With eurythmy, a new art form has appeared that can be extended and developed in the most manifold ways, and as it gradually unfolds, it can be connected with the other arts, even confronting them with this or that significant contrast.

I have pointed out that in eurythmy, we see moving sculpture. Eurythmy can also be described in another way. If one seeks the arts that are most closely associated with human speech, one realizes that, in contrast to speech, music and song must be thought of as reaching into our inner life. And indeed, when the human soul gives itself up to the melodies and harmonies of music, the significance of this musical involvement lies in the fact that music does not relate to anything so definitely as does speech. One can even say that the conscious path from musical activity to speech activity is, in a sense, a process of waking up. When we speak, we feel awakened as compared to our feeling in the musical element.

It cannot be denied, however, that waking and sleeping are relative concepts. One who has formerly had no experience of the spiritual world, but who gradually gains such a connection, feels at first that, compared to daily life, experience of the spiritual world is like sleeping. [Jan] Stuten[288] mentioned something similar this morning. If, however, we maintain complete presence of mind as we proceed from ordinary day consciousness into the other world, we experience, in what for another person is sleep, actually a higher level of wakefulness. Thus we can also say that when someone begins to experience the more extensive, cosmic significance of music as compared to mere speech, we can regard this experience likewise as an awakening. One can think of a melody being more and more compressed and squeezed together in time. Then, finally, through the intensity of the compression, a vowel or a consonant can actually result. Then the music that lies inherent in the speech is no longer perceived; the speech sound is in reality a melodic or harmonic element that has been compressed. Just as one can feel this objectively about the relation of music to speech, one can also express it by saying that music is nearer to human feeling, while poetry is nearer to human thought. And the expression of thought, of inner pictures, is what resides in the linguistic element with regard to poetry.

We can also raise up perception itself. The senses themselves that do the perceiving lie still farther outside than thought—that is, at the very periphery—and this can also be raised to an artistic level. In music, we live in a sea of flowing spirit, as it were. In speech, it is as if we had reached the shore of the spiritual sea. Thought is what lives on the shore between water and earth. But when we come out of the water and really give ourselves over entirely to the sensory world, at the same time perceiving the spirit in it, we attain something that does not live through speech, but can only be made visible by the sign that lives within the human being. We reach eurythmy.

As I was able to say the day before yesterday that eurythmy is a moving sculpture. Today I can say that entirely within the human body there weaves the musical. Music is the artistic formation of the world of feeling. Somewhat nearer to the human periphery lies the poetic element. It is the formation of the world of artistic language. Outside of the world of thought, when we are already transcending ourselves, we live in perception. What is experienced not sensually but spiritually in perception is given by eurythmy. Thus, in perceiving the movements of the eurythmist, we ought actually to sense everywhere nature itself. And whoever senses nature, but spirit in nature, perceives eurythmy correctly.

We can imagine that someone seeing eurythmy might say: That eurythmic movement reminds me of an impression I had the other day when I was walking through the woods, of a fir tree swaying in the wind. If we do not simply keep to this feeling but later are able to say: Yes, eurythmy has finally given me an explanation of that fir tree; it is not standing there just to be a fir tree; it is one letter in the eternal Word that surges and weaves through the world; eurythmy explains to me how the fir tree speaks, how the spring speaks, how the lightning speaks, and so on.

This present age only uses the word "explanation" for what is given in the form of ideas as abstract concepts. But nature is not so poor or so horribly shadowy as our abstract concepts. And with regard to nature we should not believe that we in any way capture it by forcing it into this web of concepts, through which we have described it. Nature is endlessly rich, not merely extensively but also intensively. Nature is not merely rich in quantities; it is also rich in qualities. If we want to come close to her, we must make a much stronger effort than simply using our heads. Our heads know little about a fir tree. We have to bring our organism into movement, everything that is in us, if we want to bring forth from ourselves vitally the mystery of spiritual nature in every individual thing and every individual process. Only when we are able to create something out of nature through ourselves, which then arouses a feeling of awe in us for what the cosmos has formed through us, with us, in us—only then do we climb up to a truly artistic level, the level from which every art in the history of the world has grown. Out of such a mood we will also learn how to look up to a new art form such as eurythmy.

Particularly where anthroposophy is being cultivated, there should be serious concern that artistic work—especially a new artistic endeavor such as eurythmy—will be understood, be understood with warm sympathy, for in recent times, art has suffered considerably. Because people only value the knowledge they acquire from dry, sober concepts, art has gradually become a luxury of life. If this continues, a frightful philistinism will spread over the Earth. Humanity will inevitably have a benighted future unless a really fresh, new art is created from artistic sources still untapped. That is what we have tried to do here in our own field of work with eurythmy. And we yearn that the right feeling for the artistic importance of this new art should arise within the Anthroposophical Society! But one has to realize that art is creative out of its very being, and that one falls short of art the moment one begins to "illustrate."

You can have poetry that is recited or declaimed in the proper style accompanied by eurythmy. They belong together: eurythmy, in which the whole human organism is involved in movement, and recitation or declamation, concentrated for their delivery in a particular series of organs. Each of these arts has the possibility of developing a substantive life independently. But they will work together as heart and head work together in the human organism because, although they are quite different from each other, they are organized for each other.

Moreover, you can accompany instrumental music, which is revealed through the objective musical instrument, separated from the human being, with eurythmy. We have found this tone eurythmy ourselves. But you cannot do eurythmy to singing! If you did, you would only be illustrating the song through its musical content, which is something decidedly inartistic. Mere illustration is definitely inartistic. Perhaps someday, in addition to the song, or, if you will, the song accompanied by an instrument, one will also want to perform eurythmy, but it will have to be something entirely different from our present tone eurythmy and speech eurythmy. Certainly, the arts can work together, but because the wish has been expressed to do eurythmy to singing, I am obliged to speak of it. If a person really understands that in our tone eurythmy there is already singing through the movements themselves, that eurythmy is itself singing to this or that instrument or even to the orchestra, then that person will not want the singing to be doubled! That is the whole point of the matter.

So now I have again attempted to say something that perhaps is suited to point to the essence of eurythmy. I want to make an effort on the occasion of such performances, when our dear friends have gathered as they have here, to contribute something for the cultivation, the celebration, and to help further what pours forth from our sources.

The Art of Eurythmy

February 10, 1924

A visible language built up out of the human being underlies the art of eurythmy. This is revealed in movements that individual performers carry out through their limbs or that groups of people perform. We are not dealing here with a gestural, mimic, or dance-like movement, but rather with a genuine language that stands as far removed from dance, mime, and gesture as does song or spoken language itself. Individual experiences of the soul, a sensation or feeling, are not here brought together arbitrarily with a form of movement. Rather, the movement-potentials inherent in the organic structuring of the whole human organism are formed into a means of expression, just as this happens with an individual group of organs [larynx, etc.] in song and speech. And there follow from this the individual movements, just like tones and sounds in singing and speaking.

The movements that are revealed in eurythmy are also present as potentials in singing and speech (both as organic and cognitive tendencies), but there they are already transformed *in statu nascendi* into those movements that the organs of singing and speech execute. These potentials are grasped in eurythmy through sensory-suprasensory intuition. Thereby the whole human being is made into a visibly expressive organism of singing or speech.

In human language, thought and will come to expression. Thinking inhabits the artistic element thereby. In the poetic treatment of speech, the faculty of thinking is brought back to the volitional elements in meter, rhythm, figures, and so forth. Eurythmy carries this transformation through to the end. The moving human being becomes a revelation of the soul and spirit. On the one hand, eurythmy can be accompanied by music. Then it is visible singing. On the other hand, it can be accompanied by recitation and declamation. Then the true artistic and poetic content comes to immediate intuition. When they accompany eurythmy, recitation and declamation are required to restrain themselves from all prosaic accentuation of the content of the poem. Instead, they have to allow the figurative and musical, thus the genuinely artistic, to come to the fore. Besides an artistic side, eurythmy also has therapeutic and educational applications. In these, the forms that are expressed in eurythmy as an art are correspondingly transformed. We believe that this art form, which is today still at the beginning of its development, is capable of unlimited perfecting, for, in a more comprehensive sense than in other art forms, its instrument is man himself.

THE ART OF SCULPTURE AND EURYTHMY

Dornach, February 11, 1924[289]

Whoever seeks through an anthroposophical approach of the kind cultivated here at the Goetheanum to pursue the relationships between all of the potential movements of the human organism and what comes to expression in spoken language, finds not only analogies but entirely lawful connections. So that one really can say: Someone who knows these relationships actually divines, let us say, from the way that someone enters, whether it is more with the heels or with the toes, whether they bend the knee more or less and so on, what kind of particular stylization of language that person has. For it is not only the arm and hand that express themselves in the actual thinking organs that underlie all language. Rather, it is the whole human being, particularly in the intonation of speech. Whether one has a high or low pitch is expressed in the movements of the feet and the legs. The whole articulation of the poem comes to expression in the inner structure, in the rhythmic structure, even the grammatical structure, that one bestows upon one's language. Actually, the whole human being has flowed into the language. One can indeed say: In that this is so, one can contrast this eurythmy with the art of sculpture, which reveals human inwardness through the stillness of the human form. And whoever has a feeling for it will feel in the sculptural work which depicts the human being what kind of temperament, what kind of character, indeed under certain circumstances what kind of mood, inclinations, passions are in the soul that is being depicted. But one always has the feeling that it is the quiet, the silent soul, that appears in the art of sculpture.

If the soul speaks, however, then it will not reveal the quiet human form, but rather the human being in movement. Thus one can say: The art of sculpture depicts the silent soul in all its peculiarity, while eurythmy depicts the inwardly speaking soul.

Dornach, May 3, 1924 (excerpt)[290]

Indeed, we have a kind of moving sculpture. Sculpture, which is depicted at rest, actually represents the silent soul. Whoever is able to contemplate something like that in a disinterested way, senses the silent soul in sculptural works. By employing the human being here as an instrument, we bring the soul directly into gesture. In the expression that we give the human being, we make it visible. Thus the art of sculpture is the revelation of the silent soul, and eurythmy is the revelation of the speaking soul.

[Untitled}

Dornach, May 11, 1924[291]

For some time, we have been trying to create a more and more perfect form of eurythmy in the succession of lighting effects that occur on the stage. These would ideally be continuations of what happens through moving individuals or groups of people. Thus one should not look at this as something "significant" in the trivial sense, but rather as something artistic. We can also already bring much into the whole staging, but gradually we hope to bring even more.

When, for example, it suddenly becomes bright on the stage while a poem is recited and eurythmy is performed, this brightening does not occur because it stands in the poem. It is not as though the sun, for example, breaks forth. Rather, it is because in the treatment of language something of the nature of light emerges at this point. And so with this eurythmic lighting, one should look to the way the illuminations follow upon one another, just as the tones in music form a melody and so forth.

But we know that we stand at the beginning. A short while ago, I sought to elaborate tone eurythmy by a little bit by holding a course for tone eurythmy in the School of Spiritual Science. It was a course devoted particularly to tone eurythmy. As I said, we stand at the beginning, and in this regard we are our own worst critics.

The Speech Eurythmy Course

Article from the Newsletter *of July 20, 1924*[292]

In the period from June 24 to July 12, a course on speech eurythmy was held at the Goetheanum. The content of the course was a repeated presentation of much that had been given in this field and at the same time a deepening and broadening of what was already known. The artists who practice eurythmy as an art at the Goetheanum and subsequently in many other places, those who teach in this field, the teachers of the Eurythmy School founded and directed by Marie Steiner in Stuttgart, the teachers of eurythmy at the Waldorf School and the School of Continuing Education at the Goetheanum, therapeutic eurythmists, and a number of other personalities who, through their profession as artists or scientists, are interested in eurythmy in different fields, took part in the course.

Eurythmy makes it possible to bring the artistic as such in its essence and its origins to visibility. This was a particular focus of this course. Only those can work as artists in eurythmy who creatively develop a sense of art out of an inner calling and inner enthusiasm. In order to reveal the possibilities of form and movement inherent in the human organization, it is necessary that the soul be completely filled with art. This universal character of eurythmy was the basis of all presentations.

Whoever wants to do eurythmy must have penetrated into the essence of speech formation. Above all, he must have come to the secrets of the creation of sounds. In every sound, there is an expression for an experience of the soul. In the vocalic sound, such an expression is given for a revelation of the soul in thinking, feeling, and willing. In the consonantal sound, an expression is given for the way in which the soul makes an external thing or a process into something concrete.

This expression in language remains for the most part completely subconscious in ordinary speech. Eurythmists must get to know it in a very exact way, for they have to transform what becomes audible in speech into still and moving gestures. Thus the inner structure of language was uncovered in this course. The phonetic meaning of the word, which everywhere underlies the conceptual meaning, was made clear. From the eurythmic gesture, many things in the laws of language can be brought to light, which at present, when speech is carried out in a strongly abstract state of mind, are little recognized. This has been done in this course. Thereby, it may be hoped, it will also have given teachers of eurythmy the guidelines they need.

Eurythmists need to devote themselves to the smallest of gestures, so that their presentation really becomes a self-evident expression of the soul. They can only form the large gesture when this smallest thing has first become conscious and then, eventually, has become a habitual expression of the soul's being.

We have considered how the gesture as such reveals soul experience and spiritual content, and also how this revelation relates to the expression of the soul that is realized audibly in spoken language. In eurythmy, one can learn to appreciate the technique of art, but it is also in eurythmy that one can be deeply penetrated by the way in which technique must shed all externality and be completely seized by the spiritual, if the truly artistic is to live. People who are active in any field of art often speak of how the soul should work behind the technique, but the truth is that the soul must be active in the technique.

In these lectures, special emphasis was placed on showing that the aesthetically sensitive person perceives the soul directly in a very clear way in the truly formed gesture. Examples were given which illustrated how a content in the soul's constitution can be seen in a certain form of gesture in a self-evident way.

It was also shown how all forms of speech, which are revealed in grammar, syntax, rhythm, poetic tropes and figures, in rhyme and stanzaic structure, also find their corresponding realization in eurythmy.

The participants in this course should not only be supported in the knowledge of eurythmy, but they should experience how all art must be carried by love and enthusiasm. Eurythmists cannot detach their artistic creation from themselves and present it objectively to the aesthetic connoisseur as the painter or sculptor does. Rather, they remain personally within their presentation; one sees in them whether art lives in them like a divine, cosmic content or not. In the immediate artistic present, the eurythmist must be able to present the artistic to the human being as visible beingness. This requires a special inward and intimate relationship to art. The course wanted to help the participants understand this. It wanted to show how feeling, sensation is ignited in the soul when beholding the gesture, and how this sensation then leads to the experience of the visible word. Much that can only be imperfectly expressed in the audible word can be brought to full revelation through the eurythmic gesture. The audible word in recitation and declamation together with the visible word then gives a total expression, which can bring about the most intense artistic unity.

❀

List of Abbreviations

CW — the Collected Works of Rudolf Steiner in English

CW 260 — The Christmas Conference for the Foundation of the General Anthroposophical Society 1923/1924: The Laying of the Foundation Stone: Lectures and Addresses; Discussion of the Statutes: Dornach, 24 December to 1 January 1924 (Hudson, NY: Anthroposophic Press, 1990).

CW 277A — Eurythmy: Its Birth and Development, trans. Alan Stott (Weobly, Herefordshire: Anastasi, 2002). Some items from GA 277a are included in CW 277b, CW 277c and CW 277d.

CW 277B — the present volume.

CW 277C — The Early History of Eurythmy: Rehearsals and Performances of Rudolf Steiner's Mystery Dramas, of the Oberufer Christmas Plays and of Goethe's Faust: Addresses, Notes, Programs and Chronologies, ed., transl. and intro. Frederick Amrine (Great Barrington, MA: Steiner Books, 2014).

GA — Gesamtausgabe, the complete works of Rudolf Steiner in nearly 400 volumes, published by the Rudolf Steiner Verlag, still incomplete. This is the standard edition in German, and even scholarship in languages other than German will often refer to it.

GA 36 — Der Goetheanumgedanke inmitten der Kulturkrisis der Gegenwart: Gesammelte Aufsätze aus der Wochenschrift «Das Goetheanum» 1921-1925, 2nd edn. (Dornach: Rudolf Steiner Verlag, 1993). This volume has not been translated into English.

GA 40 — Wahrspruchworte, 9th edn. (Dornach: Rudolf Steiner Verlag, 2005), which has been translated partially as Breathing the Spirit: Meditations for Times of the Day and Seasons of the Year (Sophia Books, 2007). Breathing the Spirit does not include the address of August 29, 1915.

GA 260A Die Konstitution der Allgemeinen Anthroposophischen Gesellschaft und der Freien Hochschule für Geisteswissenschaft: Der Wiederaufbau des Goetheanum, 2nd revised and expanded edition (Dornach: Rudolf Steiner Verlag, 1987). GA 260a includes material that was originally intended to be included in GA 37, but that number never was issued. GA 260a has not been translated into English.

GA 277 Eurythmie: Die Offenbarung der sprechenden Seele: Eine Fortbildung der Goetheschen Metamorphosenanschauung im Bereich der menschlichen Bewegung: Ansprachen zu Eurythmie-Aufführungen aus den Jahren 1918 bis 1924 mit Notizbucheintragungen und dazugehörigen Programmen (Dornach: Rudolf Steiner Verlag, 1972). Reprinted in 1980 and 1999. Not previously translated into English. See CW 277b, CW 277c, and CW 277d above.

GA 277A Die Entstehung und Entwickelung der Eurythmie (Dornach: Verlag der Rudolf Steiner-Nachlaßverwaltung, 1965). Revised 2nd edition 1982; 3rd edition 1998. Thoroughly revised 5th edition 2022. See CW 277a above.

GA 279 Eurythmy as Visible Speech (London: Rudolf Steiner Press, 1984).

GA 301 Die Erneuerung der pädagogisch-didaktischen Kunst durch Geisteswissenschaft, 4th edn. (Dornach: Rudolf Steiner Verlag, 1991). The latest English translation is: The Renewal of Education, Foundations of Waldorf Education 9, trans. Robert F. Lathe and Nancy Parks Whittaker, intro. Eugene Schwartz (Great Barrington: Anthroposophic Press, 2001). This translation is also available from Amazon as a Kindle e-book. There is also a somewhat older British translation of this volume: The Renewal of Education through the Science of the Spirit, trans. Roland Everett (Forest Row: Steiner Schools Fellowship Publications, 1981). This volume contains, in addition to the addresses on Eurythmy listed below, fourteen lectures presented to Swiss teachers in Basel from 20 April to 11 May 1920.

HAHN An Introduction to Eurythmy: Talks given before sixteen eurythmy performances, translated by Gladys Hahn (Hudson, NY: Anthroposophic Press, 1984). This selection includes one address from GA 277a, plus fifteen others that had been published prior to the first editions of GA 277a (1965) and GA 277 (1972) under the title Eurythmie als Impuls für künstlerisches Betätigen und Betrachten (Dornach: Rudolf Steiner-Nachlaßverwaltung, 1953).

XR unpublished in German, but marked by the editors of GA 277 as a "repetition," presumably of an address included in either GA 277 or GA 277a.

[XR] published in German, but outside the GA, and not included in either GA 277 or GA 277a, presumably because it was felt to be a "repetition."

XT unpublished, awaiting transcription

XX unpublished in German because no transcript exists

* abridged

Endnotes

1 GA 277a, 5th ed., pp. 341–48; also in GA 40, pp. 61–69 (complete). The new translation of this important early address is heavily indebted to previous versions by G. Karnow and A. Wulsin (Rudolf Steiner, *Twelve Moods* [Spring Valley, NY: Mercury Press, 1984]), and by Alan Stott [CW 277a, pp. 158–60].

2 *Entwerden*, literally "un-becoming" or "devolution." This neologism was coined by the Rhineland mystics (see the following note) to capture the goal of their striving for oneness with God.

3 Here Steiner adduces two members of the great trinity of "Rhineland" mystics: Eckhart or Eckhart of Hochheim (*c.* 1260–*c.* 1327) and his students Johannes Tauler (*c.* 1300–*c.* 1361) and Heinrich Suso or Seuse (*c.* 1300–1366). Of the three, Meister Eckhart was the profoundest by far: his thinking is sophisticated and his language is intensely poetic. Many consider him an important philosopher as well.

4 *in ihrer Fülle*, literally "in its fullness."

5 John 1:1

6 *Gerippe*, literally "skeleton."

7 The text printed in the 3rd edition of GA 277a, as translated by Stott in CW 277a, has deleted everything from this point through the beginning of the seventh paragraph, "What are we trying to accomplish...?" The 5th edition of 2022 has restored this omission.

8 Based on the translation by Hans and Ruth Pusch in *Twelve Moods* (Mercury Press, 1984).

9 The seven lines of each verse go with the planets in this sequence: Sun, Venus, Mercury, Mars, Jupiter, Saturn, Moon.

10 *wesend*, a strong neologism in the form of a present participle founded upon another neologism, the implied gerund *wesen*, "to enact Being."

11 *Libra*, from Latin, meaning "scales." In German, Libra is called simply *die Waage* (the scales).

12 *Auftakte*: movements, forms, and gestures performed by eurythmists before a poem as a kind of introduction to the mood of the whole piece.

13 Jan Stuten (1890–1948) later composed music for the "Twelve Moods."

14 GA 277, pp. 564–65. See the related piece of April 3, 1921.

15 *Palmström.—Das erste Gedicht: Das böhmische Dorf.* Steiner may have been holding up the book containing the poems to be performed.

16 Steiner's architectural masterpiece, which was burned to the ground by an arsonist of New Year's Eve 1922/1923. See the note on the address of January 25, 1924.

17 GA 277, pp. 23–26.

18 The materials relating to the origins of eurythmy have been collected and published as CW 277a, *Eurythmy: Its Birth and Development*, trans. Alan Stott (Anastasi, 2002).

19 See Rudolf Steiner, "Das Goetheanum in seinen zehn Jahren" [The Goetheanum after a decade] (Dornach, 1961), which was originally published in the newsletter of the Anthroposophical Society, *Das Goetheanum.*

20 *als Begleiter des Wortes*. Already in 1908 Steiner asked the painter Margarita Woloschin, hinting at the possibility of eurythmy, whether she could dance the opening of the Gospel of St. John. Hence another possible translation resonates here (which would be identical in German, given that all German nouns are capitalized): "to accompany the Word."

21 *Bildekräfteleib*. This is one of Steiner's later, anthroposophical terms for the etheric body.

22 GA 277, pp. 30–34.

23 Clara Smits-Mess'oud Bey (1863–1948). See CW 277a, *Eurythmy: Its Birth and Development*, trans. Alan Stott (Anastasi, 2002).

24 Goethe, entry of September 5, 1787, in *Italian Journey*, trans. W. H. Auden and Elizabeth Mayer (1970; London: Penguin, 1992).

25 *veranlagt*, a word that usually refers to an inherent psychological disposition or talent.

26 "As something that become visible" is a very free translation of the fraught German phrase *für sich*, which has a long and subtle history within German Idealism. The term was borrowed by Hegel from Fichte

to signify consciousness laboring under the subject-object split. The dialectical progression is from "*an sich*" to "*für sich*" to "*an-und-für-sich*."

27 "And represent that only" is an interpretive translation of a single German word here, the adverb *ganz* ("completely," "entirely," "thoroughly") modifying what corresponds to "are images."

28 Goethe, journal entry, Rome, January 28, 1787, in *Italian Journey*:

The second line of inquiry is concerned exclusively with the art of the Greeks: What was the process by which these incomparable artists evolved from the human body the circle of divine formation that is perfectly complete, and in which not one incidental, essential, or transitional feature was lacking? My instinct tells me that they followed the same laws as Nature, and I believe I am on the track of these.

29 GA 277, pp. 47–51.

30 Goethe, *The Metamorphosis of Plants* (1790). The English-language edition of choice is now Johann Wolfgang von Goethe, *The Metamorphosis of Plants*, trans. Douglas Miller (Cambridge, MA: MIT Press, 2009), with an introduction and beautiful color photographs of the species Goethe describes by Gordon L. Miller.

31 GA 277, pp. 52–57.

32 *Maxims and Reflections*, no. 719: "Beauty is a manifestation of secret natural laws, which would have remained hidden from us forever had they not appeared as art."

33 *Offenbarung*, the German theological term for "revelation."

34 *das Werden und Weben des pflanzlichen Organismus*, literally "the becoming and weaving of the vegetal organism."

35 Goethe, *The Metamorphosis of Plants* (1790). The English-language edition of choice is now Johann Wolfgang von Goethe, *The Metamorphosis of Plants* (Cambridge, Massachusetts: MIT Press, 2009), trans. Douglas Miller, with an introduction and beautiful color photographs of the species Goethe describes by Gordon L. Miller.

36 From Goethe's essay, "Simple Imitation, Manner, Style," in *Essays on Art and Literature*, ed. John Geary, vol. 3 of *Goethe: The Collected Works* (Cambridge, Massachusetts: Suhrkamp, 1986; reprint Princeton University Press), p. 72.

37 Many consider the German art historian and classical archaeologist Johann Joachim Winckelmann (1717–1768) to be the founder of modern art history, and Goethe was among the first to appreciate his importance. Goethe's essay is a widely admired classic. For more on Winckelmann himself, see Alex Potts, *Flesh and the Ideal: Winckelmann and the Origins of Art History* (New Haven: Yale University Press, 1994).

38 Here Steiner is quoting Goethe's aforementioned essay directly.

39 GA 277, pp. 58–61. This new translation is indebted to Hahn, pp. 7–10.

40 *Gemütsbewegungen*, movements of the *Gemüt*, a word with no English equivalent that refers simultaneously to one's thinking, feeling, sensibility, and temperament, all bundled up together.

41 GA 277, pp. 64–69. Revision of a translation originally published in Hahn, pp. 11–16.

42 The quote is from Goethe's essay on Winckelmann. See the note on the address of March 13, 1919.

43 That is, the Goetheanum.

44 "The eurythmy term for choreography." [Hahn]

45 Goethe's verse play *Iphigenia in Tauris* was completed in 1786. Goethe, *Verse Plays and Epic*, Collected Works, vol. 8 (Princeton UP, 1995).

46 GA 277, pp. 72–77.

47 Founded in Stuttgart, Germany, in 1919 by Emil Molt, and led by Rudolf Steiner until his death [in 1925]. After the ceremonial opening of the School, Emil Molt wrote to Marie Steiner: "Now that the Waldorf School has been founded, and eurythmy has become a central component of the curriculum, we entreat you cordially to direct the instruction and to help in the teaching through frequent visits."

48 From Goethe's essay on Winckelmann:

> In that we human beings have been placed at the pinnacle of nature, we see ourselves as a whole nature unto ourselves, within which it is our task to raise up another peak. We climb upward towards that goal by permeating ourselves with all perfections and virtues—we summon all the discretion, order,

harmony and meaning that we can, and eventually we rise up to the production of the work of art.

49 Steiner is alluding to the lecture "The Seven World Riddles," given by du Bois-Reymond before the Berlin Academy of Sciences in 1880. Emil du Bois-Reymond (1818–1896), an important German scientist who is credited with having founded the discipline of electrophysiology.

50 GA 277, pp. 87–88.

51 From *Goethe's Sayings in Prose:* "The Idea is eternal and unique: it is mistaken to use this word in the plural as well. Everything of which we are aware and about which we can speak is a manifestation of the Idea. What we express are concepts, and in that sense the Idea is itself a concept." Goethe published these in 1819. A good English-language edition of this and other similar material was edited by D. J. Enright under the title *The Sayings of Goethe* (London: Duckworth, 1996).

52 See CW 2, *Goethe's Theory of Knowledge: An Outline of the Epistemology of His Worldview* (Great Barrington, Massachusetts: SteinerBooks, 2008), where Steiner argues that the organic cannot be reduced to the inorganic and requires a completely different approach.

53 GA 277, pp. 92–112.

54 Before the beginning of the performance, the lights went out in the Carpenters' Shed, where Steiner was holding the lecture, for an extended period of time.

55 The predecessor to the School for Spiritual Science that was founded in 1924 by Rudolf Steiner. The School for Spiritual Science is organized into departments, called "sections," for the purpose of conducting spiritual-scientific research within various fields of human endeavor.

56 See Wassily Kandinsky, *Concerning the Spiritual in Art* (New York: Dover, 1977). Kandinsky and the other members of The Blue Rider were students of Steiner's in Munich before the outbreak of World War I.

57 *beweisen*, to "demonstrate" or "prove" in the sense of logic or rigorous science.

58 *Knowledge of the Higher Worlds* (CW 10), also published as *How to Know Higher Worlds.*

59 Nicolaus Copernicus (1473–1543) was the first astronomer to publish a comprehensive and persuasive heliocentric account of the universe, *On the Revolutions of the Heavenly Spheres* (1543).

Galileo Galilei (1564–1642), the Italian physicist, astronomer, and philosopher, is of course better known by his first name in the English-speaking world.

Giordano Bruno (1548–1600), an Italian Dominican philosopher, scientist, and theologian, was burned at the stake by the Catholic Church on February 17, 1600. See the classic study by Frances Yates, *Giordano Bruno and the Hermetic Tradition* (Chicago: U of C Press, 1964).

60 An important cosmogonic theory known as the "nebular hypothesis," and the ancestor of our contemporary "solar nebular disk model." It hypothesizes that the solar system was formed when a primordial nebula began to spin and formed planets through the resultant centrifugal force. Many found the explanation compelling because it seemed to explain the planets' circular and roughly coplanar orbits moving in the same direction as the Sun's rotation. It was first expounded fully by Immanuel Kant in his *Universal Natural History and Theory of the Heavens* [1755; multiple English editions available]. Pierre-Simon, marquis de Laplace (1749–1827), the great French mathematician and astronomer who extended the Newtonian paradigm in his five-volume *Celestial Mechanics* (1799–1825) and other writings, developed the same theory independently and published it in his *System of the World* [1796; many English translations available]. Steiner often derides this hypothesis, so often demonstrated in school classrooms, for failing to account for the teacher-demiurge who sets the nebula in motion in the first place.

61 Herman Grimm (1828–1901), the son of the famous linguist and folklorist Wilhelm Grimm, wrote extensively on literature and the history of art. He was widely read in the later nineteenth century. See Herman Grimm, "Studium der Naturwissenschaften – Die natürliche Tochter – Die Wahlverwandtschaften" [Study of the natural sciences – The natural daughter – The elective affinities], lecture 23 in *Goethe: Vorlesungen an der Universität in Berlin* [Gothe: Lectures at the University in Berlin], vol. 2 (Cotta, 1903), pp. 160–199.

62 The allusion is to Plato's *Phaedo* 87c–e.

63 *Maxims and Reflections*, No. 720.

64 The reference is to the lifting of the veil of Isis. See Pierre Hadot, *The Veil of Isis: An Essay on the History of the Idea of Nature* (Cambridge, Massachusetts: Harvard UP, 2006).

65 The quote is from Goethe's essay on Winckelmann; see the note on the address of March 13, 1919.

66 The German original has "two scenes" here, but there is only one scene entitled "Midnight" [lines 11384–11510], so presumably it was two separate episodes within this (relatively short) scene that were performed. This would fit with Steiner's description of the program as a "sample" [*Probe*] rather than a full performance.

67 Goethe's *Italian Journey*, entry dated Rome, January 28, 1787:

> The second line of inquiry is concerned exclusively with the art of the Greeks: What was the process by which these incomparable artists evolved from the human body the circle of divine formation, which was completely enclosed, and where not one incidental, essential, or transitional feature was lacking? My instinct tells me that they followed the same laws as Nature, and I believe I am on the track of these.

68 Goethe, *Verse Plays and Epic*, Collected Works, vol. 8 (Princeton University Press, 1995).

69 Theodor Vischer (1807–1887), most famous as the author of a ponderous treatise on aesthetics that appeared in four volumes from 1846–1854. He also lampooned the second part of Goethe's *Faust* in his own imagined continuation, *Faust: Part Three* (1886). Steiner refers to him as many contemporaries apparently did, as "the Swabian Vischer" or "V-Vischer" in order to distinguish him from the many scholars named Fischer (both variants are pronounced the same in German).

70 *höhere Töchter*, "young ladies" (as opposed to lower class women), literally "higher daughters." Steiner then mocks Vischer by calling him a "higher Philistine." This doesn't work in English so I have substituted a similar English idiom that would have the same appeal to a working-class audience.

71 Translated by Burley Channer.

72 Adolf von Wilbrandt (1837–1911), Artistic Director of the Burgthe-

ater in Vienna from 1881 to 1887.

73 Otto Devrient (1838–1894), directed Goethe's *Faust I and II* in Weimar, 1876.

74 Eduard Lassen (1830–1904), composer, set Goethe's *Faust* to music.

75 *hineingeheimnißen*, literally "insert as a mystery into"; here Steiner echoes a famous neologism Goethe used with reference to the composition of *Faust*.

76 See the note above. The actual title of this scene is simply "At Midnight" [*Um Mitternacht*]; in Arndt's definitive English translation, it is simply "Midnight" (Johann Wolfgang von Goethe, *Faust: A Tragedy*, 2nd revised edition [New York: Norton, 2001], p. 323).

77 In this scene from the Second Part of *Faust*, the Four Gray Crones appear as avenging furies. One of them, Care, breathes on Faust, blinding him.

78 GA 277a, (3rd ed., 1998) pp. 116–19. This translation is heavily indebted to Alan Stott's [CW 277a, pp. 118–21].

79 See T. S. Eliot: "It seems to me that Goethe had a compass of consciousness which far surpassed that of his nineteenth-century contemporaries. Rudolf Steiner expressly upheld this, and I do too" Nordwest-Deutscher Rundfunk [Northwest German Radio] (September 1959). Note by Alan Stott in CW 277a, p. 211.

80 Here Steiner is paraphrasing the quote from Goethe's essay on Winckelmann that recurs throughout the addresses. See the note on the address of March 13, 1919.

81 The program for December 14 indicates that the four poems were performed by Tatiana Kisseleff.

82 Luke Howard (1772–1864), a British scientist who has been called "the father of meteorology." He first proposed what has become the basic nomenclature for clouds in 1802, and then published his definitive account as *Essay on the Modification of Clouds* in 1803. Howard's work inspired not only Goethe but many other artists as well.

83 Revision of Hahn, pp. 23–27. The German original was not included in either GA 277 or GA 277a.

84 The quote is from Goethe's essay on Winckelmann: see the note on the address of March 13, 1919.

85 Johann Gottfried Herder (1744–1803) was one of the most seminal thinkers of the eighteenth century. Goethe was still a student when he met Herder by chance in Strasbourg; the older man would become his most important mentor. How appropriate that the name of the inn where they met was *Zum Geist*, "At the Sign of the Spirit"! Isaiah Berlin's study *Vico and Herder: Two Studies in the History of Ideas* (New York: Viking, 1976) is deservedly considered a classic work of intellectual history. See also the outstanding first chapter, "The Aims of a New Epoch," in Charles Taylor, *Hegel* (Cambridge: Cambridge University Press, 1975). It is hard to overestimate Herder's influence on Goethe.

86 GA 277, pp. 132–33. Although it seems to refer to the same program and sounds nearly identical in a few passages, this address seems to be different from the immediately preceding text that is available only in Hahn's translation.

87 *in dem Stimmlichen*, a strong neologism that would translate literally as something like "in the voicedness."

88 GA 277, pp. 155–56.

89 Marie Steiner, née von Sivers (1867–1948), Russian-German actress, close collaborator with Rudolf Steiner in the development of the arts of eurythmy and creative speech.

90 GA 277, pp. 173–74.

91 Johann Wolfgang von Goethe, *Scientific Studies*, vol. 12 of the Suhrkamp Edition [in English], edited and translated by Douglas Miller (New York: Suhrkamp Publishers, 1988), pp. 3–5.

92 See "Zu dem 'Fragment' über die Natur," in GA 30, *Methodische Grundlagen der Anthroposophie 1884-1901: Gesammelte Aufsätze zur Philosophie, Naturwissenschaft, Ästhetik und Seelenkunde* [Methodological foundations of anthroposophy 1884–1901: Collected essays on philosophy, science, aesthetics and psychology] (Dornach: Rudolf Steiner Verlag, 1989), pp. 320–327. Only a few items in this volume of Steiner's early essays have been published in English translation; this has not. Because Goethe included this text in one of his journals, he was long thought to have been the author, although Goethe told his secretary late in life that he could not remember having written it. The scholarly consensus is now that the author was Johann Georg Christoph Tobler (1757–1812), a

Swiss theologian whom Goethe knew. Goethe also told Eckermann that in any case the "hymn" captured very well his own thinking at the time.

93 Steiner seems to have been holding up the Sunday supplement of the newspaper *Schweizer Zeitung* in which an article had been published arguing that Goethe had not written the hymn, but rather Tobler (GA 277, p. 173).

94 "Positive" and "comparative" in the grammatical sense.

95 GA 277, pp. 181–87, and also GA 301. This new version is indebted to earlier translations of GA 301.

96 Schiller, *Tabula Votivae* (Musen-Almanach, 1797).

97 Spoken by the character Homunculus in Part Two of Goethe's *Faust* [line 6992].

98 *durch sinnlich-übersinnliches Schauen*; the allusion is to Goethe's "Sensory-Moral Effect of Color" in his *Theory of Color, Scientific Studies*, vol. 12 of the Suhrkamp Edition [in English], ed. and trans. Douglas Miller (New York: Suhrkamp Publishers, 1988), pp. 278–297.

99 See GA 280.

100 GA 277, pp. 570–72.

101 *Hochschulkurs*. This course was inaugurated on September 26, 1920; the main event was Rudolf Steiner's lectures collected in GA 322; *The Boundaries of Natural Science*, translated by Frederick Amrine and Konrad Oberhuber, foreword Saul Bellow (Spring Valley, NY: Anthroposophic Press, 1983).

102 Dr. Rudolf Treichler (1863–1972), one of the first teachers at the Waldorf School in Stuttgart.

103 I.e., a "primordial" or "archetypal" eurythmy. See Goethe's *Urpflanze*, "archetypal plant."

104 See the note to the address of July 22, 1923.

105 *müssen ... konstatieren. Konstatieren* is an ambiguous verb that can mean either "confirm, establish" or "investigate." So it is unclear whether Steiner intends this sentence as a confirmation of his assertion based on his own research, or a call for research that might (further) confirm it, or both. Surely he was aware of this ambiguity, which would argue that he was implying both.

106 The allusion is to Goethe's *Zahme Xenien*: "Were the eye not sun-like / It never could gaze upon the sun." "Wär' nicht das Auge sonnenhaft, / Die Sonne könnt' es nie erblicken."

Goethe is referring to Plotinus (205–270), *Enneads* I.6.9: "No eye ever saw the sun without becoming sun-like. . ." (Plotinus, *Porphyry on Plotinus; Ennead I*, Loeb Classical Library [Cambridge, Massachusetts: Harvard University Press, 1966], p. 261).

107 *"verluftigend"*; quotation marks in the original. A very rare German verb that does not appear even in the compendious *Grimms Wörterbuch*, here in the form of an adverbial present participle. Steiner may have in mind, or in the back of his mind, a fragment by the German Romantic philosopher and poet Novalis [Friedrich von Hardenberg, 1772-1801] in which the verb appears as a gerund in apposition to *ein Ätherisieren* ["an etherealizing"] and *ein Vergeistigen* ["a spiritualizing"]. This is the only other instance of the verb I have been able to find.

108 I have translated this cryptic sentence as literally as possible. What Steiner may be describing is the genesis of consciousness (which is arguably "spiritual" relative to bare life itself) in the deadening of the etheric by the physical. Consciousness "eats the seeds" of the etheric body rather than allowing them to grow, which is, according to Steiner, why we must sleep each night.

109 *gebannt*, suggesting a magic spell

110 GA 277, pp. 197–203.

111 Latin, literally "in the state of being born"

112 *Gemüt*. See the note on the introduction of May 6, 1919.

113 *Verprosaischung*, a strong neologism

114 *das Wie der Gestaltung*; the allusion is to Goethe's *Faust*, line 6992.

115 See *Four Mystery Dramas* (CW 14).

116 GA 277, p. 565. See the related piece of January 15, 1916.

117 Johann Fercher von Steinwand (1828–1902), Austrian poet beloved by Steiner.

118 Christian Morgenstern (1871–1914), now widely beloved as one of the greatest German humorists, was an anthroposophist whom Steiner expressly admired. Hence it's not surprising Steiner set so many of his

nonsense poems to eurythmy. Morgenstern's masterpiece has been translated by the famous American poet W. D. Snodgrass and Lore Segal as *Gallows Songs* (Ann Arbor: The University of Michigan Press, 1967), an edition which includes drawings by Paul Klee.

119 GA 277, pp. 241–44.

120 GA 277, pp. 244–47.

121 *Sprachgestaltung* is the name Steiner gave to this renewed art form, just as "eurythmy" is the name of his new art of movement. It is also known as "creative speech."

122 *Maxims and Reflections*, #720.

123 The quote is from Goethe's essay on Winckelmann: see the note on the address of March 13, 1919.

124 GA 277, pp. 266–68.

125 *On December 25, 1921.*

126 Emil Abderhalden (1877–1950), a Swiss physiologist and chemist.

127 GA 277, pp. 274–77.

128 See *Four Mystery Dramas* (CW 14), trans. Ruth and Hans Pusch (SteinerBooks, 2007); also *The Four Mystery Plays*, trans. Adam Bittleston (Rudolf Steiner Press, 1982) and *Four Modern Mystery Dramas*, trans. Richard Ramsbotham (Rudolf Steiner Press, 2023).

129 Here Steiner is surely alluding to the Spirit of Gravity [*Geist der Schwere*] in Nietzsche's *Thus Spoke Zarathustra* (1883–1891).

130 *das den Menschen Herunterziehende*, another unmistakably Nietzschean echo.

131 See CW 272, *Anthroposophy in the Light of Goethe's* Faust, trans. Burley Channer, introduction and commentary by Frederick Amrine (SteinerBooks, 2014) and CW 273, *Goethe's* Faust *in the Light of Anthroposophy*, trans. Burley Channer, introduction and commentary by Frederick Amrine (SteinerBooks, 2016).

132 GA 277a, p. 122. This translation is a substantial revision of Alan Stott's [CW 277a, pp. 123–24]. It was given on the occasion of the performances during the West-East Congress, Vienna, 1922.

133 GA 277, pp. 292–95.

134 Emil Abderhalden; see the note on the introduction of December 28, 1921.

135 Elsewhere, Steiner distinguishes "pedagogical" from "curative" eurythmy, which seem to be conflated here.

136 Revision of Hahn, pp. 49–53. The full text of this address was included neither in GA 277 nor in GA 277a; however, a brief excerpt (the sixth paragraph below) was included in GA 277 under the rubric "Lighting for Eurythmy" (p. 579).

137 See the note on the address of November 8, 1919.

138 The quote is from Goethe's essay on Winckelmann: see the note on the address of March 13, 1919.

139 GA 277, pp. 333–38. Substantial revision of Hahn, pp. 55–60. The Pedagogical Course has been published as CW 306, *The Child's Changing Consciousness as the Basis of Pedagogical Practice* (Anthroposophic Press, 1996).

140 Marie Steiner, née von Sivers (1867–1948), Russian-German actress, close collaborator with Rudolf Steiner in the development of the arts of eurythmy and creative speech.

141 Käthe Mitscher (1892–1940) initially performed the recitations during rehearsals, which released Marie Steiner to work upon the program. She was a member of the Section for the Performing Arts of the School of Spiritual Science, specializing in eurythmy.

142 GA 277, pp. 339–40.

143 Revision of Hahn, pp. 67–74. This address was included neither in GA 277 nor in GA 277a.

144 See the extraordinary book by Serge Maintier, *Speech: Invisible Creation in the Air* (SteinerBooks, 2016). The publication includes a DVD with high-speed photos showing the patterns made by speech sounds in the air.

145 See the note to the introduction of May 15, 1920.

146 *Schwung*, translated "verve" below

147 Marie Steiner, née von Sivers (1867–1948), Russian-German actress, close collaborator with Rudolf Steiner in the development of the arts of eurythmy and creative speech.

148 GA 277, pp. 342–48.

149 See CW 282, *Speech and Drama*, trans. Mary Adams (Anthroposophic Press, 1960) and CW 129, *Wonders of the World, Ordeals of the Soul, Revelations of the Spirit*, trans. Dorothy Lenn and Owen Barfield (Rudolf Steiner Press, 1983), lecture seven.

150 *Begreifen*. Some recent neurological research has discovered a firm connection between the action of manual grasping and the evolution of language. See Giacomo Rizzolatti and Michael Arbib, "Language within Our Grasp." *Trends in Neuroscience*, Vol. 21 (1998): 188–194.

151 The English cognate "grasp" is transparent in exactly the same way. See also the etymology of the word "comprehend," literally "to get your fingers around something."

152 *handgreiflich*, a wonderfully concrete and vivid German adverb, literally "handgraspingly"

153 Demosthenes (383–322 BC), the greatest orator of antiquity.

154 Demosthenes famously practiced speaking with stones in his mouth in order to overcome a speech impediment, and he found that it greatly improved his diction generally.

155 *das Malerische in der Sprache*, literally "the painterly in the language"

156 Marie Steiner, née von Sivers (1867–1948), Russian-German actress, close collaborator with Rudolf Steiner in the development of the arts of eurythmy and creative speech.

157 GA 277, pp. 349–56.

158 See CW 282, *Speech and Drama*, trans. Mary Adams (Anthroposophic Press, 1960), lecture one.

159 Fritz Mauthner (1849–1923), is most famous today for his three-volume *Kritik der Sprache* [Critique of language] (Stuttgart, 1901–1903), largely because Wittgenstein claimed it had influenced him in the writing of his *Tractatus*. The *Kritik* seems not to have been translated into English, but for an extensive recapitulation and discussion of the argument, see Gershon Weiler, *Mauthner's Critique of Language* (Cambridge: Cambridge University Press, 1971). Mauthner had studied with Ernst Mach in Prague, so he had philosophical and scientific pretentions,

but (apart from Wittgenstein) the academic world rejected his *magnum opus*. Mauthner also wrote fiction, and he wrote journalistic feuilletons and satirical pieces for the *Berliner Tageblatt* in the 1890s, when Steiner was also active in Berlin. Steiner invokes Mauthner frequently and seems to have viewed him as an archetypal philistine.

160 See Steiner's own explanation of this neologism immediately following. The reference is to *Der Atheismus und seine Geschichte im Abendlande* [Atheism and its history in the West], vol. 1 (Stuttgart and Berlin: Deutsche Verlags-Anstalt, 1922), the chapter on "immortality," which is for the skeptic Mauthner a misuse of language.

161 Oswald Spengler (1880–1936) was an amateur historian whose book *The Decline of the West* (1918 and 1922) became a bestseller in the German-speaking world. Spengler's cultural pessimism, biologism, and nationalism were highly influential; Steiner criticizes him harshly in many places.

162 *Der deutsche Monistenbund* was a scientific society founded in Jena in 1906 under the leadership of the eminent biologist Ernst Haeckel. It was a complex organization with competing factions, but its general tenor was materialist and anti-religious.

163 *Johanni-Imagination (Rötliche Gestalt mit Sonne und Mond)*. Pastel sketch 1923.

164 GA 277, pp. 357–62.

165 See the note on Serge Maintier above.

166 *Lallen*, onomatopoetic, the first sounds that infants make.

167 There is a finite verb missing in the very long and syntactically complex sentence I have rendered as three English sentences here.

168 Here Steiner is quoting a famous line from Goethe's *Faust* [line 1740].

169 Marie Steiner, née von Sivers (1867–1948), Russian-German actress, close collaborator with Rudolf Steiner in the development of the arts of eurythmy and creative speech.

170 The first Waldorf school, founded in Stuttgart in 1919.

171 *das Klinisch-Therapeutische Institut*, which exists to this day.

172 GA 277, pp. 365–70. This is a substantial revision of Hahn, pp. 75–80.

173 See the lecture of March 11, 1923 in CW 222, *The Driving Force of Spiritual Powers in World History* (SteinerBooks, 2023).

174 *ganz peripherisch*, both adverbs, literally "entirely peripherally"

175 Marie Steiner, née von Sivers (1867–1948), Russian-German actress, close collaborator with Rudolf Steiner in the development of the arts of eurythmy and creative speech.

176 GA 277, pp. 388–96. Substantial revision of an incomplete translation by George Adams (edited by H. Collison) that appeared in the British journal *Anthroposophical Movement: Weekly News for English-speaking Members of the Anthroposophical Society*, vol. 5, No. 37 (September 9, 1928).

177 Max Müller (1923–1900) was a German-born philologist and Orientalist who lived most of his life in England. He was instrumental in founding the fields of Indian Studies and Comparative Religion. "Bimbam" is how German speakers describe the sound of a tolling bell onomatopoeically; hence Müller refers to it derisively in English as the "dingdong" theory. M. P. Sinha has summarized succinctly Müller's discussion of the two theories to which Steiner is referring here, plus two others that he does not mention:

Max Müller rightly derided the different theories posited by his predecessors as ding-dong theory, bow-wow theory, pooh-pooh theory, and sing-song theory. The so-called ding-dong theory argued that every object has its specific sound. Man in his primitive stage possessed the ability to produce a special sound when he came in contact with an object. Thus in the beginning there were about five hundred sounds which later on became speech sounds. Max Müller rejected this theory that the possession of such a gift is purely imaginary. Bow-wow theory believed that man produced sounds in imitation of the sounds of nature. It based its argument on onomatopoeic words. It was rejected on the ground that only a limited number of words are onomatopoeic. Pooh-pooh theory, which posited that language came into being when man expressed his strong emotion in words like "oh," "ah," "o," etc., was rejected by scholars on the ground that the expressions of strong emotions are not the same all over the world. Sing-song theory believed that language had its origin in singing sports. The musical rhythm later on became phonemes and syllables. This theory was purely hypothetical and was immediately rejected. (*Modern Linguistics* [New Delhi: Atlantic, 2005], p. 13)

178 *I* (*ee*) as in "deep"; *E* (*a*) as in "day"; *U* (*oo*) as in "food."

179 *Faust*, line 6992.

180 Marie Steiner, née von Sivers (1867–1948), Russian-German actress, close collaborator with Rudolf Steiner in the development of the arts of eurythmy and creative speech.

181 GA 36, *Der Goetheanumgedanke inmitten der Kulturkrisis der Gegenwart: Gesammelte Aufsätze 1921–1925 aus der Wochenschrift "Das Goetheanum"* [The idea of the Goetheanum within the present cultural crisis: Collected essays 1921–1925 from the weekly *Das Goetheanum*]. A translation by Erna McArthur was published in *Eurythmy: Essays and Anecdotes* (Roselle, IL: Schaumburg Publications, 1980), pp. 91–96. This version has been revised substantially by F. Amrine. Steiner wrote out this text for the translator in advance; hence it was readily available for reprinting in *Das Goetheanum* as part of the report on the tour.

182 See the lecture of October 9, 1920, in CW 288, *The First Goetheanum: Architecture as Living Form and Organic Style*, trans. Frederick Amrine (SteinerBooks, 2017).

183 Marie Steiner, née von Sivers (1867–1948), Russian-German actress, close collaborator with Rudolf Steiner in the development of the arts of eurythmy and creative speech.

184 GA 277, p. 402.

185 Here Steiner is referring to the group of young people studying at the Goetheanum who also guarded the grounds—especially after the burning of the First Goetheanum.

186 Ela Dziubanjuk (1881–1944), eurythmist and painter; member of the stage group at the Goetheanum; taught with Tatiana Kisseleff at the "Ecole d'Eurythmie Rudolf Steiner" in Paris.

187 Marie Steiner, née von Sivers (1867–1948), Russian-German actress, close collaborator with Rudolf Steiner in the development of the arts of eurythmy and creative speech.

188 This text is a thorough revision of Johanna Collis' translation, originally published in CW 260, pp. 33–36.

189 See CW 275, *Art as Seen in the Light of Mystery Wisdom* (London: Rudolf Steiner Press, 2012).

190 Intuition, inspiration, and imagination are three faculties of higher knowledge described by Rudolf Steiner in, for example, *Knowledge of the Higher Worlds* (CW 10).

191 *A* (*ah*), as in "father." *E* (*a*), as in "day."

192 See CW 315, *Curative Eurythmy*, lecture of April 12, 1921, and CW 279, *Eurythmy as Visible Speech*, lecture of June 26, 1924.

193 The shorthand report ends here. The eurythmy performance began after a few more words about that day's program.

194 GA 277, pp. 419–22. Also included in *The Christmas Conference for the Foundation of the General Anthroposophical Society 1923/1924: The Laying of the Foundation Stone: Lectures and Addresses; Discussion of the Statutes: Dornach, 24 December to 1 January 1924* (Hudson, NY: Anthroposophic Press, 1990).

195 See the note on the introduction of June 10, 1923.

196 See CW 282, *Speech and Drama*, trans. Mary Adams (Spring Valley, NY: Anthroposophic Press, 1960), lecture 19.

197 *The Dream Song of Olaf Åsteson* is a Norwegian folk epic that was recorded by Landstad in 1850. It tells the story of a man who fell asleep for thirteen days and nights, and then awoke to tell of the initiatory experiences he had. See CW 158, *Our Connection with the Elemental World: Kalevala – Olaf Åsteson – the Russian People: The World as the Result of Balancing Influences* (Rudolf Steiner Press, 2017).

198 GA 277, pp. 422–27.

199 CW 284, *Rosicrucianism Renewed: The Unity of Art, Science, and Religion: The Theosophical Congress of Whitsun 1907*, trans. Marsha Post (Great Barrington, Massachusetts: SteinerBooks, 2007), pp. 300–304.

200 See CW 284, *Rosicrucianism Renewed.*

201 This was the term for officially recognized local groups within the Theosophical Society, and Steiner continued to use it after he broke away to found the Anthroposophical Society.

202 *E* (*a*), as in "day."

203 GA 277, pp. 429–30.

204 *in ihrer Schnelligkeit*, literally "in their quickness"

205 *hineingeheimnisst*, literally "inserted as a mystery into"; here Steiner echoes a famous neologism Goethe used with reference to the composition of *Faust*

206 Revision of Hahn, pp. 95–100.

207 GA 277, pp. 439–44.

208 Emil Abderhalden; see the note to the introduction of December 28, 1921.

209 Ita Wegman (1876–1943), medical doctor and close collaborator with Rudolf Steiner. They co-authored the book *Extending Practical Medicine: Fundamental Principles Based on the Science of the Spirit* (CW 27).

210 GA 260a, pp. 215–216. This translation is heavily indebted to Alan Stott's [*Eurythmy: Its Birth and Development*, p. 130].

211 See the following address. "Words of Wisdom" refers to the Foundation Stone verse itself.

212 GA 277, p. 447; GA 260a, pp. 216–217.

213 The Christmas Conference took place in Dornach from December 24, 1923, to January 1, 1924, as a refounding of the Society. The central event was Rudolf Steiner's recitation of the Foundation Stone meditation, laying it in the hearts of the membership. Rudolf Steiner also assumed leadership of the Society, which he had avoided up to that point. See CW 260, *The Christmas Conference for the Foundation of the General Anthroposophical Society 1923/1924: The Laying of the Foundation Stone: Lectures and Addresses: Discussion of the Statutes: Dornach, 24 December 1923 to 1 January 1924* (Anthroposophic Press, 1990).

214 GA 277, pp. 449–55. Substantial revision of a translation by an unknown translator, edited by H. Collison, that was published originally as a pamphlet by the Anthroposophical Publishing Company (London) and the Anthroposophic Press (New York) in 1928.

215 Presumably Steiner held up the program itself at this moment. The image to which he is referring is "Easter, Three Crosses," watercolor, April 7 and 19, 1924.

216 CW 278, *Eurythmy as Visible Singing*, trans. Alan Stott (Rudolf Steiner Press, 2020).

217 See Joseph Beuys' "expanded concept of art."

218 Anton Alexander Graf von Auersperg (1806–1875). This is Steiner's paraphrase rather than a verbatim quotation.

219 GA 277, p. 457.

220 CW 278; see the note to the previous introduction.

221 *Beleuchtungseurythmie.* For an account of the development of lighting for eurythmy, see Ehrenfried Pfeiffer, *A Modern Quest for the Spirit*, ed. T. H. Meyer (Mercury Press, 2010).

222 "From the 'parting words' by Rudolf Steiner at the Second International Summer Course in England, the following words stand out: 'For art, for eurythmy, there was in a certain sense an extremely loving concern in these Summer Courses, so that this eurythmy—meaningful, as I believe it is for the present and the immediate future and drawn from esoteric intentions—could appear here. The spiritual, the artistic element, can indeed especially come about through this eurythmy.'"

223 GA 277a, 4th edition, p. 136. This translation is heavily indebted to that of Alan Stott [*Eurythmy: Its Birth and Development*, p. 136].

224 GA 277a, 4th edition, p. 61.

225 Steiner is referring to what has come to be called the First Goetheanum.

226 GA 277a, 4th edition, pp. 110–113.

227 This is Clara Smits, mother of the first eurythmist, Lori Maier-Smits.

228 Richard Wagner (1813–1883) was a German composer and theorist who is especially well known for his operas or "music dramas," as he called them. He is considered a late Romantic. Among his most important works are *The Ring of the Nibelungs*, *Tristan and Isolde*, and *Parsifal*.

229 The foregoing ungrammatical passage has been translated literally instead of interpretively.

230 GA 277, pp. 26–30

231 "The mysteries" is the Greek term for schools and rites that were esoteric in the strong sense: neophytes were forbidden from divulging their teachings—in some cases (such as the Pythagoreans) on pain of death. The most important mystery centers were in Eleusis, Samothrace, and Ephesus.

232 See, e.g., CW 275, *Art as Seen in the Light of Mystery Wisdom* (Rudolf Steiner Press, 2012) and CW 271, *Art and Theory of Art: Foundations of a New Aesthetics* (SteinerBooks, 2021).

233 GA 277, pp. 555–563

234 The consciousness soul is evolving during the current historical epoch, which Steiner sees as having begun *ca.* 1413—i.e., with the Renaissance.

235 Emmanual Geibel (1815–1884).

236 Ernst von Wildenbruch (1845–1909).

237 GA 277, pp. 566–567

238 GA 277, pp. 567–568

239 GA 277, pp. 80–85

240 GA 277, pp. 113–115

241 GA 277, pp. 134–140

242 Many consider the German art historian and classical archaeologist Johann Joachim Winckelmann (1717–1768) to be the founder of modern art history, and Goethe was among the first to appreciate his importance. Goethe's essay on Winckelmann of 1805 is a widely admired classic. For more on Winckelmann himself, see the splendid study by Alex Potts, *Flesh and the Ideal: Winckelmann and the Origins of Art History* (New Haven: Yale UP, 1994).

243 "The Rock Spring Wonder" is a fairy tale told by Felicia Balde to Capesius in Scene Five of Steiner's second mystery drama, *The Soul's Probation* (CW 14).

244 GA 277, pp. 141–147

245 GA 277, pp. 148–155

246 Rudolf Steiner wrote and directed four Mystery Dramas: *The Portal of Initiation* (1910), *The Soul's Probation* (1911), *The Guardian of the Threshold* (1912) and *The Souls' Awakening* (1913). See GA 14, Rudolf Steiner, *Four Mystery Dramas*, trans. Ruth and Hans Pusch (SteinerBooks, 2014); also *Four Modern Mystery Dramas*, trans. Richard Ramsbotham (Rudolf Steiner Press, 2023).

247 GA 277, pp. 158–165.

248 Albrecht von Haller (1708–1777), scientist, physician, and poet.

249 This poem by Goethe is called "Allerdings" [By all means].

250 GA 277, pp. 166–172.

251 Steiner is referring to World War I.

252 GA 277, p. 568.

253 GA 277, p. 569.

254 GA 277, p. 189.

255 GA 277, pp. 205–208.

256 Emil Abderhalden (1877–1950), a Swiss physiologist and chemist.

257 GA 277, p. 573.

258 GA 277, pp. 214–220.

259 GA 277, pp. 573–574.

260 GA 277, pp. 237–240.

261 *Sprachgestaltung*, literally "speech formation," also known as "creative speech." This is the art of recitation developed principally by Marie Steiner.

262 GA 277, pp. 277–279.

263 Fercher von Steinwand (1828–1902), Austrian poet, personal acquaintance of Rudolf Steiner.

264 GA 277, pp. 279–280.

265 GA 277, pp. 577–578.

266 GA 277, p. 578.

267 GA 277, p. 579.

268 GA 277, p. 580.

269 GA 277, pp. 309–314.

270 This famous poem is by Goethe.

271 Arthur Schopenhauer (1788–1860), a post-Kantian German philosopher known especially for his profound pessimism. Although Schopenhauer's magnum opus, *The World as Will and Representation* [*Die Welt als Wille und Vorstellung*] was first published in 1819, it was only decades later that Schopenhauer became widely read and influential.

272 GA 277, pp. 316–320.

273 GA 277, pp. 323–324.

274 GA 277, pp. 580–581.

275 GA 277, p. 581.

276 Revision of a translation by Gladys Hahn, originally published in *An Introduction to Eurythmy* (Anthroposophic Press, 1984), pp. 61–66. GA 277 does not include this address.

277 Ibid., pp. 81–87.

278 Marie Steiner-von Sivers married Rudolf Steiner on December 24, 1914, becoming his second wife. She became a close collaborator in all things, but was especially important in developing "creative speech" (also known by the earlier designation "speech formation"). She was especially well suited to this task because she was multilingual (her native language was, in fact, Russian), and she had trained as an actress. See especially CW 281, *Poetry and the Art of Speech*, trans. J. Wedgwood and Andrew Welburn (London School of Speech Formation, 1981) and CW 282, *Speech and Drama*, trans. Mary Adams (Anthroposophic Press, 1960).

279 GA 277, pp. 372–378

280 As in "father."

281 As in "day."

282 As in "glee."

283 *Blatt*, pronounced "ah" as in "father."

284 GA 277, pp. 380–386. Revision of a translation by Vera and Judy Compton-Burnett, originally published in CW 279, *Eurythmy as Visible Speech* (1931; Rudolf Steiner Press, 1984), pp. 281–287.

285 As in "glee."

286 As in "day."

287 GA 277, pp. 413–418.

288 Jan Stuten (1890–1948), an anthroposophical composer and conductor.

289 GA 277, p. 432.

290 GA 277, p. 16.

291 GA 277, p. 582.

292 GA 277, pp. 469–471.